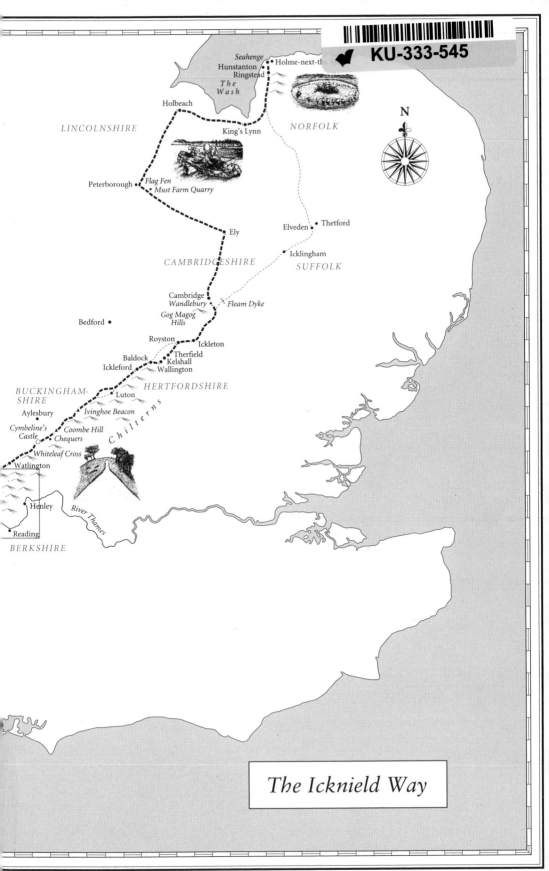

N

Seahenge
Holme-next-the-
Hunstanton
Ringstead
Holbeach
The Wash
King's Lynn
LINCOLNSHIRE
NORFOLK
Peterborough
Flag Fen
Must Farm Quarry
Elveden • Thetford
Ely
Icklingham
CAMBRIDGESHIRE
SUFFOLK
Cambridge
Wandlebury *Fleam Dyke*
Gog Magog
Hills
Bedford
Royston
Ickleton
Baldock
Therfield
Kelshall
Ickleford
Wallington
BUCKINGHAM-
SHIRE
HERTFORDSHIRE
Luton
Aylesbury
Ivinghoe Beacon
Cymbeline's
Castle
Coombe Hill
Chequers
Chilterns
Whiteleaf Cross
Watlington
River Thames
Henley
Reading
BERKSHIRE

The Icknield Way

The Green Road
into the Trees

Also by Hugh Thomson

The White Rock: An Exploration of the Inca Heartland

Nanda Devi: A Journey to the Last Sanctuary

Cochineal Red: Travels through Ancient Peru

Tequila Oil: Getting Lost in Mexico

50 Wonders of the World

Hugh Thomson

The Green Road into the Trees

An Exploration of England

preface
publishing

Published by Preface 2012

10 9 8 7 6 5 4 3 2 1

Copyright © Hugh Thomson 2012

Hugh Thomson has asserted his right to be identified as the author
of this work under the Copyright, Designs and Patents Act 1988

Map © John Gilkes
Illustrations © Adam Burton

First published in Great Britain in 2012 by Preface Publishing

20 Vauxhall Bridge Road
London, SW1V 2SA

An imprint of The Random House Group Limited

www.randomhouse.co.uk
www.prefacepublishing.co.uk

Addresses for companies within The Random House Group Limited
can be found at www.randomhouse.co.uk

The Random House Group Limited Reg. No. 954009

A CIP catalogue record for this book is available from the British Library

ISBN 978 1 84809 332 4

The Random House Group Limited supports The Forest Stewardship Council (FSC®),
the leading international forest certification organisation. Our books carrying the
FSC label are printed on FSC® certified paper. FSC is the only forest certification
scheme endorsed by the leading environmental organisations, including Greenpeace.
Our paper procurement policy can be found at www.randomhouse.co.uk/environment

Typeset in Centaur MT by Palimpsest Book Production Limited,
Falkirk, Stirlingshire
Printed and bound in Great Britain by
Clays Ltd, St Ives PLC

For Daisy, Owen and Leo

Illustrations by Adam Burton

Contents

Out on that almost trackless expanse of billowy Downs
such a track is in some sort humanly companionable:
it really seems to lead you by the hand.

'The Romance of the Road',
The Pagan Papers, Kenneth Grahame

Mi casa es su casa, 'my home is yours'.

South American proverb

Chapter 1

The Stranger's Welcome

Hamlet: 'But this is wondrous strange.'
Horatio: 'And therefore as a stranger give it welcome.'

I stumbled into the English spring sunshine after a deep sleep. An unnatural sleep, a jet-lagged sleep. I had spent the months before travelling around South America and the long flight back across the Atlantic from west to east, against the sun, had wound my body up and then down. Now I was emerging after what seemed like a hibernation. The river meadows were flooded with purple bugle and fringed with white hawthorn blossom. My neighbour's apple orchard was also gleaming with blossom, underplanted with daffodils; it led down to the river which still ran fast with the old rains of winter. Back inland, towards the Chilterns, a flush of yellow was spreading across the year's first crop of oilseed rape.

Mole at the start of *The Wind in the Willows* realises that spring has arrived without his noticing. I felt the same way. When I had left for South America, it had been bitter February weather, with snow on the ground and the only colour coming from a woodpecker or robin.

Needing a strong coffee and with no food in the house, I cycled to the local market town. The sound of Abba's 'Dancing Queen' being pumped out by a brass band could be heard for some way before I arrived. A celebration was in full swing. Red and white bunting hung from the church, matched by the small flags the children were waving and by the icing on the teacakes sold in the market place; near by was a puppet stall where Punch was setting about Judy with ferocity. The children watching had their faces painted to look like lions or tigers.

Tattoos snaked out of the busts and jeans of the farmers' wives queuing at the ice-cream van, which had been painted in neon orange with a 'chill-out' logo, and was dispensing Skyrockets, Mr Magics, Daddy Cools and Blackcurrant Peep-Ups. A quiff-haired teenager ostentatiously did a wheelie right across the Market Square on his bicycle pimped up with double shocks and chunky chrome spokes. Oblivious to the fairground stalls and the noise, an elegantly overdressed older lady with sunglasses, light wool coat and malacca cane was stooping against the spring breeze, leaning into it.

The band had finished 'Dancing Queen' and were now playing a more stately jig. I noticed not so much the music as their hats: a pink stetson playing the guitar, a bowler manning the cello, a Pete Doherty-style pork-pie perched on the lead guitarist and there, on the drummer's head, an unmistakable panama, just as I had seen and bought at a small market on the Ecuadorian coast only weeks before.

England has become a complicated and intriguing country. In truth it's always been one, but perhaps I'm just noticing it more now. The familiar is looking very strange. It may be the jet lag, or the sudden immersion in all this noise, colour and confusion after a deep sleep, but I am seized with a sudden desire to explore England. The few other times I've ever had really bad jet lag – the sort where you walk in a trance, as if under water and sedation – have been when I've travelled abroad, not travelled home. The only cure then has been total immersion in the new culture.

So I feel like plunging in – and to do so by the darker, underground ways, again like a mole, tracking the older paths into the country.

My usual pattern is to travel abroad to an exotic location, then rest up at home to write about it and try to cultivate my tomato plants in the insipid English sun. And then repeat the process.

Suddenly I like the idea of doing it all in reverse.

*

I was on my third cup of coffee, when a dog caught my eye before I noticed its owner. Not to disparage the owner, who was large and wearing shorts and a brightly coloured pair of Crocs. But it was the dog that drew my attention: it had the wiry, attractive qualities of a natural rat catcher, a smooth-haired fox terrier with unusual markings, its face black and white in an exactly symmetrical way, black on one side, white on the other, as if wearing a harlequin's mask. And as such, a natural conversation opened with its owner, not that Simon, said owner, needed much excuse.

Even South Americans don't introduce themselves so fast. Within ten minutes, Simon had told me his entire medical, matrimonial and financial history, which could be summarised as 'crocked, divorced and bust'. Not that he was letting this get him down.

He made his living by being an artist and a poacher; the two seemed complementary. I was more interested in the poaching, having read Richard Jefferies' books on the subtle arts and skills, and occasionally brutal encounters, of the poaching world.

Simon supplemented his portrait painting by foraging for truffles and mushrooms that his dog found for him in the woods, and the odd larger bird or fish tickled out from under a gamekeeper's nose. At forty-nine, he was almost exactly my age, with a touch of the overgrown schoolboy, exacerbated by his shorts. He was large with a hint of vulnerability; he certainly had plenty to be vulnerable about. A car crash (or rather a car crashing into him when he was parked) had broken his neck and left him with back pain, which he took morphine for, along with other pain-killers. As he talked, he apologised for occasionally repeating himself: 'It's all these drugs I keep having to take.'

I asked him more about the poaching. I couldn't help noticing the badge on his jacket lapel: it was for the Countryside Alliance.

'I like to call it "supplying wild produce". Rabbits, pheasants, squirrels, deer, mushrooms, truffles, crayfish. It's all in these woods. And a lot of the time if I didn't have it, it would just go to waste.'

He got out a catapult to show me, keeping his hands well below the café table. It was a beautifully crafted piece from birch, that he had made himself, with a thick industrial rubber band and a supply of lead musket balls that he kept in a pouch.

'Incredibly fast, incredibly accurate. Totally legal. And the best thing is that I can get it out quickly. Sometimes I'll get to a field and it's in those first few minutes that the best game presents itself, before I can get out a gun. With this little beauty I can pop off a rabbit straightaway.'

Simon ate a lot of rabbit and provided it for his son who lived with him. 'Skinning a rabbit is easy. Make one incision and you just unzip the thing. Get the guts out and you're away. Although like they say, there's plenty of ways to skin a rabbit. Not like a squirrel. Squirrel has a pelt so thick it's unbelievable. I look down the barrel of a gun sometimes when shooting a rabbit and you see the pellet pass straight through the skin, the flesh, the skin and out the other side. But with a squirrel the pellet never gets out again. Skinning a squirrel is a bastard.'

'Is squirrel good to eat?' I wondered, mindful of the old adage that they were just rats with tails, and conscious too that with the jet lag I was not at my sharpest.

'Squirrel? Very tasty,' said Simon loyally. 'But what I really like is deer. Plenty of muntjac around. To the extent that it's a pest. Beautiful deer, of course. I love the way they move. You know the best way to skin a deer?'

This was purely rhetorical.

'Wrap some rubber bands around the handle of a golf club. Work the golf club down the spine of the deer when it's suspended from a tree and tied to the ground. Then attach a lead from the golf club to the tow bar of your pick-up truck. Reverse very, *very* slowly.' (Simon stressed this, as if concerned that I might rush the job.) 'And the skin will peel off like a baby's nappy. But the deer has to be fresh.'

I nodded.

'Not so much any more, but there was a time when I was supplying a lot. Local hotels, restaurants, places up in London. They loved it. All my stuff was organic, free range – and local. That's probably what they put on the menu. "Local free-range venison." You bet it was free!

'I had a good run with crayfish. They're not on this year. Something wrong with the river. I tried the usual beats. A couple of years ago they were jumping into my hands. The other day though, I found a lovely stretch for eel. They're coming back. I was going down in the boat and we passed plenty of perch. But what I liked the look of were the eel. Good, thick ones. Eel only put on a pound a year, so they're slow-growing. Some of the butchers over in Henley and Maidenhead, towards London, have started to sell a lot of smoked eel.'

Simon ordered another cappuccino.

'I live on air really. Painting doesn't pay much. My life is about survival.' This complaint – which sounded well rehearsed – was undermined when he showed me copies of his paintings on an expensive iPad he drew from a capacious pocket. The paintings were excellent. Some were of horses, commissioned by their owners. Some were large oils of patterns cast on water. 'I did these from looking out over the river so much, for fish. You get fascinated by the way the light plays on the water. There's always a patch beyond the trees where the light is slightly different.'

After a brief silence, he changed tack abruptly.

'I learned one thing from that car crash. All you have in this life is time. All that matters is time, and how you use it. Nothing else matters. Possessions don't matter. I lost everything after the crash. And I realised that nothing else is real. Your clothes, that magazine you're reading, that sandwich you're eating. Your marriage. None of it. None of it is real. All that matters is your time and what you do with it. I've wasted a lot of my life.'

Simon had gone from being very talkative to subdued. He explained that he had these sudden mood swings. 'It's the medication.'

✳

It was easy to live in the countryside, as I did, and not know what was stirring beneath its surface. Most rural dwellers in England are blithely unaware what the farmers around them are doing, let alone the poachers. If I made a journey, as well as being an investigation of the deepest past, I wanted to explore what was happening now – how the countryside was changing.

The question was which journey to make. There were many old trackways threading their way around England. Not far from me ran one of the oldest and most intriguing, the Icknield Way.

Unlike many of the older paths, this had not been commodified into a long-distance trail with accompanying guidebooks, signposts and people to hold your hand. For much of the Icknield Way's long route from the south coast near Dorset diagonally across the country to Norfolk, it was still half covered by bramble and tunnelled by elder, beech and oak, forgotten and ignored. This prehistoric track dissected England in a way no modern major road did, since most ran arterially out of London. A century ago, one of the poets I most admired, Edward Thomas, had tried to follow its traces.

That same afternoon, I went over to an escarpment near by. Across the fields of oilseed rape, the clearest of paths showed the Way continuing up to the hills beyond.

It was a path I knew well: I had cycled, ridden and walked it many times, with dogs, friends and neighbours. From where I stood, the path led up into the Chilterns, one of the largest forested areas in England when the Anglo-Saxons arrived, as it still is. Before the Saxons came, this had been part of Roman Britain, but more lightly colonised because of the rougher terrain: south of Romanised Dorchester, the River Thames makes a great horseshoe sweep down from the crossing at Wallingford and around below Whitchurch and Mapledurham to reach Henley. The Chilterns sprawl out from the centre of this horseshoe in a mess of wooded valleys.

It was the West Saxons, the Gewisse, who colonised this area, a group less civilised than the East Saxons of Kent, resisting Christianity until much later. Their original name, the Gewisse, is thought to mean 'the trusties' – or as we might put it, 'the heavies'; one historian described them as 'a strong-arm gang controlling weaker neighbours by brute force'. Only later have they been labelled more sedately as 'the West Saxons'. The eponymous kingdom they founded of Wessex is often associated with the south-west coast and Thomas Hardy's novels, but it was first centred here in Oxfordshire and the upper Thames.

Under the veneer of commuter respectability – for Henley in particular lies within striking distance of London and is much prized by Jaguar owners for its regatta and gentility – you do not need to go far into the woods to find traces of a less polite past.

Entering the Chilterns along the Icknield Way I came to Berins Hill, at the start of what locals called 'the Ipsden triangle', a dense patch of woodland in which both motorists and walkers were forever getting lost; it also had no mobile phone signal, which I found satisfying.

Berins Hill was named after the Italian bishop, Birinius, who in AD 631 came on a missionary expedition to convert those Saxons like the Gewisse who had not succumbed to the earlier charms of St Augustine. Birinius was successful and baptised the king of the Gewisse at nearby Benson.

Benson had now been taken over by the RAF, who performed helicopter manoeuvres over the fields. It was a place of security compounds, breeze-block buildings and shaved heads.

But Berins Hill was still wild. I came in from the fields and entered its wooded flanks. Because the beech trees were climbing up the side of the hill, they had to grow even higher to reach the sunlight. The effect was spectacular, the tall beeches disappearing for nigh on a hundred feet up into the canopy, the great height of the tree trunks accentuated by the delicacy and smallness of the beech leaves floating like maidenhair. With the large ferns guarding the entrance to the wood, the effect was Amazonian; not for the first time, I reflected on how exotic we would find a horse chestnut in flower, or beech forest in spring, if we came across them in Brazil rather than Buckinghamshire.

As I got higher onto the hill, the ground thickened with holly and there were pockets of dense wildwood. And then to my surprise I came across something I had never noticed in all the years of passing, perhaps because, in the old maxim, you only ever find what you are looking for: off to one side, on the north, close to a small road but invisible from it, a broad, deep ditch had been dug, wide enough to be a substantial moat, a hollow way that did not feature on any map. And why was this called Berins Hill? Was it because from here the bishop could survey the broad sweep of the West Saxon heartland, both the farms in the valley and the woods up above?

Certainly St Birinius, as he later became, made a judicious if odd decision when it came to dividing up the parishes. Rather than doing so in the usual compact shape, he created long, thin strips that ran down from the hills to the river, so that each parish should enjoy access to the woods at one end and the River Thames at the other. The fact that they all look like Chile on the map has confused both priests and parishioners ever since: my own church lies many miles inland from the river villages it serves.

In the following centuries the West Saxons were forced south out of Oxfordshire by their neighbours to their north: first the Mercians and later the Vikings. This has always been a martial frontier, as evidenced by the much earlier Grim's Dyke near by, which marked a similar divide of the Iron Age. The hills that bisect the county are a natural border point. The centre of Wessex headed south, towards the coast. After Birinius, the bishops moved their see from Dorchester to Winchester – and the Chilterns and Berkshire Downs became savage and disputed frontier lands. They were the scene of many battles, one of the most important being the battle of Ashdown, not far from here, which Alfred the Great fought against the Vikings in 871, a battle that deserves to be remembered as much as Agincourt, Waterloo or El Alamein.

It was Grim's Dyke that I joined just a little further to the north where the Icknield Way crossed it, a high embankment with a defensive ditch which once ran west and east from the

Thames for hundreds of miles. This was one of the best-preserved stretches of the Dyke, as it entered the Chilterns.

The bluebells in the beech woods that surrounded and disguised the embankment came as a shock. I had forgotten that they would be there, a soft purple rather than blue, as I came in from the bright sunshine of the fields and saw waves and islands of them spreading below the trees, not so much lighting up the forest as glowing within it: purple shadows.

They spread across the ridge. A heavy-seeded plant, bluebells travel slowly across the ground: it had taken many, many generations for them to cover such distance. The carpet of blue flowers managed to be a celebration both of the transience of spring and of the permanence of the English landscape.

Along the top of the Dyke, I followed a path that was covered with beechmast and threaded through with white wood anemones. Looking down through the trees at the wheat fields to either side, with the young wheat still tight in bud, the stalks shimmered blue under the green of their tops, so that when viewed from certain angles they looked like water, an effect exaggerated when the wind blew across the fronds and sent a ripple of green-yellow across the underlying blue.

The Dyke took me back to an older heritage than the Saxon world; it was built by the Celts of the Iron Age in about 300 BC, for reasons that, if archaeologists are honest, remain mysterious – to the point that there has been some argument as to whether it was for southerners to keep northerners out, or vice versa. To my lay eyes, it seemed probable that it was designed to keep the north out, with the ditch on that side of the embankment; but more crucial for me was the acceptance of a mystery. I was used in Latin America to ancient earthworks whose purpose or meaning remained resolutely obscure, and I liked that. Keats's idea of 'negative capability', that we should be humble in the face of what we do not understand, does not always sit well in the world of archaeology, where forcibly expressed hypotheses and the denigration of rival theories are the norm.

Perhaps because we understand so little about it, you never hear Grim's Dyke mentioned in the same breath as Offa's Dyke on the Welsh border. Yet it was also a substantial achievement and wherever traces of it remain, as they do on the high horse country below Wantage and even around Watford and suburban London, it is a reminder of how insistently north and south were divided in this country, a fatal fault line that ultimately allowed the Normans to conquer the Anglo-Saxon world.

It was along Grim's Dyke as it rose from Mongewell by the Thames over to Nettlebed (named at a time when nettles were much appreciated as a resource) that the bluebells were at their finest. I walked here in 'courting days' when I was eighteen, too shy to kiss the girl I was with and so kept talking of music instead, a male displacement activity long before Nick Hornby identified it; and I walked here more recently thirty years later when I had fallen in love again after a difficult divorce (aren't all divorces difficult?) and was trying to rebuild.

I found the bluebells in the woods had a mesmeric quality, one of darkness as well as of light, along this old earthwork trackway whose purpose was still not clear, that collated different impulses together for me: the mystery of the path; the mystery of love that after thirty years I had still not understood; and the bluebells spreading underneath the beeches in purple shadows that would last just a few weeks but had taken centuries to establish.

✳

There is nothing like taking a walk to make up your mind. Or for making you accept an obvious solution, however challenging it might be.

I knew that I could base myself at home and launch excursions to various different trackways and drovers' paths around the country; cherry-pick them, so to speak.

But how much better to make a journey from coast to coast? To be bold. To begin at the Atlantic and end at the North Sea. To travel from Dorset to Norfolk. To follow the Icknield Way not just for a few, familiar miles, but for its entire length right through rural England: the ancient, prehistoric way to cross the country, along its spine and following the hills.

There was a geographical appropriateness to the plan. Locals were fond of saying that we lived in the area that was furthest from the sea. I suspected that this was debatable and a contested national title – like the accolade of being the wettest place, for which I've seen many candidates – but it was undoubtedly very landlocked; it was also almost exactly at the midpoint of the Icknield Way. By travelling from coast to coast, I would be connecting the place I knew so well with the country's furthest edges.

That same night, I looked out some maps and gathered the things I needed for such a journey. Truth to tell, as I had not unpacked, this was hardly difficult. My down jacket, tent and boots stood ready to go from my travels in Peru. The teabags and blister-kit were still in the backpack.

The cure for a hangover was to keep drinking. The cure for jet lag was to keep travelling.

I was on the train to Dorset next morning.

*

Can there be a finer place in all England to start a journey?

I'm at St Catherine's Chapel on the Dorset coast. A square-cut Norman chapel with immensely thick four-foot walls, it stands isolated on a hilltop, with magnificent views sweeping down the

Atlantic along Chesil Beach to Portland Bill. Behind me are the folds of Dorset, undulating away with their coombs and copses and small English lanes, made more drunken than usual by a toponymy that even locals find confusing.

The chapel was built in the fourteenth century by the monks of the nearby Abbey. They constructed it in stone throughout, including the roof, because of the fear of fire from both lightning and the French invaders who made regular incursions along the coast.

The chapel was abandoned for centuries. It has now been restored to its bare essentials and the walls repaired, but there is nothing inside – no pews, no altarpiece, no stained glass. Once a year at Christmas there is a small service held by candlelight for a few devoted souls.

As an emblem of both continuity and neglect, it could not serve me better. St Catherine was perceived as the Athena of the early Christian world: calm, dispassionate, intellectual and courageous; dying as a martyr to a cruel Roman emperor, tied to the wheel that still bears her name and is lit up every Guy Fawkes Day. Her story made for an alluring myth – and myth it properly was. She was removed from the list of official saints by the Vatican in 1968 because 'she probably never existed'.

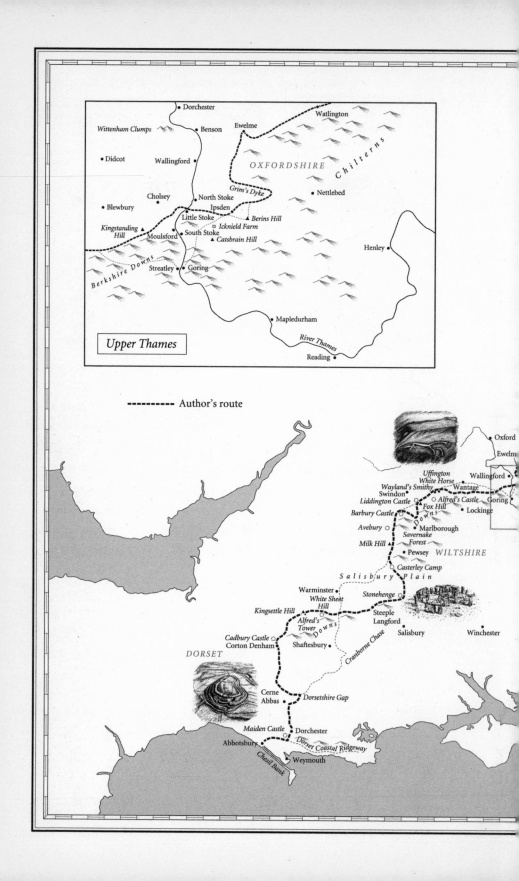

Upper Thames

------- Author's route

Map 1 (Upper Thames):
Dorchester • Wittenham Clumps • Benson • Ewelme • Watlington • Didcot • Wallingford • OXFORDSHIRE • Chilterns • Cholsey • North Stoke • Grim's Dyke • Nettlebed • Blewbury • Ipsden • Little Stoke • Berins Hill • Kingstanding Hill • Icknield Farm • Moulsford • South Stoke • Catsbrain Hill • Henley • Berkshire Downs • Streatley • Goring • Mapledurham • River Thames • Reading

Map 2 (Author's route):
Oxford • Ewelm • Uffington White Horse • Wallingford • Wayland's Smithy • Wantage • Swindon • Alfred's Castle • Goring • Liddington Castle • Fox Hill • Lockinge • Barbury Castle • Downs • Avebury • Marlborough • Milk Hill • Savernake Forest • WILTSHIRE • Pewsey • Casterley Camp • Salisbury Plain • Warminster • Stonehenge • White Sheet Hill • Kingsettle Hill • Steeple Langford • Alfred's Tower • Downs • Salisbury • Winchester • Cadbury Castle • Shaftesbury • Cranborne Chase • Corton Denham • DORSET • Cerne Abbas • Dorsetshire Gap • Maiden Castle • Dorchester • Abbotsbury • Dorset Coastal Ridgeway • Chesil Bank • Weymouth

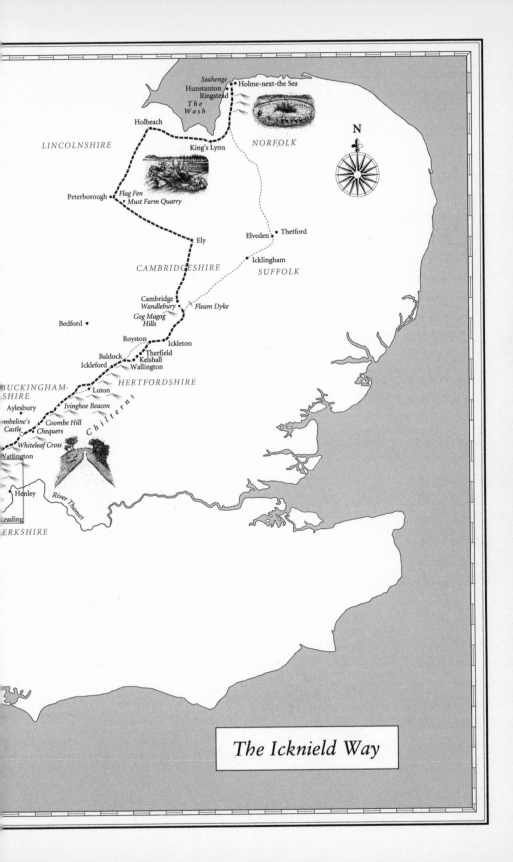

The Icknield Way

The last chapel to St Catherine I visited was in the Sinai desert. This chapel has an equally wild beauty. Thomas Hardy described it as being 'in a fearfully exposed position'. The chapel seems to be dedicated not to the church but to the sea.

I won't see the sea again for another 400 miles or so, when I emerge on the Norfolk coast. I will be following as near as I can the old road of the Icknield Way, which has some claim to be the most ancient route in England. It linked the world of the Mediterranean, whose traders landed along the coast from here to Cornwall, with the world of those northern Europeans who came to East Anglia – a prehistoric highway between these two points of entry to England, slicing diagonally across the country from Dorset to Norfolk, with lay-bys at all the great prehistoric sites: Maiden Castle, Stonehenge, Avebury, a string of hill-forts and finally, on the Norfolk coast, Seahenge.

London and the South-East were completely avoided; only later, with the Roman invasion, did all roads start there and Dover become such a principal port. But that suits me fine. I want to take the temperature of England as a country not a city, and to slice across it from the South-West to East Anglia is the perfect way to do so. London can stay off my map.

Perhaps because of the later Roman reorientation of English roads out of London, far more traces of the Icknield Way survive than one might expect: it has not simply been built over and tarmacked. Nor was the route taken by prehistoric man one that now favours the motor car. The old path often follows the hill-tops, not the valleys; it is more concerned with natural ford points of rivers, with keeping above the flood plain and with following the grain of the landscape.

Dorset has always been a good launching-off point into England; so much so that Walter Raleigh concentrated on Weymouth for his defences against the Armada, as he suspected that, if Philip of Spain had any tactical sense, that was where he would land. In the event, Philip had no tactical abilities whatsoever and south-westerly winds blew the Spanish fleet into the Channel.

Directly below St Catherine's Chapel, on the semi-saline waters of the Fleet Lagoon, protected from the Atlantic by the thin strip of Chesil Beach, I can see the old Swannery, established by the same Benedictine monks who built the chapel. It is one of the last surviving swanneries in the country, testament to the medieval appetite for roast swan (preferably with another bird stuffed inside), although now benignly managed to preserve, rather than eat, the birds. Daniel Defoe was much taken with it when he came this way in the eighteenth century: 'The famous swannery, or nursery of swans, the like of which I believe is not in Europe'.

When I descend there from the chapel, one of the women workers tells me they have just completed the biannual count of mute swans. Seven hundred and forty were tagged as their own, as opposed to any 'freeloading royal swans' belonging to the Queen that might come as visitors. She showed me some arresting photographs of the local villagers of Abbotsbury wading into the waters of the Fleet to help hold and tag the swans, as they have always done.

What is it about the incongruence of humans holding swans? Many of the pictures of Leda and the Swan gain their power from the sheer anatomical disjointedness of the species. It certainly puts a new spin on the idea of 'necking'.

In the photos, the villagers are putting on a brave face. The English countryman or woman is expected to deal with most things with aplomb: holding a live ferret, dealing with a dead sheep, breaking down in their 4x4 on the middle of Dartmoor. But holding a live swan, with a neck like an articulated python and a wing powerful enough to break a man's arm, is a whole different order of magnitude.

My path leads inland from the old Swannery. It's a good way to start getting into my stride: an old ropewalk, with a stream bubbling beside it, hart's tongue ferns in the banks, and roses in the cottage gardens I pass.

But any sentimentality is banished in Abbotsbury – as it should have been by the ropewalk, which was a brutal industry, a medieval sweatshop in which the endless tying of material into rope along a straight path would lose any charm if actually witnessed.

Abbotsbury is a testimony to destruction. Where the abbey once stood is a gaping void, with just the odd gatepost left. All that remains of what must have been a quite wonderful medieval building is the outpost of St Catherine's Chapel behind me on its hill, spared by Henry VIII at the Reformation only as a useful landmark for the navy of which he was so proud.

England's green and pleasant veneer – nowhere more seductive than in Dorset – has always hidden its capacity for sudden and brutal change. The winding roads that so picturesquely lead inland were the ones that killed T E Lawrence on his motorbike.

*

My teenage children get embarrassed because, when walking, I have the most un-English habit of buttonholing complete strangers and asking them the time of day and what moves in their neck of the woods. While my children pretend that I am some stray father who has got attached and is just tagging along, the accosted stranger, after the surprise of being addressed by someone who hasn't known them for at least five years and is saying more than hello, will do that other very English thing: launch into a long tale. For it is a national characteristic that we have the boldness of the very shy. We keep ourselves zipped up but given the opportunity – the licence – and it will all pour out.

A few words to a farmer in Abbotsbury and I find myself

hearing a story that needs a longer sit-down and a cup of tea, in a farmhouse with a horse yard and chickens that has managed to stay in the centre of the village without being redeveloped.

David Young was born in 1937. A shrewd and gentle man, he had lived his whole life in Abbotsbury. He practised mixed farming until the late 1960s, but then concentrated on dairy farming until 1998 when he retired, although he told me he wasn't sure 'whether he gave up dairying or dairying gave up on him'.

The whole village has always had one landlord: the Ilchester estate, which also owns the Swannery. Apart from some new shared-equity accommodation, put up by the Salisbury Trust, the Ilchester estate has completely controlled the village for as long as he could remember.

The old Lord Illchester had a paternalistic interest in keeping the village uniform. 'Anyone painted their door a different colour, he would put them right.' He died in 1964, but both his sons had already been killed: one in a shooting accident when still a schoolboy; the other on active service with the army in Cyprus. The title then passed to a fourth cousin, which is about as distant as it gets in the peerage. The most recent holder had been called Maurice Vivian de Touffreville Fox-Strangways to his friends, Lord Ilchester to the neighbours.

When David was a boy, he and the other children in the village were always conscious of the power of the Ilchester estate.

'It was like a pistol pointing at your foot. No one would step out of line. As kids, all of us in the village would make dens, like kids do, but we never dared go into the woods, even though they were all around us. That would have been sacrilege, disturbing the pheasants.'

They had to be careful where they went anyway. The same reasons that might have made this Dorset coast attractive to Philip and his Armada applied equally in the Second World War. The beach and surrounding area were heavily mined. I had seen the remains of pillboxes and barbed wire scattered along Chesil

Beach, together with what the locals called 'dragons' teeth', large concrete blocks put up as tank traps.

David remembered that when they were children, the local gamekeeper had been blown up when he stepped on a mine.

'The estate had to bring an older keeper out of retirement. We weren't exactly scared of him, mind, but he was what you would call authoritative. No one wanted to get on the wrong side of him. Of course, in those days we respected people who had authority.'

This didn't stop David going out with his father to poach the odd pheasant for the family Sunday pot, particularly during the long years of rationing.

'We took a sponge and a bamboo and some ammonia. Put the soaked sponge under a roosting pheasant in a tree – and plop, there was Sunday lunch. No shots, no weapons. I was only a lad tagging along with Dad when he did it. Some of the locals used a different technique: they would pierce a dried pea with a needle, right through, and tie it to a stick. If any pheasant took the bait, they couldn't get loose. A bit cruel, that was. I never did it.'

David won a place to the grammar school in Dorchester. In those days there was still a train line from Abbotsbury. Now there are just a few intermittent buses.

'I used to get the last train back from Weymouth. Often I was the only passenger. I got to know the driver and he would let me drive the train. Think of that! You wouldn't get away with a boy being allowed to drive a train these days.'

David's father had been a reluctant farmer.

'His heart was never in it, not really. He should have been a carpenter. He was good with his hands. But that was like a lot of people around here. They'd have a small dairy herd, say thirty cows – enough to earn a living and have a drink in the pub. Everyone around here was a farmer when I was growing up. Then my friends started to do different things. One went off and joined the fishing boats in Weymouth.'

David was more enthusiastic about staying. He took over his father's farm, and built up the dairy herd. That was in the days of the Milk Marketing Board, whose passing he, like many farmers, regretted.

'The Milk Marketing Board was a monopoly. That's why they had to get rid of it later. But it protected the farmers. They had the power to dictate prices to the big supermarkets. Soon as that went, the big five supermarkets could turn round and dictate prices to individual dairies.'

'When the milk quota came in around '84, it almost did for me. I had just started expanding the herd. Then I had to cut back again, so as not to go over the quota. I was taking milk up the back of the fields and dumping it so that I didn't get fined for overproduction. That was heartbreaking.'

'They have a much better system on the continent, where the quota system goes with the cow, not the land. But here we had the House of Lords controlling the bill as it went through Parliament. Vested interests. So of course they tied the quota to the land, to the owner. That meant that if they kicked a tenant farmer off, they could still keep his quota.'

David had now retired from running the farm, which had gone 'back-in-hand' to the estate. The yard at the back of the house was still busy with horses, chickens and ducks. His wife and daughters were active horsewomen. Just the week before, the family had suffered a bad burglary. Someone had broken into the tack room: 'While we were watching telly, they jemmied the door off and wheelbarrowed away nine thousand quid's worth of saddles and gear.'

He still had a business looking after hedges and fences for other farmers, so saw a great deal of the surrounding area and its changes.

'This used to be a very sleepy farming part of the world. The land didn't suit big farms. Too hilly. Not like those prairies up in East Anglia. But all the small tenant farmers are going or gone. The estate runs most of the old farms now as one big business.

'A lot of people in the village have come from elsewhere to retire. Some of them have been here twenty years. They like to think of themselves as Abbotsbury people,' he laughed kindly, 'but they're not. Not like us. We don't have many second homes. Too far from London or the cities.

'In some ways I suppose farming has lost its soul a bit. But I can still do a day's hedging and be proud of it. And I've never wanted to live anywhere else. There are times when I come down from the back road on a summer's evening, and I've got a spare five or ten minutes. Then I stop and look around. I get a lot of pleasure from that. As much pleasure as for an art connoisseur at an art gallery. There's always something different to see, whether it's the boats over towards Weymouth Bay or what's changing in the hedgerows.

'I wouldn't have had my life any other way.'

*

The butcher's in Abbotsbury sold me a pie for the day's walking. I'm a great believer in the power of the pie; in the Lake District I used to try to reach the summit of peaks with a pie still hot in my pocket from the Keswick shop.

I was taken aback, however, when I asked the farmer's wife running the shop which of the various pies she recommended.

'Oh, I couldn't say. I'm a vegetarian.'

How could a vegetarian run a butcher's shop? It was not a question I liked to ask outright, although I suppose eunuchs were always good at running harems.

If the lost abbey of Abbotsbury had been a geographical and historical landmark of the most familiar sort, given that

English schoolchildren were still force-fed 'Tudors and Stuarts' like geese for foie gras, then my next destination, at the top of the back road where David had his farming epiphanies, was exactly the kind of place I wanted to investigate. Set back inland from Abbotsbury, and a brisk walk up the coast path, was the Kingston Russell stone circle, a place so off the map that even Aubrey Burl didn't list it in his authoritative gazetteer, *Rings of Stone*.

In a corner of a farmer's field, the stones lay a little forlorn. There were seventeen of them, arranged in a careful, elliptical shape mirrored by other stone circles along the Atlantic coast. They had been there some 5,000 years.

The stones had all fallen over. English Heritage, who nominally administered the site, hadn't put up so much as a board to inform visitors what they were looking at. While I was there, three couples passed at intervals, heading for the coast path. They would not have noticed the circle if I hadn't pointed it out.

Yet the stones had a majesty, and much of that came from their position. The slight rise in the land meant that there was a clear sight line to the round hills of Beacon Knap and other similar knolls heading west along the coast. I was accustomed to the prehistoric love of mimicry, the circle reflecting the shape of the hills beyond.

Making a landscape yours, stamping ownership on the land by showing that you too can shape it, is a primal human instinct. The power of the sacred landscape, and in this case of the sea as well, can be refracted by a sense of placement, of concentration. There was a feeling at the stone circle of great deliberation – that this was precisely the right place for these stones.

Only a week or so before I had been in Peru, at one of my favourite sites: the White Rock, Chuquipalta, which lay in the heart of the Vilcabamba and was the title of my book on the Inca heartland. This huge granite boulder lies in a remote valley in the eastern Andes, a place likewise steeped in prehistory.

The rock had been sculpted by the Incas to give a similar concentration of place, of significance. Around it too were scattered other stones, although these were building blocks left by the Spaniards when they destroyed what they thought of as 'an idolatrous temple'. Many prehistoric sites in Britain had suffered the same fate or neglect – Avebury being a prime example – and not just because of Church disapproval; there has always been a perception, still current today, that British history begins properly only when the Romans lit the touchpaper and that anything prior is dull or inconsequential.

It is as if Peruvian history began only when the Spaniards arrived, for they, like the Romans, were the first to write anything down, the Incas being as illiterate as Iron Age Britons.

To walk along the high escarpment facing the sea, sometimes called the Dorset Ridgeway, was a reminder of the sheer depth of British prehistory. The Kingston Russell stone circle was an emblem of Neolithic Britain and the late Stone Age, with its megaliths and barrows. Further along the Ridgeway, I passed the burial tumuli of the succeeding Bronze Age, which lasted from 2500 BC to 800 BC and was a very different culture, a rich one that we were barely beginning to understand. And ahead of me lay Maiden Castle, the largest Iron Age hill-fort in Europe; an Iron Age that was far more problematic than the arrival of a new technology might suggest, lasting from 800 BC to the arrival of the Romans.

When I travelled in Peru, or Mexico, or the Himalaya, what interested me most was their prehistoric past, their Inca, Aztec or Buddhist inheritance, both because it was so different from the present, but also so formative; moreover new technology was allowing archaeologists to reveal far more about that past.

I wanted to follow the same line of pursuit in England, although there was a significant difference. In those countries, they revered their prehistory; here we patronised our earliest history by homogenising it. The Neolithic, Bronze and Iron Ages were all very distinct cultures; yet we think of them, if we think of them at all, as if they were one long and bad Ken Russell movie – a bunch of savages in woad, with a few Druids chanting. It always reminded me of the famous *New Yorker* cover cartoon by Saul Steinberg of the view from Manhattan's 9th Avenue, in which nearby streets get labelled but everything beyond the city boundaries and the Hudson is ludicrously foreshortened.

It could be said that the history of England – or the formation of England – should end in 1066, rather than beginning then. Everything since has been our present.

I admit to having at times shared this myopia. My problems with early English history were: that the subject was approached with mind-numbing academic boredom, made worse by long quotes in Anglo-Saxon and peer-language archaeology; or conversely that it was co-opted by New Age preachers who used it to sell me ley lines and a crystal through which to peer dimly at the Celtic twilight.

This journey, in good Buddhist spirit, would attempt the middle way. Recent revisionist work by archaeologists and historians showed that early English history was less straightforward and more interesting than popular preconception might suggest. I realised, though, that there was a little work to do to overcome the stumbling blocks that others might share with me.

My youngest son Leo had been appalled when I told him my plan. 'Exploring England!' he said. 'That sounds incredibly dull. We live here anyway. Why can't you do something like that writer friend of yours you made a film with, the one with the large stomach who lisps slightly – what's his name?'

'William Dalrymple.'

'Yes, like him. Why don't you do a book about somewhere mysterious, like India?' He had started to speak louder, as he does when he feels an eleven-year-old sales pitch coming on. 'You could call it – you could call it *Secrets of India*. Now that would really sell!'

✳

This Dorset coast was Thomas Hardy country – so much so that some of the locals were heartily sick of the man – but while people remember him for his fatalism and the harshness of the countryside life he described, they forget his interest in the prehistoric. *Tess of the d'Urbervilles* has a memorable scene set at Stonehenge, and Hardy found and erected a sarsen stone at his home, Max Gate. More remarkably still, he built the whole house within the late Neolithic enclosed circle of Flagstones.

All along the ridge from here to Maiden Castle, tumuli and barrows were scattered like confetti. They were easy to miss as the view out to sea was so fine: the thin strip of Chesil Beach extended out along the headland towards Weymouth, capturing the waters of the Fleet behind its defences; beyond rippled the Atlantic.

'The number, size and types of monuments in the area around Dorchester is only paralleled by the rich complexes at Stonehenge and Avebury,' had written Niall Sharples, the most recent investigator of Maiden Castle. There was a reason the 'archaeological record' was so good along the Dorset Ridge and had been preserved. Prehistoric man farmed here extensively; the light topsoil lying over the chalk was much easier to work than the heavy clay of the valleys below. But they over-farmed. The thin topsoil was depleted, meaning that some areas, particularly to the east of Dorset, are agricultural wastelands that have still not recovered, and others have reverted to pasture, preserving the barrows and monuments underneath: nothing disturbs the archaeological record more than a plough. There had even been a period in the early Bronze Age when the interior of Maiden Castle was cultivated, although likewise this soon exhausted the topsoil. Over-farming is not a modern invention.

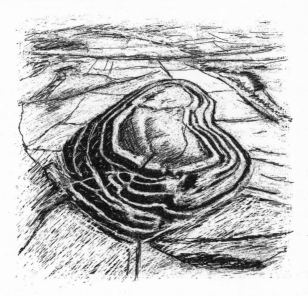

The hill-fort of Maiden Castle is as monumental as an aircraft carrier. Several aircraft carriers, in fact. It lies to the south-west of Dorchester, running over two connecting hilltops. By the time I arrived, the afternoon sun was marking deep ripples of shadow along the banks, bringing out both the shape and texture of the ridges. The houses of Dorchester in the distance looked placid and dull by comparison, like the sheep in the intervening field.

Hardy described it well, as 'an enormous many limbed organism of an antediluvian time, lying lifeless and covered with a thin green cloth, which hides its substance while revealing its contour'.

It is not the top of Maiden Castle that is remarkable – once you're up there it feels just like an empty plateau, and a large one of some forty-seven acres – but the giant ramparts and ditches that flow in sinuous folds around the hill for almost exactly a mile.

'Hill-fort' is really a misnomer, although academics continue to use it as a convenient term. Archaeologists now think these enclosed places were used for a whole variety of purposes – as settlements, as granary stores, as displays of power, as places of spiritual significance. Local farming communities could have gathered there for a whole variety of reasons, of which defence was only one.

The over-elaborate ditches of Maiden Castle may have been as much for ostentation as military use. I was fascinated by Niall Sharples' suggestion that limestone had been brought from some distance to face one of the entrances, rather than using more local stone; this was an idea I was familiar with from Peru, a way of deliberately harnessing the power of a different part of the landscape to your own. It is something to which archaeologists have only recently become attuned. When the great mass of man-made Silbury Hill was first excavated, no one thought to question where the infill had come from; it was just assumed to be local. Only now has it been shown that gravel and sarsens were fetched from some considerable distance for no functional reason – but almost certainly a symbolic one.

By the end of the Iron Age, Maiden Castle was the largest hill-fort in England, a reminder of a time when Dorset was the crucial point of entry from the Mediterranean and southern Europe. Wine, precious stones and other goods from as far as Egypt arrived all along the coast here, from Hengistbury Head to Seaton; they might have been exchanged for bracelets made from the polished black Kimmeridge shale, sourced locally at Purbeck, or whetstones and querns from Devon, or slaves.

The Icknield Way serviced the trade by providing a route inland and over to a principal access point from northern Europe, the Norfolk coast. London was bypassed and became important only with the arrival of the Romans; Dorset's importance fell away and it turned into a relative backwater in the nation's affairs – one of the few counties, as locals like either to complain or boast, without a motorway. Just a few years after the Roman invasion, even the local coinage was devalued.

It is easy to forget how excited archaeologists were in the 1920s and 1930s when they started to excavate these Iron Age hill-forts. There is a fine photograph of Sir Mortimer Wheeler from the time, wearing his characteristic plus fours and tilted trilby. A small gathering of society observers has formed behind him as he stands proprietorially on his excavated site; a woman wears a flapper hat, with her coat rakishly askew.

Sporadic work on Maiden Castle had been done before, but Wheeler's excavation between 1934 and 1937 was the first large-scale investigation of the interior of a hill-fort. Such was his dashing appeal that he was able to fund the project with donations from the public, and he set off a veritable 'iron rush' among fellow archaeologists. By 1940, some eighty other hill-forts around the country had been excavated.

The tale that Wheeler told captured the popular imagination. His excavations uncovered the bodies of fourteen people who had died violently. There was a layer of charcoal, and signs of Roman occupation. Wheeler put all this together and suggested that Iron Age defenders of the fort had died when the Roman general Vespasian, who later became emperor, defeated the Durotriges tribe; the Romans then burned their fortress.

As archaeological stories go, it was perfect. Heroic British defenders, a historical name that could be attached (the Emperor Vespasian had star value), and a clear conclusion to the story: a burning.

It was also wrong. More recent excavations conducted by Niall Sharples in the 1980s, with the benefit of radiocarbon dating, show that the layer of ash was left from earlier production of iron on the site. Far from burning Maiden Castle, the Romans used it as their own fort for some time. Bodies may have been buried there, but did not necessarily die there.

However, for fifty years Wheeler's theory was accepted as pioneering and bold archaeology. The novelist John Cowper Powys was living in Dorchester at the time of the excavation.

He had already drawn on the interplay between landscape and the history of ideas for *A Glastonbury Romance*. Wheeler's excavations unfolding at nearby Maiden Castle were a gift and Powys produced a novel of that name, wanting it to be 'a rival to *The Mayor of Casterbridge*'.

No one would pretend that *Maiden Castle* is an easy read. Critics like George Steiner and Margaret Drabble ('He is so far outside the canon that he defies the concept of a canon') have championed Powys as one of the great lost figures of twentieth-century literature. Yet his monolithic Wessex novels — *Weymouth Sands* along with *A Glastonbury Romance* and *Maiden Castle* — now stand like desolate tors, ignored and unvisited.

Perhaps it is because the books are so rooted in place, as the titles suggest. Landscape for Powys had a brooding, psychic force that the modern reader can find oppressive. We like our history to be weightless and free; our towns connected by open roads. The postmodern novel delights in being fictive and elusive; the travel book as a glove-compartment guide that can move the reader at speed between counties, countries and continents. Our writers 'divide their time' between New York and Delhi; Hollywood and London; the South of France and Harvard — let alone cyberspace.

Not so Powys. Landscape is held over his characters like a hammer over an anvil. No one seems able to leave. Maiden Castle is a brooding presence in the novel it dominates. As the breathless blurb declared on its cover, 'even as the characters in Dorchester struggle with the perplexities of love, desire, and faith, it is the looming fortress of Maiden Castle that exerts the otherworldly force that irrevocably determines the course of their lives.' When Powys died, his ashes were scattered on Chesil Beach.

There was a brief vogue for his books in the 1970s, after his death, when Picador published the novels in paperback and he was part of the post-hippie 'cult of Avalon'; although Powys would have hated the association and in his earlier and best-known novel, *A Glastonbury Romance*, lampooned any attempt to commodify the Grail legend.

I was then at school. An inspirational teacher, Christopher Dixon, persuaded me to read Powys and not just the Wessex novels. I tried *Porius*, a late work of such dense historical confusion that even his warmest admirers have hesitated to cut through its hedge of thorns. The book is set in Wales in AD 500 with Druids, giants, Merlin, a Pelagian monk and various characters who have forgotten to go back to Rome with the legionaries. Margaret Drabble commented that 'the reader may wander for years in this parallel universe, entrapped and bewitched, and never reach its end'. Powys never reread or edited any of the novels. It shows.

But if the plots wander, some of the set pieces and detail within each novel are extraordinary. For *Maiden Castle*, Powys's diaries show that he attended a lecture by Mortimer Wheeler in 1935, having toured the site earlier that same day. In the novel's climactic scene, the hero, Dud No-Man, walks up to the castle with a character called Uryen (Powys had a fondness for baroque names), who, he discovers during the walk, is actually his father.

The shock of this revelation means that he looks at Maiden Castle – or rather, 'this Titanic erection of the demented mould-warp man' – with an intensity of response one could only find in a John Cowper Powys novel:

Dud stared in fascinated awe at the great Earth monument.

From this halfway distance it took all sorts of strange forms to his shameless mind. It took the shape of a huge 'dropping' of supermammoth dung.

It took the shape of an enormous seaweed-crusted shell, the shell of the fish called Kraken, whom some dim notion of monstrous mate-lust had drawn up from the primeval slime of its seabed.

It took the shape of that vast planetary Tortoise, upon whose curved back, sealed with the convoluted inscriptions of the nameless Tao, rested the pillar of creation.

But above all as he surveyed that dark-green bulk rising at the end of the long, narrow road, he was compelled to think of the mysterious nest of some gigantic Jurassic-age bird-dragon, such as, in this May sunshine, he could imagine even now hatching its portentous egg.

Looking at it in equally strong spring sunshine, I felt my own imagination distinctly underpowered by comparison. If anything, I reacted against the tendency of writers and artists to regard Maiden Castle as a strange, inexplicable phenomenon, or Wheeler's similar attempt to give it a human narrative. For me, the hill-fort was remarkable enough for a far simpler reason: that an Iron Age tribe should have invested so many patient man-hours in building such elaborate earthworks, and that they had the considerable resources needed to do so. It was a statement of confidence.

There was something else that struck me. Maiden Castle is remarkable for the complexity of its entrance: the ditches weave backwards and forwards, almost like a maze, before you can gain access. It may not have exclusively been a fort, but the Iron Age when it was built, the first millennium BC, was certainly a time of conflict. The Celtic influence that had come to Britain from the continent with the new technology of iron created far more pressure for existing resources and, almost certainly, divisions and territorial claims. Maiden Castle was a Celtic status symbol, to which you could only gain access if you were allowed.

The idea of the Celts is at best a complicated construct, hedged round by all sorts of romantic and nationalistic longing. They are sometimes thought of as the indigenous people who were pushed out to the margins by waves of later invaders – Romans, then Anglo-Saxons, then Vikings – but kept the flame of true Britishness burning in Cornwall, in Wales and in the Gaelic lands. This ignores the fact that they were themselves Iron Age invaders who partially disrupted what appears to have been a peaceable Bronze Age society – and also ignores the process of gradual assimilation rather than invasion that at times took place. We have always been a polyglot society. And the idea of 'the original Britons', the Celts, is as dangerous and delusive a myth as any.

✳

The walk from Maiden Castle to Dorchester was odd. You left the ramparts of a prehistoric fort to cross the modern equivalent, a town's ring-road.

As I reached the centre of town, I was struck by the tawdriness of what had once been Hardy's Casterbridge, with its South Street a pedestrian mess of ugly fascias and badly fitting pavements. At least a street market brought a flicker of energy. Stalls were selling bric-a-brac from around the world – cheap scarves, leather hats, earrings, 'charms', glass beads, silver chains, hematite, lockets, amethyst, lapis and above all silver – not so different from traders who had landed on the Dorset coast with their Egyptian faience beads or prestige Beaker pots.

An Iron Age traveller would have enjoyed – and needed – the nearby Body Shop with its unguents, lotions and aloe vera deodorant. The busker outside, with a lurcher dog and a flute, was playing Paul McCartney's 'Mull of Kintyre'. I gave him some change, on the condition that he chose another song.

But worse lay ahead. My route lay through Poundbury, the Prince of Wales's controversial new model urban estate on the edge of Dorchester. I had hoped that this might prove counter-intuitive; that despite or because of the outcry from all those modernist architects whose noses the Prince had put out of joint – 'carbuncled' – this might be a defiantly different experience. A place that ran to its own, more organic rhythm.

The reality was very different. It looked like the village in *Shrek*. The open loggia of the Town Hall with its mock medieval wooden gate was bad enough – but just opposite was a house with a ludicrous Chippendale front. Giant urns had been placed on the roofs of buildings as if they were empty mantelpieces that needed filling. The townhouses ressembled ornamental carriage clocks. In the square that was supposed to be at the heart of this new, more human town planning stood a fountain, topped by a mermaid wearing fishscale stockings that looked suspiciously as if they might have come from the Ann Summers shop. Across the empty square from the fountain was an empty café.

The tragedy was not just that of a wasted opportunity – and chance to jolt complacent modernist architects out of their normal glass-and-buttress conformity. The tumulus of Poundbury's own Iron Age fort had been obscured in the process.

Poundbury Hill-Fort lies north of Maiden Castle and is substantial in its own right. John Cowper Powys described a memorable scene here in his diary when he attended a jubilee bonfire in the 1930s:

We did enjoy the fireworks and the enormous bonfire. It became a personality – this great fire – as it whirled and swept and curved up . . . And the fireworks were striking but the best thing was to see the crowds silhouetted against the sky. They might have been the old Neolithics under the crescent moon.

It was ironic that the Prince of Wales, who had so often and rightly lamented the hemming in of St Paul's Cathedral by the horrors of Paternoster Square, should have ignored the Iron Age monument on his doorstep when designing Poundbury.

*

The passing of so many cattle and men over the years has hollowed out the lane to a remarkable degree. It looks like a bobsleigh run as it shoots away from me down the hill, its banks covered with hart's tongue ferns, sloes, brambles and a wet greenness that glows in the shadows.

I've reached one of Dorset's wildest and empty stretches – the Dorsetshire Gap, where a number of old drovers' roads meet in a valley that allows access through from the north of the county to the south and the sea. The only nearby house at Folly was once an old drovers' pub, the Fox, although it is now in private hands.

It seems an empty stretch of countryside, but look closely and it glows with the tracings of the time when this was a thoroughfare. There is an old Roman fort up above on a plateau called Nettlecombe Tout, although no footpath leads there and it has never been excavated. The drovers' road drops down from the Dorsetshire Gap to the ghost medieval village of Higher Melcombe, whose buildings can be traced as faint outlines on the farmland. At the farmhouse there is an old chapel which is disused but still has its stained-glass windows in place. Beyond lie the ruins of the Benedictine abbey at Milton Abbas.

Close as well to the Gap, there are many Bronze Age cross-dykes built to divide the land into plots – particularly around Lyscombe Bottom, a valley or coomb scooped out of the ground so that the surrounding ridge encircles it, a place that must have been pleasingly obvious as a settlement centre for prehistoric man as the valley was naturally protected.

The land is still protected, but now as a wildlife reserve and well-managed farm. On this spring morning the meadows are covered in early gentians and fragrant orchids, although it is too early for the Adonis Blue, which has always fascinated me because of the unusual courtship ritual that gives this chalkland butterfly its name. The silvery male of the species flies coquettishly along; the drab brown female gives chase and tries to catch it.

When Daniel Defoe made his tour of England, he was much taken by the quality of the local Dorset pasture and the sheep it fed; so much so that he returned several times in his narrative to the 'fine carpet ground, soft as velvet, and the herbage, sweet as garden herbs, which makes their sheep be the best in England, if not in the world, and their wool fine to an extream'.

It was the same pastureland that drew prehistoric man to the area, and right through to the twentieth century, Dorset sheep, together with cattle, were taken along the Icknield Way to distribution points like Banbury Fair in Oxfordshire, where, Defoe reported, the sheep had such a reputation that butchers came from all over the country to source them.

This is grass that has been fine-cropped by sheep for millennia, which is why it is such a beautiful green sward now. Well-managed sheep farming can create a hillside like a lawn as those sharp teeth nibble neatly down.

Another traveller this way, the naturalist W H Hudson, noted how the local plants had adapted by growing as low as possible to avoid the attentions of the sheep. I was a great admirer of Hudson and had visited the house where he was born in Argentina, overshadowed by an enormous *ombu* tree: a strange tree which is more like a giant shrub and needs to have its branches supported on crutches across the ground, so that it resembles a giant spider. He brought to his studies of England, in particular *A Shepherd's Life* about these Dorset and Wiltshire Downs, a sense that England was just as strange and exotic as the pampas; also a sense of how short rural memories are. He told an odd story of how a farmer puzzled over finding a disused well full of sheep heads with horns, when none of the local breeds were horned; and how Hudson had to tell him about the old Wiltshire breed of sheep, with horns, which had died out only a generation or so before.

I see not a single walker through this stretch of Dorset, even though parts of it are waymarked 'the Dorset Ridgeway'. There are so many long-distance paths now across the country that they have become devalued. The only way of knowing that others have passed this way is a thoughtful tin that someone has left at the crossing point of the Dorsetshire Gap; inside is a notebook wrapped in a bag, in which passers-by have left comments over the years. These tend to the inconsequential, 'a charming place', or the paradoxical, 'just sorry that we are disturbing the stillness and solitude by being here ourselves'; but there is an attraction in this slow accumulation of comment, like a cairn to which every traveller has added a stone.

We think of southern England as being overpopulated. In the fine photos NASA has taken of the Earth from space at night, we are one of the brightest spots on the planet as we burn our office and home candles at both ends. Yet there are still wonderful lacunae of emptiness such as this. A lesson I learned long ago in South America is that however much people think of an area as being known and explored, they are invariably talking about the principal points of a map – the rivers, mountaintops, settlements. There are always 'the places in between', as Rory Stewart called his study of rural Afghanistan, that we rarely visit.

*

At this point the more curious reader might ask where I'm spending the night. It would be good to report that I unrolled the mat from my knapsack and stretched out under the Dorset stars. I do have a mat and tent with me — and there will be times when I do just that, or face an additional ten-mile walk to some overpriced bed-and-breakfast with doilies on the washstand.

But by great good fortune I have friends living near by who can put me up. Even better, they are believers in the good life and have a well-stocked cellar and a hot tub they've built on the garden hilltop above the house so they can take in the sunset while sipping a New Zealand Sauvignon Blanc and wondering which red wine to drink over dinner.

There are times when it is wonderful and austere and bracing to sleep under the stars. That time will come. For now, a pleasant bed, good wine and the prospect of a cooked breakfast send me to sleep very happily.

But not before a confession. I've taken many expeditions to the Andes, sometimes with people I didn't know that well beforehand, if at all. There may come a moment when, after a few days, you find yourself alone together at the campfire or by the roadside, and they turn with a 'There's something I've got to tell you.'

In a relationship, those words would be the blue screen of death. From someone you've known for a couple of days, it's just something they are nervous about hitting you with on Day One. That they are insulin-dependent, bad at altitude, a recovering alcoholic, or once voted for Richard Nixon.

There's a moment that is just right for such an admission — some days into a journey, but before you've gone too far and it's absurd that you didn't know earlier. So at this point I need to look the reader in the eye and draw a little closer. You see, there is a reason we're doing this whole journey on foot, and not necessarily the one you thought it was. It's not just the lyrical intensity of a walking experience, although I can have my own occasional epiphanies. It's because I have to. Not to put too fine a point on it (and here I would lean a little closer, and perhaps touch your arm), the thing is, Reader, I have just lost my driving licence.

This may not come as a complete surprise to those who sat with me in the passenger seat through *Tequila Oil: Getting Lost in Mexico*. But it certainly came as a surprise to me. One moment I had a spotless driving record of twenty-five years without a single point. The next they were coming at me like Space Invaders.

I was not alone. Speed cameras at the entrances to villages were tripping up the most sober and upright of countryside citizens. I knew of at least three worthies — a county councillor, a captain of industry and the owner of a large local estate — whose Range Rovers were on nine points and hanging over the cliff edge, like *The Italian Job*. Some people had got wives or penniless students to take their points for them; or hired expensive solicitors to get them off on technicalities.

I faced up to the magistrates, feeling a little like Toad when he was sentenced to jail for motor offences and the Clerk 'rounded up the sentence' to twenty years to make it neater.

'To my mind,' observed the Chairman of the Bench of Magistrates cheerfully, 'the ONLY difficulty that presents itself in this otherwise very clear case is, how we can possibly make it sufficiently hot for the incorrigible rogue and hardened ruffian whom we see cowering in the dock before us.'

(*The Wind in the Willows*)

Although in my case it was a Chairwoman of the Bench, with one of those low, soft voices ('Mr Thomson, would you mind telling us how you came to be travelling at 34 mph in a 30-mile zone') that meant trouble. Her two male colleagues looked as if they had just lunched at the Rotary or golf club, and were contemplating a post-prandial liqueur to celebrate the sentence they were about to dish out. The courtroom could have been designed by Terry Gilliam, with a vast height and expanse rearing up above the dock to the magistrates sitting in the gods above and looking down. They may all have come on from a session of housebreaking and were in hanging-judge mood. Between them, they tried to give me a suspension of one year. 'One year' echoed out above my head like a voice of doom. The Clerk had to remind the court that: my points were all for small 'trip-wire' offences; the maximum suspension was six months anyway.

Even with this reprieve, my car was languishing at home.

Although the need to walk everywhere had proved salutary: it had been a reminder of how shoddy public transport services were in the country, where buses ran to some villages only when there was an 'r' in the month; and like slow cooking, there was nothing like being on foot for getting the true taste of a journey.

*

'You work all day and half the night and where does it get you?'

Mike had sharp blue-grey eyes and a farmer's way of holding your gaze while he spoke. I met him when I passed a sign for eggs at the end of a lane, and fancied boiling some up for the journey; at the other end of the lane were Mike and his open-sided barn, where he kept a dozen or so young calves and a few chickens. It was not so much a farm as a smallholding and Mike lived in nearby Sherborne now but, as he tells me, once he had far more.

It was a sad story, although it started off well. Mike had been born in the country to a family of modest means. He left school at sixteen and married young. For many years he made ends meet through a variety of jobs, from working on the dustcarts to helping a farmer in the local village, Poyntington.

The farmer was elderly and came to depend on his younger labourer for help. He had no children himself. When he died, he left Mike the farm, much to the anger of the farmer's nephew and family, who were cut out of the will. They tried to sue Mike, but he survived this. Slowly, he built up the stock of cattle to some 100 head.

Very few farm labourers ever end up owning a farm. Social mobility is still painfully slow, and land prices high; banks will rarely lend substantial amounts to a labourer.

Mike's particular skill was bringing on young cattle. He would buy them at just a few weeks old, for only £30–£40, then grow the calves on and sell them at five times the amount when they reached six months.

For more than ten years he worked 'all the hours God gave me' to build up his herd. But then came disaster. His marriage of thirty-seven years collapsed. As part of the divorce settlement he had to sell the farm. At fifty-six, all he was left with now was six acres of land and a few cattle; he needed to lay hedges for other farmers to earn a living.

I asked him if he felt at all bitter.

'If I'd lost the lot, then I really would be sick. But at least I've still got this bit of land.'

When he hears that I'm walking from Dorset to Norfolk, he insists on giving me half a dozen eggs for free. As in South America, the people who are most generous to travellers are always those who have the least to give.

*

That afternoon saw me reaching the windswept ridge of Corton Hill. Looking behind me I could see the passes around the Dorsetshire Gap leading back to Dorset and the coast. When I reached the end of the ridge, I looked ahead and there, as if arising like an island from the plain, was Cadbury Castle, the closest we have to Camelot, the centre of Arthurian legend and tradition. Even respected archaeologists like Leslie Alcock had endorsed Cadbury Castle as Arthurian.

I had been well set up to this moment with a Bloody Mary of savage and potent force from the Queens Arms in Corton Denham, the village just before this hill. The barman made it for me with chilli vodka, grated raw horseradish and an additional kick of sherry. One advantage of losing your driving licence was that there were no longer any worries about drinking at lunchtime. Together with their excellent home-made pork pie, I now felt I could fly over the valley to Cadbury Castle, or at the very least imagine a knight leading his horse, damsel and page across in a troupe.

But I should at once declare my position on all matters Arthurian. I would be bitterly disappointed if it was ever proved

– which looks unlikely – that there was a historical Arthur. One of the great triumphs of the English literary imagination is that the cathedral of prose which is the Arthurian cycle was built up over centuries on empty ground.

Even so, on arriving at Cadbury Castle I could see why such sober heads as Leslie Alcock, who had excavated here in the 1960s, should have succumbed to its charm: the ring of trees around the banked hill; the approach up through them along a hollow way; the emergence onto a plateau commanding views across to the Somerset Levels and Glastonbury. Moreover it was close to the River Cam, and had the villages of West Camel and Queen Camel just to the west, so encouraging the identification with 'Camelot'.

When Alcock excavated here, he established that the hill-fort was built in the Bronze Age, with later Iron Age usage, and that it was substantially enlarged and occupied just after the Roman withdrawal from Britain in the fifth century – much more so than other comparable hill-forts. The fifth century was precisely when Arthur was supposed to have emerged to lead the British against the Anglo-Saxons.

With great good luck, Alcock discovered a 'Great Hall' from this period, measuring some sixty-five feet long; good luck, in that his team of archaeologists allowed themselves only a relatively small part of the plateau to excavate, so to find anything was providential. Perhaps it was this that tipped Alcock over the edge into making the identification with King Arthur, which brought Cadbury Castle to worldwide attention at a time, the late 1960s, when a generation were searching for a lost and future king. It cost him a great deal of respect from his peers, who questioned the historicity of Arthur. There are no contemporary accounts of his reign and the first chronicle describing his deeds dates from 600 years later – but then, argued Alcock, there are hardly any fifth-century contemporary accounts of anything in the first place.

The power of the Arthurian myth is intense, and I can see how archaeologists could succumb to that sheer power, like those who open burial chambers with toxic fumes.

After Geoffrey of Monmouth created the story in the twelfth century (although he may have used sources that have since been lost), the tale grew in the telling over the following centuries as it was passed between the English and the French. With their perennial fascination for adultery, the French elaborated the story of Lancelot and Guinevere, and stressed the romance of the tales; the British built up the patriotic and nation-building elements – 'the Matter of Britain', as the epic became known.

As with *Star Wars*, in order to expand the cycle new writers had to keep creating prequels. The finale to the story – the death of Arthur at the hands of Mordred, and the disintegration of the Round Table – was one of the first elements in its telling. Only by going further back could they create new material, spinning out fresh adventures for different knights, embroidering the Grail Quest and delving earlier into Arthur's boyhood – a process that has continued right up to the present, with T H White's influential *The Sword in the Stone*. In the BBC's recent *Merlin* series, even the wizard is imagined as a young boy, which really does put the story into reverse. Next we can expect *Merlin's Mother*.

But over the thousand years in which the story has been retold and expanded, one account stands out with diamond clarity. Sir Thomas Malory's *Le Morte d'Arthur* combines a journalistic matter-of-factness in his retelling of events – one lecturer of mine at Cambridge observed that you can read the accounts of jousts like cricket fixtures and see certain knights advancing slowly up the 'prowess-ranking' – with an underlying elegy for the passing of an age.

Malory had notoriously seen the rougher side of life. He was imprisoned numerous times, on charges that included theft, rape and attempted murder. Attempts have been made to rehabilitate his reputation and show that many of these charges may have been politically motivated – that, for instance, it was a jealous husband who accused Malory of rape when Malory absconded with his wife; but the authorial tone is not that of someone who has led a cloistered existence. When his knights fight, it has all the gritty exhaustion and confusion of a bar brawl that starts up all over again just when everyone thinks the protagonists have calmed down.

He wrote it during the Wars of the Roses, in which he played a part. Those self-destructive and brutal wars circle under Malory's disintegrating Round Table. The age of the lance and halberd was giving way to that of gunpowder and the arquebus. Edward IV could give a chivalrous speech and then massacre his Lancastrian opponents sheltering inside Tewkesbury Abbey.

Malory divided his original manuscript for *Le Morte d'Arthur* into eight books, most of which are very familiar to us: the tales of Arthur and Merlin, of Lancelot and Guinevere, of Tristan (which he tells at Wagnerian length) and of the Holy Grail. His great achievement was to take this disparate set of stories and unify them into one overarching narrative, adding link passages, which are called 'explicits'.

The book that I've always liked most is the least familiar – that of 'Sir Gareth of Orkney'. It is the sole book for which there is no obvious source. Critics have suggested the source is lost, but I like to think that this was the one part of the story Malory made up.

The plainness of the tale is characteristic of him. He is not drawn to the flowery romance of Lancelot and Guinevere – he underplays their adultery as much as possible – or the more abstract theological points of the Grail legend. What Malory likes is grittiness of character and, in characteristic English style, a good story about class difference. 'Gareth of Orkney' could be a Mike Leigh film. He is the only one of Arthur's knights whose name you can still find in a playground today:

calling a child Galahad, Percival, Lancelot or Gawain would mark them for life.

Gareth arrives at King Arthur's court incognito, a big, raw-boned lad of great strength; *'large and longe and brode in the shoulders'*. For reasons that are unclear, he does not announce himself as a prince of royal blood; but he is in truth the son of King Lot of the Orkneys and the much younger brother of Sir Gawain, who has been away from home so long chasing damsels and dragons that he fails to recognise his own brother.

Gareth asks that King Arthur grant him a boon. Arthur, who always falls for such open-ended requests, agrees, but is disappointed when all that Gareth asks is that he be given food and drink for a year. The disagreeable High Steward Kay points out that Gareth could have asked for horse and armour and become a knight, and that this proves he's a *'vylane born'*, just a peasant. Kay nicknames Gareth *'Beaumains'* ('Fair Hands') – more malicious for being in French – because he looks as if he's never done any manual labour, and sends him to the kitchen as a galley boy.

After a year in which Gareth is fattened up *'like a porke hog'*, a damsel arrives with the customary tale of woe and need. Lancelot, who can spot a prince dressed as a frog, knights Gareth and he is sent off to help the damsel – who is none too pleased. She had expected a more upmarket, Premiership knight. The names of Tristan, Gawain and Lancelot himself are mentioned.

The damsel's name is Lynette and she would undoubtedly be played by Alison Steadman. As Gareth makes his way across country to help rescue her besieged sister, Lynette gives a non-stop commentary on how Gareth 'smells like a kitchen boy' and is 'nothing but a ladle-washer'. Even the various knights Gareth defeats she describes as easy pickings: 'That first knight you killed – his horse just stumbled; and as for the second knight, you came up behind him!'

The effect is to make Gareth fight even harder. With the true masochism of an Englishman, it is her scolding that drives him:

the chivalric code forbids talking back to a lady, so he can only become yet more violent in his fighting.

Although Malory is likewise gentlemanly about this, it's clear that bossy Lynette is not much of a looker; but her sister Lyonesse, who needs rescuing, turns out to be a stunner when she unwimples her visage – or, as Gareth puts it, '*the fayryst lady that ever I lokyd upon*'.

Gareth launches a frenzied assault upon her captor, the Red Knight, that lasts an entire day.

At first light the opponents joust, but both fall to the ground, stunned. They engage again on foot, buffeting each other around the head with their swords, leaving pieces of shield and harness strewn around them. This goes on for some hours, until they are winded and stand there swaying, '*stagerynge, pantynge, blowynge and bledying*'. Gareth and the Red Knight run at each other again like boars, clashing heads and '*grovelynge*' to the earth. They are so stupefied by the struggle that, Malory reports, they pick up each other's swords by accident. Come the evening and most of their armour has fallen away, leaving them half naked.

And then occurs one of those moments of genius that Malory's deceptively simple prose style allows him to slip into his narrative. The two men agree to rest and find two molehills to sit on '*besydes the fyghtynge place*'. They unlace each other's helmets and literally have a breather. They '*take the cold wynde*'.

The armistice pause is broken when Gareth glimpses Lyonesse at the window and remembers what he's there for. Egged on by sister Lynette – 'Where's your courage, man!' – Gareth rips off his adversary's helmet, about to kill him, when the Red Knight manages a long, exculpatory monologue. He explains that he is avenging some damsel whose brother was killed by Lancelot or Gawain, although he's not sure which. It's a lame story; nevertheless, given that a woman is behind it all, Gareth feels he has to stay his hand.

So Gareth gets the girl. Even here, Malory can't resist throwing in some bedroom farce. The young lovers arrange to meet at night '*to abate their lustys secretly*'. Because they are young and inexperienced in such matters, notes the older and wiser Malory, the plan doesn't stay secret. When Lyonesse arrives at Gareth's bed wearing nothing but a coat lined with ermine – about as hot an image as the fifteenth century could manage – her jealous sister Lynette sends a knight with an axe to stop them.

Although the bold Gareth sounds more like a Monty Python character at times, Malory weaves him into the fabric of the tale so that his death unpicks the whole great tapestry. When Lancelot accidentally kills Gareth later, Gawain's revenge for his brother's death precipitates the collapse of the Round Table. Gareth is the very human and English keystone that Malory adds to his great narrative arch.

As I left Cadbury Castle and made my way across to the landmark of Alfred's Tower at Stourhead, which marked the ascent of the Icknield Way to Salisbury Plain, it was hard not to think of this Somerset country as a castellated plain. Many of the hills were surmounted by an Iron Age fort or earthworks – or in the case of the most dramatic of all, Glastonbury Tor, which I could see behind me, by a tower rearing up foursquare.

Unlike Leslie Alcock and the historians, I had no need to worry about the truth of Arthur's existence; but I had an absolute belief in the truth of the Arthurian story as story – that it satisfied a very English need for stoicism in the face of adversity, for a lost Golden Age, and illustrated a perennial truth: that rather than face a damsel with a sharp tongue, most Englishmen would fight an army, or a dragon, or go on a quest to the other side of the world.

*

From Cadbury Castle I was following the old drovers' road east, directly towards the rising sun on Salisbury Plain. There were times when the old lane had been superseded by modern roads;

but a surprising amount of the Icknield Way, or this loop of it, was still traceable. It gave me pleasure to rejoin a grassy lane, the sort that one would hardly notice out of the corner of an eye if driving, yet once resurrected as part of a greater road had real resonance. The Long Lane, as it is sometimes called in this part of Somerset, glowed green for me: 'the Long Lane' because it led on to the North Sea.

It was impossible anyway to get too lost over the next ten miles as ahead lay the landmark of Alfred's Tower on Kingsettle Hill. This three-sided folly rose up like a giant triangulation point. It was erected as a supremely self-confident monument by the eighteenth-century banker, Henry Hoare, for his Stourhead estate. The tower commemorated the historical likelihood that here in 878 King Alfred raised his banner to summon his troops for one last stand against the Vikings, who had penetrated this far into Wessex.

The tower stands 160 feet in height and dominates the surrounding landscape; it 'commands Somersetshire nearly as far as the curvature of the earth allows', wrote Edward

Thomas. Much of its triumphalism can be understood if one remembers that the tower was built when George III had just ascended the throne – a king with a background as equally Germanic as Saxon Alfred – and that Britain had recently defeated those other Scandinavians, the Swedish, in the Seven Years War.

The myths about Alfred were as complex as the ones about Arthur and the bold statement over the Tower's entrance was one I would untangle as I journeyed further into the Berkshire Downs ahead:

> Alfred the Great
> AD 879, on this summit
> Erected his Standard
> Against Danish Invaders.
> To him we owe the origin of Juries;
> The establishment of a Militia;
> The creation of a Naval Force: –
> Alfred, the light of a benighted age,
> was a philosopher and a Christian;
> the Father of his people,
> The Founder of the English
> Monarchy and Liberty.

Certainly Alfred managed to rally the English for a final push back against the Vikings, and having walked here, I could see why this was a supremely good place for him to have done so. His subjects in the burghs to the west of Salisbury Plain would all have known how to reach this spot along those same drovers' paths I had followed. There would, too, have been a sense that the Vikings had reached the inner keep of Wessex; if the Saxons could not hold the drawbridge into Somerset, where, in the celebrated story, Alfred had hidden when on the run as a failed baker, then it was all over. They would get no support from Celtic Cornwall.

Some have suggested that if this was indeed Arthurian country – or already associated with him – then there could have been no more symbolic place for Alfred to raise his standard. But they forget that Arthur was a symbol of the Romano-British who had originally resisted the Saxons, so may not have been the best role model for Alfred. Come to that, Arthur may not yet have been invented.

The tower was not quite as monumental and unchanged as it looked. An American plane – ironically, a de Havilland Norseman – had flown into one of the tower's turrets in 1944, killing all the crew, when low fog had crept up from the Somerset marshes and hidden the tower. It had taken forty years to repair the damage.

But my thoughts on climbing the 200 steps of the tower were not of Alfred, nor of plane crashes. Because I had come here before, with my wife and children, when I was still married.

It had been for a picnic, on a convenient day's excursion from Bristol. What concerned me, as I climbed the steps again, with a diamond lattice of light illuminating each sweep of the spiral staircase as it passed a narrow window, was that I could remember almost nothing about that first visit. This had been some five or six years earlier – I could not be certain exactly – but not that long ago. And yet other than the bald fact that we had all climbed the tower, the experience had been wiped clean from my memory.

You can sometimes get that same feeling looking at an old photo album. Why am I smiling in the picture when I can't even remember the day, the hour, the occasion? In this case exacerbated by a subsequent separation and divorce.

It wasn't that the last time I climbed the tower I had been with three children running around me; it was that I couldn't remember what they had done. What we had all done. Was someone told off for going too close to the edge at the top? Undoubtedly. Or for running back down again?

This had, admittedly, been part of a larger outing. We had visited the main Stourhead estate as well. But it gave a certain melancholy to the view as I gazed back at Glastonbury Tor and Cadbury Castle in the distance. How the past can get wiped so clean. And an empty tower with a spiral staircase was a powerful receptacle for the loss of memory.

*

The next day, I was cheered by the discovery that there was a pub directly on my route up onto Salisbury Plain, despite the isolated country. The Red Lion was an old drovers' inn. The name was a giveaway: it indicates a pub of great antiquity; the red lion was an emblem on John of Gaunt's fourteenth-century coat of arms. I was to pass many more Red Lions in my journey along the Icknield Way.

Even better, there was a quite superb stretch of the Long Lane leading there, grassed over and hedged by hazelnut.

'Yes, it's Roman,' the pub landlord told me. 'There's more Roman stuff up on the hills above.' I didn't like to tell him that both the road and the remains on White Sheet Hill were thousands of years older than the Romans; I was used to the assumption that anything old must be Roman.

And there were more important matters to discuss: no less than five pies to choose from, heaven for a pie fancier. I asked the landlord for his thoughts. 'They're all good, but the lamb and leek smells the best,' he told me. It was an eccentric recommendation and all the better for it.

The landlord had a beard, the sure sign of a fanatic of some sort. Most publicans with beards I've encountered over the years have been obsessed by CAMRA, or a particular football team, or kept unfeasibly large dogs on the premises. But this one was subtler and more unconventional. He darted around the tables as his customers ate their assorted pies, more like a maître d' at a good restaurant, checking that his charges were enjoying themselves.

Sometimes his small talk ran a little off-key. With one couple, he complimented the woman on the very short skirt that she was wearing. A conversation ensued as to whether the skirt would or would not be suitable for work. When the woman got embarrassed and the conversation dried, the landlord quickly added, 'But of course I really like your top as well.'

Fortified by my pie, I set off up White Sheet Hill, my entrance to the heights of Cranborne Chase and Salisbury Plain. At the bottom of the hill was a curious set of artificial mounds which the Normans had constructed to encourage rabbits, a good cash crop. Weaving its way around them, the chalk path took me onto the hill. A south-westerly wind had got up and White Sheet Hill was not a hospitable place, but I saw a lone figure standing on top of what even at a distance was clearly a Bronze Age barrow. He had various boxes of kit open.

For a moment I wondered whether I'd stumbled on that rare thing, an archaeological dig, but the man turned out to be a member of the local model aeroplane flying club.

I admired his model aeroplanes, which were all in the boxes. He told me he came to the same spot every day, whatever the weather.

'The barrow must be a convenient place to fly them from,' I suggested.

'What barrow?'

Almost completely forgotten today, for 4,000 years White Sheet Hill was a convenient beacon for first Neolithic, then Bronze Age and finally Celtic travellers, all of whom left their mark on the hilltop. There was a Neolithic causeway, various other Bronze Age barrows and one large Iron Age hill-fort in close proximity to one another. The local water board had sympathetically built a small reservoir almost on top of the Iron Age fort – which seemed gratuitous when they had an entire open hillside near by to choose from.

It was as I headed on from the hill over Cranborne Chase that the magic took hold. I had a book in my knapsack, which I had referred to frequently since the coast. Ever since I had managed to find an old copy of *Ancient Trackways of Wessex*, written in 1965 by the husband-and-wife team of H W Timperley and Edith Brill, I had wanted to follow some of the old drovers' ways they laboriously tracked. It was only with their help that I had negotiated a route through the complexities of the Dorset valleys, as the Icknield Way has many variants.

Most of the time they kept to a dedicated route-finder approach, for which the reader needed an OS map beside them at all times. But when it came to this stretch, which they described as 'the Harrow Way', a loop of the Icknield, they allowed themselves a rare moment of lyricism:

> This is the most splendid and – in feeling if not in actual number of feet – the highest stretch of the Harrow Way, and one of the loneliest downland walks in Wiltshire.

The wind was buffeting around my head as I advanced down the old lane into the wide-open expanses. I could see for miles and there was not a single person. For Cranborne Chase as it leads into Salisbury Plain is the vortex of England, the great emptiness at its heart, sucking it in.

This was where Arthur and his knights finally disintegrated: the setting for the battle of Camlann where Mordred and Arthur killed each other. Malory tells it all with a bleak beauty: how it was resolved that the two armies 'should meet upon a down beside Salisbury, and not far from the seaside'.

Throughout the *Morte d'Arthur*, Malory shows a keen sense of geography, going out of his way to give the epic a scope ranging right across the British Isles, from the Orkneys to Kent. At one point Lancelot offers to make a bare-shirted journey on foot from Sandwich to Carlisle as penance for having unwittingly killed Gareth. It is after this accidental killing that Gareth's brother Gawain swears vengeance on Lancelot and will not allow Arthur to make peace, however much the king would like to; Arthur has a glorious aside to the effect that 'I can always get another queen, but not such a brotherhood of knights.'

For the final battle on Salisbury Plain, Malory must surely have drawn on his own experience of civil war of the most vicious sort during the Wars of the Roses. He is careful to show that the conflict was not an inevitable outcome of opposing views, but came rather from a series of very human failings and misunderstandings. What other writer would allow his king to faint with the knowledge of the carnage that lay ahead? There are more manly tears in the last book of *Le Morte d'Arthur* than a Mills and Boon novel: Malory's knights are in touch with their feminine side. But they are also capable of creating violent mayhem.

I thought of Yeats's poem 'Meditation in Time of Civil War' in which, while recounting violence similar, the poet notices with most intensity the honeybees building their nest outside his window. Malory likewise tells us that the conflict begins in spring, when every heart should *'flourysheth and burgoneth'*. Instead a *'grete angur'* has been born. As Yeats wrote of his own time, suddenly there was 'more substance in our enmities than in our love'.

Whereas Malory's main source for his account of the battle, the earlier French thirteenth-century *Le Mort le Roi Artu*, makes much of the fact that Merlin had once foretold that the kingdom of Logres would end in a cataclysmic battle on Salisbury Plain, Malory omits this prophecy completely; as he does much of the lengthy heraldic list of kings and their exploits in the battle chronicled by the anonymous French writer.

He keeps his description terse, like a foreign correspondent, but makes sure that the figure of 100,000 dead stands out, a number that was not inconceivable by the European standards of his own time.

What he does introduce is a human detail of startling simplicity. The two armies have originally agreed to meet in truce on the Plain but, as each distrusts the other, they are equally ready to draw their swords in defence if the other side should raise theirs. An adder comes out of the bushes and bites a knight on the ankle, who not unnaturally responds by killing it, and '*thoghte none othir harme*'. Cue trumpets, horns and bloodshed.

Malory describes the chaos of such a battle. '*There was but rushynge and rydynge, foynynge* [thrusting] *and strykynge.*' When the dust clears, the survivors can hardly see each other for the bodies. Arthur kills Mordred, but in a Mexican stand-off the usurper manages a last, mortal blow at the same time, and the king falls to the cold earth.

As night arrives, the grievously wounded Sir Lucan sees looters and robbers creep out by moonlight to strip dead knights of their rings and jewels, and kill any who are injured for their horse harnesses and riches. A time of darkness has come.

I spent many hours walking on the Plain, which is not as flat as it sounds. W H Hudson once compared it to an open hand, 'with Salisbury in the hollow of the palm, placed nearest the wrist, and the five valleys which cut through it as the five spread fingers'.

After crossing over one of these valley ridges, I came to an old beech copse, with a holly tree at its entrance and more brush-holly underpinning the trees. Called 'Hanging Langford Camp', the ancient woodland settlement dated from the late Iron Age and the Arthurian Romano-British period. Brooches from that time had been found under the trees, particularly when any had been uprooted by the wind. From there, the old lane swept down out of the copse towards the bottom of the Wylye Valley along one of the hardest of flint roads I had yet walked on, a penitential track.

What I liked about following this old road across England was not just the necklace of prehistoric sites that accompanied it, but the way they could be so hidden unless you knew where to look. Brush away what appeared to be a normal bit of British countryside, as here, and to my right, hidden under the beaches of Castle Hill, was a tumulus; I had just left a Roman camp and road on the ridge behind me, along with the earthworks of Grim's Dyke. And now I came over the brow of West Hill, again with its early earthworks, I could see the Langford Lakes laid out before me, next to the medieval village of Steeple Langford.

The lakes were protected as a bird reserve and the terns were circling overhead with their swept-back wings. The odd shaft of light through the dark clouds was picked up by the surface of the water. Coarse fisherman had set up day camps along the reed banks.

Malory never identifies the lake to which Arthur returns his sword when he is dying. The king asks Sir Bedivere, one of his stewards and one of the few survivors of the battle, to take Excalibur and throw it in the lake. Twice Sir Bedivere takes the jewel-encrusted sword but cannot bring himself to waste it in the water. Only on the third time of asking does he not deny Arthur, and throws the sword in, 'after wrapping the belt about the hilt', Malory adds, with his usual concern for detail. He sees it grasped by the Lady of the Lake's hand as it rises up out of the water. Again, Malory keeps a telling detail from one of his sources: the hand shakes the sword three times and 'brandishes' it, before withdrawing below the surface.

As an ending that leaves the reader wanting more, it has few rivals. The sword is never explained. Arthur's body is borne off to 'the vale of Avalon' on a barge crewed by black-hooded queens.

When Lancelot learns that Guinevere too is dead, '*he wepte not greteleye, but syghed*'. Malory, sitting in his prison tower as he wrote, waiting for a reprieve that never came from Edward IV for his part in the Wars of the Roses, wanted to achieve a sense of elegy and of loss, of an England that had wasted a golden age through the quarrelsomeness of human nature.

I had been sitting by the banks of the Langford Lakes for no more than a minute when a kingfisher landed on a bare branch just a few feet away from me. I had often waited for hours to see them along stretches of the Thames. This was a gift. It gave its characteristic sweet, bitten-off cry. A slash of turquoise ran down its back, a slash that is difficult to see in flight or unless it is close. The violently red stalks of dogwood along the banks made it stand out even more.

I looked out over the water. In Greek legend, the kingfisher is the bird that harbingers the 'halcyon days', those days of calm before a storm. With the wildfowl circling and the strange reflections of both sun and dark clouds on the surface, it was easy to imagine the Arthurian end sequence as having taken place here.

Before I could get too carried away by the moment, one of the fishermen disabused me: 'They're old gravel pits. Only been filled with water for the last fifty years, if that.'

*

William Cobbett had spent parts of his childhood here in Steeple Langford, so when it came to doing his *Rural Rides*, it was natural that he should return. He was disappointed:

When I got to Steeple Langford, I found no public-house, and I found it a much more miserable place than I had remembered it. The Steeple, to which it owed its distinctive appellation, was gone; and the place altogether seemed to me to be very much altered for the worse.

Cobbett, like many a distinguished British traveller – Smollett and Johnson come to mind – loved a good disappointment. The *Rural Rides* are full of them. He managed to find the Berkshire Downs, which lay ahead of me and in some ways were the treasure trove of Wessex, bleak and equally unsatisfactory. What he liked was a good valley, like that of the Wiltshire Avon.

But his trenchant approach to poor working conditions was admirable. I particularly liked his rant when he visited the nearby village of Milton Lilbourne about how capitalist writers like Adam Smith and his followers – 'The Scotch *feelosofers*', as he called them – could do with a spot of manual labour to appreciate why the working man might occasionally need a holiday:

The Scotch *feelosofers*, who seem all to have been, by nature, formed for negro-drivers, have an insuperable objection to all those establishments and customs which occasion holidays. They call them a great hindrance, a great bar to industry, a great drawback from 'national wealth'. I wish each of these unfeeling fellows had a spade put into his hand for ten days, only ten days, and that he were compelled to dig only just as much as one of the common labourers at Fulham. The metaphysical gentleman would, I believe, soon discover the use of holidays!

But why should men, why should any men, work hard? Why, I ask, should they work incessantly, if working part of the days of the week be sufficient? Why should the people at Milton, for instance, work incessantly, when they now raise food and clothing and fuel and every necessary to maintain well five times their number? Why should they not have some holidays? And, pray, say, thou conceited Scotch *feelosofer*, how the 'national wealth' can be increased by making these people work incessantly, that they may raise food and clothing, to go to feed and clothe people who do not work at all ?

Cobbett set off on his rural rides not long after he had been living in the United States, effectively exiled there for his political views, and saw England with fresh eyes on his return at the end of 1819, just after the Peterloo massacre had given fresh impetus to the need for reform, and the new Corn Laws were making landowners rich at the expense of their workers.

He made a point of talking to as many farmers as possible, often staying with them, and was interested in new farming methods, like the revolutionary seed drill that Jethro Tull had suggested (Cobbett republished Tull's book, *Horse Hoeing Husbandry*); he inveighed against the potato, seeing it as a dangerous fad which the Tory government of the time was trying to promote; and above all he sympathised with the poor lot of the farm labourer, disliking the 'new rich', like the Baring family who had made their money from banking and had now 'bought into the country side' without understanding it.

God knows what Cobbett would have made of much of southern England now: chips sold in every pub and a banker in every large estate; a patrician ruling Tory Party; a venal House of Commons whose members had just been exposed to public condemnation for their abuse of expenses, and were driven by the dictates of lobbyists; and a victory for free-market capitalism across all the political parties that would have made 'the Scotch *feelosofers*' ecstatic.

It would be wonderful to have his campaigning and humane journalism lance the boils and excesses of the current age, just as he did those of the early nineteenth century.

Chapter 2

The Sun and the Clock

'The clock should be read by the sunshine, not the sun
timed by the clock.'
Richard Jefferies

I arrive at Stonehenge towards sunset, walking across the Plain,
coming from the west: which is strangely appropriate. In the
popular imagination, the stones are associated with the east, with
the rising of the sun for the summer solstice, when travellers,
pagans, Druids and partygoers descend on Stonehenge to see the
dawn. But in recent years archaeologists have suggested that the
winter solstice sunset in the west was celebrated more: the turning
point of the year on 20 December, when the long nights start
to shorten; the reason Christmas became such a significant festival,
building on pre-Christian traditions. As I know from my studies
in Peru (where again it was the winter solstice that was most
important for the Incas), the sun sets on the winter solstice along
the same axis that it rises for the summer one, so the orientation
is the same.

This confusion over solstices is important because it gives rise
to the misconception that Stonehenge celebrates the dawn — for
which read rebirth and renewal. One can almost hear the snare
drums and African choirs of the New Age ravers kick in.

But Stonehenge may have had a far darker, sunset orientation.
Despite recent findings by archaeologists, no one associates the
site with death. We now know from recent excavations that this
was one of the largest Neolithic burial grounds in Britain, and

used as such for centuries. The New Age ravers who flock here each summer are dancing on a graveyard.

They have already started to arrive for the solstice, although there are still some days before it is due. Among them are the Druids who lead the solstice celebrations. While New Age travellers fondly like to imagine that they are re-enacting Druid ceremonies at a Druid site, this is historically incorrect. The stones were erected many thousands of years before the Celtic prophet-priests became active around 500 BC. While perfectly possible that the Druids may have been drawn to the stones, they would have done so much in the same way as today's New Age travellers – as pilgrims hoping to tap into the spiritual energy of their forebears.

I see the travellers' vans lurking in lay-bys and along some of the sandy tracks that lead off the busy roads besieging Stonehenge in a pincer of tarmac: the A303 and A344 thunder by unbelievably close, the latter almost clipping one of the outer megaliths, the thirty-five-ton 'Heelstone'. An unattractive wire fence separates the stones from the cars that stream past.

For Stonehenge represents all that is best and worst about England.

There is the sheer imaginative leap of the decision, whether taken in a day or over several generations, to turn a ring of wooden posts into a circle of gigantic sarsen stones with – the literally crowning glory – stone lintels notched and raised onto them: a triumph of spirituality, of engineering, of ingenuity and of the sheer bloody-mindedness that has distinguished much later English history.

And there is the desultory way in which they have since been treated, with a disdain inherited from the Romans for anything prehistoric: first left partially to collapse when under private ownership; then, when 'saved for the nation' in 1918 by a benefactor, the nation repaying that gift with the indifference of someone who has not had to pay. The odd stone was propped up if in danger of falling. Archaeological digs were given scant resources and no single museum established, at the site or elsewhere, to display and interpret any findings. In my lifetime, plans have come and gone to reroute the absurdly intrusive roads — not difficult, as they are passing over a largely empty plain. On almost the day I arrived, the government announced it would withdraw the funding it had previously promised to landscape the site and house the findings in a Visitors' Centre.

Worst of all, we have fenced off the actual stones so they cannot be visited, but only viewed from afar, patrolling around them along a 'designated walkway'. This provides fine distant views of the stones but is hardly an immersive experience. Nor is it necessary on the spurious 'health and safety' grounds that are usually quoted. If visitors can approach to within inches of paintings at national galleries, surely they can do the same to far less vulnerable stone blocks.

The decision to fence them off was made in 1978, a low point of the century for much of Britain, with its strife and winter of discontent, in response to the 'Free Stonehenge' festivals and regular invasion of the site. In retrospect, one can understand the political symbolism. The government of the day was not able to control the unions, but at least it could stop long-haired hippies invading a national monument; never mind that the monument had been open to all for the previous 4,000 years. Like so many restrictive laws, it has proved harder to remove than enforce. In these less confrontational times, when the Chief Druid sits on a consultative body with the Wiltshire police, it should long ago have been rescinded.

In my pack, I have a tie, which I put on, and a clipboard. Experience has taught me that no one will ever question a man with a tie or clipboard in case they get questioned themselves. It's the end of the day and most of the coach parties have left. And so I can slip quietly inside the ring of stones.

✳

Stonehenge stands so solid and monolithic both in photographs and our imagination that it is difficult to imagine the fluidity of the changes that took place over the millennium of its main construction from around 3000 to 2000 BC.

For this was not a monument built to a simple blueprint, a snapshot of Neolithic man; rather it was a continually evolving design that met changing requirements at which we can only guess. Stonehenge remains a wonder because we do not understand fully to what purpose the great effort to raise the stones was expended.

That it was an epic undertaking can be understood by the contemplation of a single fact: the transporting of the bluestones from the Preseli Mountains on the western coast of Wales, some 240 miles away. That distance is almost incomprehensible. We marvel at the ability of the inhabitants of Easter Island or Machu Picchu to move great stone statues or ashlars respectively, again without the aid of mechanised transport; but that was over a relatively short haul of a few miles. A distance of 240 miles beggars belief, when one remembers that the bluestones weighed up to four tons each. While they were almost certainly transported some of the way by water (although that in itself raises both doubt and wonder), Stonehenge still lies inland and is hardly a convenient destination; so improbable does it appear that there have been recent inconclusive efforts to show that the bluestones may have come from elsewhere, or were left as glacial deposits.

Around 3000 BC, at a time when ancient civilisations were stirring in Mesopotamia, China, India, Egypt and Peru, the first of these Preseli bluestones were erected at the site of Stonehenge within a laboriously created circular ditch (labourers used deer antlers to scoop the rubble out and build its inner bank — deer antlers that can be dated). Fifty-six pillars were arranged in a double crescent shape within the circle. These are no longer visible; only the holes they stood in remain.

What we think of as the archetypal Stonehenge, the circle of thirty or so sarsen stones linked by stone lintels, was erected only around 2500 BC, half a millenium after the first monumental development of the site. These grey sarsen stones had come from much closer, the Marlborough Downs, about twenty miles to the north, and the lintels were carefully carved with tongue and groove notches so that they fitted together. Within this circle of grey sarsen stones were arranged a further horseshoe of five giant trilithons, each made up of two freestanding, upright stones with a third placed across the top, like the mathematical sign for pi: π.

The original bluestones were not abandoned after the arrival of the grey sarsens. They were moved from their old positions at some stage between 2280 and 2030 BC to form an outer circle and an inner oval beside the trilithons. Almost all the bluestones of this inner oval have either fallen or been removed. One of the largest fallen bluestones is now known, imaginatively if unhelpfully, as the 'Altar Stone'.

By contrast more than half of the sarsen stones are still standing in their outer circle and were sculpted and erected with unusual care and skill, with mortise-and-tenon joints connecting the uprights to the lintels.

Just this brief summary of the monument's complicated history shows the need for an on-site museum or display centre to explain its timeline and development: over the millennium of its construction, the furniture was moved around the room several times, the smaller bluestones in particular being arranged first one way, then another; once the big sarsens were in place I imagine that, like a large wardrobe, nobody would ever want to move them again.

Archaeologists like William Hawley and Richard Atkinson, who tried during the twentieth century to make sense of the complicated old post-holes and stone pits that pockmark the chalk ground, reeled back from the complexity of the task and did what most archaeologists do when faced with a conundrum: fail to publish the full results of their excavations. Only recently, in 1995, did an English Heritage project try to put together their findings; considerable controversy remains over when each stage was built and whether the outlying part of it was roofed. But it is clear that, like many a medieval cathedral, the construction took place during many centuries, from the Neolithic into the Bronze Age, during which time architectural fashions changed. If it were a cathedral (and in some ways it is), the ruins would have Gothic, Perpendicular and Renaissance sections.

British archaeologist Francis Pryor has offered the insight that for Neolithic and Bronze Age peoples the process of construction may have been as important as the result; that they were often more interested in the collaborative effort needed to build their ceremonial centres than the actual final structure. In some instances he cites evidence that they tore down part of a finished structure so that they could continue building it.

We are so used to a mindset that insists on giving primacy to the finished building that we find this difficult to assimilate; but if we accept it, then seeing Stonehenge in its current partial and complicated state may be more suitable than we realise – for this was always meant to be a work in continual progress.

My first thought when I slip inside the site is how small the bluestones are that were brought hundreds of miles from the Preseli Mountains. The lichen that has grown up over centuries (zealously preserved by English Heritage) makes it difficult to see their distinctive dolerite rock grain.

It is of course the main stones, the grey sarsens from the

nearby Marlborough Downs, that make the bluestones seem so small: whales among dolphins, they tower over them.

Because the grass is so little trod between the stones, it looks quite fresh. Oddly, given that 1 million visitors a year patrol the perimeter, the actual stones feel abandoned. I notice a few ravens who have made their homes among the lintels of the trilithons, the biggest of all of the stones that nestle at the heart of the site in a horseshoe shape. Ravens were often associated prehistorically with places of burial – and for good reason, as they would pick the corpses clean.

I recall an intriguing theory that Mike Parker Pearson put forward. Mike is head of the Stonehenge Riverside Project. His team have been investigating a separate circle down by the River Avon, dubbed 'Bluestonehenge' by the press, an unfortunate term that makes it sound like a shopping mall. He suggests that Neolithic man built in stone when commemorating death, and in wood, at sites like Woodhenge, when celebrating life. The avenue leading from that wooden circle at nearby Durrington Walls to Stonehenge might therefore have been 'a ritual passage from life to death, to celebrate past ancestors and the recently deceased': a fascinating idea which, while highly speculative, makes sense of the sacred landscape around Stonehenge.

It is through one of the stone trilithons that the sun's rays would have set at the winter solstice, but that particular trilithon has not been restored: the lintel and one shattered support lie inert on the ground, covering the so-called 'Altar Stone'. It seems irrational that other stones have been restored to their positions and not this one.

That said, if just one trilithon was standing, Stonehenge would still be a fabulous monument: to have three upright, with an outlying circle of smaller sarsens, is just out of sight, as James Brown would say.

I feel a far greater peace than I had expected. From afar I can hear the last tourists circling the ruins, the traffic on the road, even a distant helicopter from one of the airbases. But in my heart I feel grounded and centred; and that every visitor should be allowed inside.

As I leave, I glance back and see the tourists still walking around the 'designated walkway', holding the audiophone guide to their ears. At this distance they look like celebrants, in their bright neon anoraks, making a final last outer circuit around the stones.

*

I follow the processional Avenue away from Stonehenge. This broad Neolithic track heads north across the meadows and then hangs a right towards a ridge with a line of twelve burial mounds called the King's Barrows.

The barrows intrigue me because they have never been excavated; the local farmer was reluctant to let archaeologists cut down the trees to get at them. Some are buried in a beech copse at one end of the mysterious Cursus, the long depression so named because the antiquarian William Stukeley thought it was built by the Romans for chariot races, although actually it is even older than Stonehenge.

One of the King's Barrows stands out on its own in a field, with four beech trees as guards. I leave the path and make my way over. Inside the bower of the beeches, the rise of the mound is covered by cow parsley; right at the centre is a small patch of bluebells that must be a recent planting, as they have certainly had 4,000 years to spread since its unknown occupant was laid to rest in the mound.

It is a peaceful place, and after a long day walking, the temptation just to lie in the long grass and cow parsley and watch the sun descend is seductive. Fields of dandelions and buttercups lead back to Stonehenge over the meadow. The late sun coming down through the translucent leaves of the beech trees above makes it feel brighter than it really is, and when it fades, I feel a sudden lethargy and just sink into sleep, with my pack as a pillow.

When I wake, it is cold and past midnight, and I pull on extra clothes. Across the meadow, I can see the distant lights of the A303 as it passes Stonehenge, the cars gleaming like fish passing in a stream across the horizon. The stones themselves are invisible – no *son et lumière* here in the way of the Pyramids or Acropolis – but the stars above are crystal clear. The large expanse of Salisbury Plain lessens the usual light pollution of southern England. For once, I can see each star of the dagger that hangs from Orion's belt.

Lying back in my nest of cow parsley and long grass on the King's Barrow, I try to sleep again. Sleeping on a grave isn't off-putting – indeed is oddly restful – but I had forgotten how long grass always rubs you up the wrong way, even if you're sleeping in all your clothes.

Far too early next morning, and with the dew still on me, I walk up past the Cursus, stretching away for over two miles to the west. I can see why the usually reliable William Stukeley thought that it was built by the Romans, for the dimensions are both imperial and gladiatorial, and it calls out for a horse to gallop along. Archaeologists since Stukeley have always been mystified why the Cursus was built, until 2011 when a team from the University of Birmingham showed that it too may have helped mark different solstice points, and provided a way to process between them.

On a cold but sunny dawn the sheer beauty of the Cursus is unmistakable. The idea of 'a sacred landscape' is one I am used to from Peru. The great achievement of Andean civilisation was to give meaning to a harsh and difficult environment, to create a complex sacred landscape where once had been plain rock and water: the Nasca lines being the most famous example, but with plenty of others to choose from, including the Inca Trail to Machu Picchu, along which every viewpoint is designed to frame a sacred mountain or alignment.

The Neolithic culture of Wiltshire works in much the same way, but is less recognised. Gerald Hawkins, the British scholar who did most to establish the accuracy of the solstice alignment at Stonehenge and to create the discipline of archaeo-astronomy, went on to investigate those same lines of Nasca. Yet it has still taken longer for us to appreciate that Stonehenge is not an isolated monument but part of the wider ritual landscape that surrounds it: the King's Barrows, the Avenue, the Cursus, the other nearby henges. It doesn't help that, unlike the Peruvians, who have carefully preserved the Nasca lines, we have built roads through most of our sacred landscape, or made it inaccessible on private or military land.

Which is why I have tried to support the creation of a new walking trail through this landscape, to be called the Great Stones Way and linking Stonehenge with Avebury; I wrote the first article promoting the project, for the *Guardian*, arguing that it is high time we arrived at Stonehenge by the only sensible and appropriate route – on foot. The comparison that immediately comes to mind, and which I know well, is that same Inca Trail to Machu Picchu. The experience of trekking to both sites is immeasurably richer, not just 'because you've earned it', but because both sets of ruins can then be understood in the context of the surrounding landscape.

I am following that same suggested Trail now, leading me from the Cursus past the 'Cuckoo Stone', as a fallen sarsen standing alone in a field is called, and on to Woodhenge: here the original wooden posts in concentric rings have been marked by concrete pillar stumps less than a foot high that look like parking bollards.

While I understand the purist archaeological vision that wants just to indicate not re-create, I can't help wishing that a little more imagination might have been shown. What would be the harm in re-creating the wooden posts, with a clear health warning attached that this was just that, a reconstruction? No one in the Americas, from a tribal reservation in the north to Peru in the south, would have hesitated for a second. One can be too austere in these matters. I remember a well-respected American archaeologist saying, off the record, that 'British archaeologists need to lighten up. Get out of the trench once in a while and have a party.'

It is not a concern that has troubled Buddhists in Bhutan or Japan, who reconstruct their temples regularly after fires; Douglas Adams once took time out from hitch-hiking around the galaxy to see the Gold Pavilion Temple in Kyoto and was

mildly surprised at quite how well it had weathered the passage of time since it was first built in the fourteenth century. I was told it hadn't weathered well at all, and had in fact been burnt to the ground twice in this century.

'So it isn't the original building?' I asked my Japanese guide.

'But yes, of course it is,' he insisted, rather surprised at my question.

'But it's burnt down?'

'Yes.'

'Twice.'

'Many times.'

'And rebuilt.'

'Of course. It is an important and historic building.'

'With completely new materials.'

'But of course. It was burnt down.'

'So how can it be the same building?'

'It is always the same building.'

(Douglas Adams, *Last Chance to See*)

Woodhenge in its prime may have been as evocative as Stonehenge for celebrants, with circles of high wooden posts rather than stone. It is a reminder of the way in which wood had an equally central place in the Neolithic ritual world, even if for obvious reasons that wood has not survived as well. Only at sites like Seahenge on the Norfolk coast, towards which I'm heading, has a wooden monument been preserved intact by the peat until being uncovered just a few years ago.

Woodhenge, and the huge circle of Durrington Walls beside it, are far less well known than they should be. Yet excavations show this is where the builders of Stonehenge may have lived: excavations that happened only because a road was built through the area in a brutal fashion.

Looking at the concrete posts of Woodhenge and the unnecessary road running through Durrington Walls makes me feel a little melancholy. I notice a transit parked up beside the sites in the lay-by, the only vehicle. It's painted a dark forest green and looks too spruce and well kept to be your average travellers' van.

Brendan and Sue are pottering about inside, a middle-aged couple in cardigans from London who look like they too ought to be in a Mike Leigh film. Brendan is frying bacon. He notices me lurking outside, like a dog with its tongue hanging out, and takes pity. After giving me tea and sympathy (Brendan's special *masala chai*), they tell me together, in chorus, that they spend two weeks every year travelling the country to visit prehistoric sites.

'Well, it gets you out and about,' says Brendan.

'Yes it does, it gets you out and about,' adds Sue.

They are coming at me in stereo, in the way of some couples.

It emerges that they prefer Woodhenge to Stonehenge and have spent some days there. I am impressed by the purity of their approach and depressed by my own corresponding lack of imagination, which has failed to make Woodhenge come alive in the same way.

'Oh no, it's not that,' says Sue. 'It's just that the car park here is free. You have to pay at Stonehenge.'

✳

Until a few more rights of way are opened, Salisbury Plain is not easy to access. Nothing wrong with the terrain — it's wide and flat and inviting. But the army have carved a great deal out of it for their firing ranges, and if the 'red flags' are up, you can't walk across.

So I take a detour along the quiet upper Avon Valley that Cobbett liked so much and meander with the river past a series of sleepy, pretty villages: Coombe and Fittleton, with their Judas trees and millponds and dovecotes; Enfold, with its flint and stone church, and old funeral wagon waiting on standby in the nave; Longstreet, with the Swan pub appearing at just the right moment for a lunchtime reappraisal of the route.

At Fighealden (pronounced 'file-dean'), an allotment holder tells me he doesn't grow courgettes 'because they're foreign food'. An older man, he's working in his vest and trying to hoe ground that's rock hard after an unusually long period of sun. He grows spinach and potatoes mainly, with a prized asparagus bed. There is hardly a weed to be seen on his section: particularly gratifying in an allotment, as the comparison with more slovenly neighbours alongside is so apparent.

Before retiring, he used to work as a gamekeeper on one of the local estates. 'These days, of course, we encourage all the predators and raptors — the buzzards and the sparrowhawks and the red kites, although kites are more carrion. But what no one ever points out is what it's doing to the songbirds. Used to get a lot of skylarks on Salisbury Plain. Not any more. There were clouds of peewits over by the aerodrome. But they've all gone. What people don't understand is that there is a reason to control predators. You ever see a sparrowhawk come down on a garden table and take a few songbirds for breakfast? The ones hopping about on the little bird-feeders people put out, like bait. Might as well poison the blue tits and the chaffinches as lure them for a sparrowhawk's breakfast!'

I think of his words as I head up to Salisbury Plain. There

are corn buntings sitting on the fence posts, friendly and bold birds in the presence of humans, given that their numbers have likewise been much reduced in the last few decades. The 'Downland Reversion Scheme' has subsidised local farmers to restore wildflower meadows, which has helped slow their decline.

It's a far rarer bird I'm hoping to see, one that was driven to extinction in Britain by 1832 and is only now being slowly reintroduced. The male great bustard weighs in at some forty pounds, making it one of the heaviest birds in the world that can fly. The female is half the size but still hardly petite. They have strong legs and can run at great speed; they take off like Harrier jump jets, using those legs to spring high in the air before flying. Bustards can then cover distances of over 100 miles in the air.

Not surprisingly, such eminently trophyable birds attracted the attention of hunters. Henry VIII and other monarchs led hunts across the plain in search of them; you can see why Henry VIII in particular might have been so drawn to the bird, almost an avian simulacrum of himself. The local population enjoyed the attention. There is still a small hamlet called Bustard in the vicinity.

What drove the great bustard to extinction was not the hunting – although it can't have helped – but changes in farming. The female generally laid two eggs in a year, on open ground like agricultural fields. Quite apart from other predators who were attracted to the large, juicy eggs, the chances of getting hit by a ploughshare increased as farming techniques improved.

So to try to reintroduce them to the British countryside is a quixotic if wonderful venture. They are not like red kites or beavers, tough scavenger species that may well spread past their current limited reintroduction areas. The bustard is a lumbering dowager duchess of a bird, as out of place on the wilds of Salisbury Plain as a Russian aristocrat – and it is from Russia that these birds are being reintroduced, in small numbers, by a team led by David Waters.

When I arranged to see the birds, I had spoken to David on the phone and asked why they bothered to bring them all the way from Russia when there was a larger and more convenient population in Spain. 'We tested the DNA of stuffed British birds. The results were much closer to the Russian than the Spanish profile,' he told me. And so each year they visit a large *oblast* south-east of Moscow to get some birds' eggs.

David used to be a policeman before he set up the Great Bustard Group in 1998. He had become fascinated by the birds as a teenager. 'I remember thinking that all the interesting birds lived in places like Papua New Guinea. Then I saw male bustards doing their display rituals and realised that wherever you go in the world, you won't see a better sight.'

I have arranged to join a group of interested birdwatchers who are being taken by Lynne, David's colleague, to see the release area for the birds; but not, as Lynne says, necessarily to see any of the bustards themselves, as they can be remarkably elusive for such a large bird; when crouched on the ground they camouflage well. Moreover, if the army are firing on the ranges, as they generally are, the bustards have plenty of reason to 'duck and cover'. One of the more quixotic aspects of the bustard scheme is that they are being released into the jaws of the largest MOD firing area in the country.

This is a question that Andy raises. Andy has crew-cut hair and wears square, metallic glasses. He is also very angry. He introduces himself to the rest of the group as a committed Christian birdwatcher and conservationist, which raises a few interesting questions in my mind: how are Christian conservationists different from any other type? Do they believe in an avian afterlife? Or, quite interestingly, that there is an afterlife for extinct species? I start to wonder in all seriousness about the theology of this – which just shows what happens when you have been walking by yourself too long and sleeping on the tombs of dead kings. Luckily, before I can ask Andy, he fires off a stream of his own questions at Lynne.

How does the Trust stop bustards flying into power lines? (Answer: if there are enough 'incidents' – i.e. deaths – the electricity company will put up safety decoys.)

How are farmers persuaded to leave female bustards in peace when hatching, given they need so much undisturbed breeding space? (Answer: a cash reward if they inform the Trust and leave an area round the bustard unploughed – although they do have to spot the bustard before their combine harvesters reach the egg.)

The affable Lynne deals with these and other questions with an easy manner. She is a cheerful-looking blonde soul who would not be out of place in a Beryl Cook painting. But Andy is clearly a driven man. Others in the group shift a bit uneasily at his continued inquisition.

In my occasional encounters with twitchers, I've come across this before. The idea that the calm observation of birds flying freely in the air might in itself bring serenity and happiness is far from true. Britain's most famous birdwatcher, Bill Oddie, has revealed that he is riven with neurosis and insecurity. Those obsessed with building their species lists drive up and down the country to outdo each other; they are monitored by a fact-checking jobsworth who has taken it upon himself to verify the sightings made by competing birdwatchers. There must be more joy in train-spotting. Which is why I have always remained a strictly amateur bird fancier.

Andy leans forward, the metallic frames of his glasses reminding me of the ones Laurence Olivier wore as a dentist when he tortured Dustin Hoffman in *Marathon Man*. He fingers the long telescopic barrel of his scope as he goes for the killer punch.

'And how can you possibly justify *single-species* conservation?' He says '*single-species*' with a sibilant hiss. Lynne flinches as if an adder has appeared in the grass. Single-species conservation is the *bête noire* of the eco-warriors. It implies a distressingly narrow focus on just one animal – often a glamorous one like, it must be said, the great bustard – to the exclusion of the wider ecosphere and smaller species ('Has anyone thought about the plankton?' goes the plaintive cry). Single-species conservationists are seen as the stalkers of the eco-world, driven, compulsive and ever so slightly sad.

Lynne blushes, like a nice girl who's been asked if she has an unsuitable boyfriend. 'I thought you might ask me that. But we do have stone curlews as well. They enjoy the same habitat. They're part of our programme.'

Andy goes quiet. We all get in the Land Rover that Lynne has brought to take us to the release area. The atmosphere remains tense and oppressive, perhaps from the combined warmth of the fleeces all the birdwatchers are wearing (even in summer they rarely moult).

I feel pleased that I have arranged for my friend Peter Buxton to join us for moral support and, more practically, to bring some extra binoculars so that I'm not going naked to the party. Peter has worked as a counsellor and is adept at pouring oil on troubled waters. He is also, unlike me, a serious birdwatcher.

'So Andy,' he asks, 'have you seen the *jibaro* bustards in Spain?'

Andy lightens a little. 'Ah yes, wonderful birds, the *jib-aros*.' He ever so slightly rasps and stresses the Spanish 'j' in *jibaro* a little more than Peter had, to show his full possession of the species. I manage to stop myself from giggling, but only just. Andy's face has darkened anyway as he stares out of the Land Rover window at the clouds of smoke that are rising from the MOD firing ranges. 'But the *jib-aros* hate disturbance.' Pause. 'Like the great bustards,' he adds ominously. Lynne hunkers down over the steering wheel and does not answer.

Peter tries Andy again: 'Do you ever see a Dartford warbler in your part of the world? I came across one near here on Pewsey Hill.'

At this Andy almost purrs, like a difficult cat who has finally been tickled in the right place. 'As it happens, I know a lot about Dartford warblers.' He proceeds to tell us. My mind drifts. Not only have I never seen or heard of a Dartford warbler, but it sounds more like a criminal than a bird. ('The Boston Strangler? No it's the Dartford warbler wot done it.')

I ask Lynne quietly how often the army uses the firing range. 'All the working week and one weekend per month.' Which leaves only about six days a month when the birds are not being potentially shelled. When we stop, I read the MOD notice guarding the range, which informs me that *'projectile'* means any shot or shell or other missile or any portion thereof', and that over much of what we're looking at you're liable to be bombarded by one. You can also be arrested without a warrant.

There are fires burning on the slopes where Lynne had hoped to show us the bustards. 'In this dry weather the ordnance can set them off,' she explains. I feel sorry for her. Andy's face looks like that of a priest who has just heard confession. There is, unsurprisingly, not a single bustard to be seen. 'Let's go and have a look at the stone curlews instead,' says Lynne brightly.

'Is that a stone curlew over there?' asks Andy, pointing to the distance.

'No,' says Lynne, with far less satisfaction than I would have brought to the answer: 'That's a calf. It's just very far away, so it looks small.'

I leave them to it and begin the next stage of my walk across the Plain, skirting the firing grounds along the proposed Great Stones Way route to Avebury. It has yet to be approved by all the 'stakeholders', one of those horrible words like 'gatekeepers' that means those with the power to obstruct – in this case the MOD, various parish councils and the village of Avebury itself, which is curiously hesitant to attract walkers.

At the moment, without a trail to follow, hardly anyone comes up onto this area of Salisbury Plain. The work avoiding firing ranges is off-putting. Not a single garage or shop along the Avon Valley bothers to sell local maps, so few are the walkers who come to the heartland of Neolithic Britain.

It's a shame, as the Plain has a bleak beauty along with its history. Just across from the great bustard release site is the biggest unexcavated tumulus in Britain; and back over the river lies the East Chisenbury midden, a monumental dumping ground for late Bronze Age artefacts which was recognised as such only in 1992 – it's so large that it had always been mistaken for a hill. The find prompted an academic paper with one of my favourite titles, 'East Chisenbury: ritual and rubbish': it contains the sober assessment that, 'in terms of scale, the midden dwarfs other contemporary sites; this is clearly an important pile of rubbish.'

Some way into the Plain I am passed by the only other person I see in this area, a smartly dressed, lone woman wearing Dolce and Gabbana sunglasses, who is heading determinedly towards the shooting area; the red flags are up to signify that it's a 'live' day. I'm hesitant to approach her, as she has the very English air of someone minding their own business, but in an equally English way she seems pleased when I open a conversation; given we are the only two people in sight for miles around, it would be absurd to ignore each other.

In a Kensington and Chelsea accent, she tells me she regularly drives down from London to walk right *inside* the firing range, as it's one of the few places 'where you don't run the risk of meeting anybody else'. I murmur that this might be because they worry they'll get shot.

'Oh, I love all that. It gets my endorphins going. I got back to the car once and found it ringed by military police. When I told them I just enjoyed the walking, they didn't believe me. They said, "How can you possibly claim to enjoy walking when you don't have a dog?"'

She strides away towards the red flags on the horizon. I suspect she won her last argument with the military police, and will again.

An old cattle drovers' road leads me on from an isolated farm; the farmers here are paid an additional subsidy because of the disruption caused by the firing ranges. I always love the width of an old cattle track, particularly one like this which has become disused: the way its ruts attract the cow parsley; the unevenness of the grass across its ledges. Of course there is an intimacy to a small and narrow path – but there is also a propulsion that comes from feeling you are walking behind many herds of cattle that once came this way. The very name 'Icknield Way' may derive from 'Ichen', meaning 'cattle', according to the antiquarian John Aubrey; although it may also derive from 'Iceni', the tribe who lay at the end of the long trackway across England, in Norfolk.

A little later I come to the edge of the firing area at Casterley Camp, an Iron Age hill-fort that now adjoins a guardhouse. The soldier on duty looks at me warily, but like the woman wearing Dolce and Gabbana sunglasses, opportunities for conversation do not come along that often on Salisbury Plain and we get to talking. An older man, in his fifties, he tells me that at one time the army were in trouble for riding roughshod over some of the smaller tumuli and barrows with tanks, largely because local commanders didn't know or care that they were there. With 2000 monuments listed over the Plain, this was not surprising. So they stuck large marker stakes in the middle of the tumuli; this only annoyed the archaeologists even more. Now they section them off completely.

We are looking back over the Plain. There are fires rising from some sections. 'The ordnance can catch in this hot weather, particularly the small-arms and tracer fire,' says the guard. He says it in the same neutral, observational way that Lynne had earlier, as if it were a perfectly natural human activity to bombard a hillside with material that may set it ablaze.

✢

I'm lying on a mossed and tussocked mound that pillows out from Old Adam Hill at a perfect angle, allowing me to write and look back down south over the way I have come, from Salisbury Plain and the beautiful and isolated Vale of Pewsey. Somewhere just below me is a horse cut from the chalk, which, while I am now too close to see it, has been guiding me across the valley as I came. The heads of the wild grasses are waving in the wind and just catching the light in the same way that the white marks left by the seed driller are doing in the fields below.

This area of Pewsey is delightfully empty now – no major roads, not even a 'designated long-distance footpath', and little written about despite its beauty. As if to demonstrate the isolation, a young badger passes me in broad daylight, not ten feet away, and potters up the hill towards its sett.

The white horse carved on the hill below me is a later tribute to a prehistoric past. The horse has a prancing, kinetic energy, the tail lifted, which recalls those first images of horses on prehistoric British coins and the more famous white horse at Uffington.

A middle-aged woman passes me with hair down to her waist and a white parasol. She says she has been visiting all the four white horses close to Avebury and that they are placed at the cardinal points – surely, she muses, a deliberate act by a prehistoric society. I feel almost guilty telling her that, apart from Uffington, all the other white horses on the Downs – and there are nine of them – are much later creations, mostly from the eighteenth and nineteenth centuries, and were cut as homages to the earlier ones.

To my mind this makes them almost as moving as the real thing – evidence of a continuity that stretches for thousands of years: the power and appeal of a moving horse on landscape and of 'leucippotomy', a wonderful word, the art of carving white horses in chalk upland areas. As artworks, the best of them – like this one on Old Adam Hill, one of the highest points in Wiltshire – are remarkable, for etching a horse as part of the landscape is very different from a drawing or a sculpture. The horse has to be seen from multiple vantage points; one or two of the less successful horses look as if they were done from a flat drawing and so are foreshortened when seen from below.

This particular chalk horse was designed in 1812 by a travelling painter called John Thorne, who was commissioned by a local farmer for the then princely sum of £20 both to draw and to cut it. Although he did the drawing, he absconded with the money before carving the horse; the farmer had to pay someone else to see his project finished. John Thorne was caught and found guilty of a series of crimes, for which he was hanged. The story would have been a gift to Thomas Hardy.

The parking spot at nearby Milk Hill is full of revellers heading for either Stonehenge or Avebury, in the days approaching the summer solstice, and the travelling community, the old hippies and the young ravers, are all making their way across country to an appropriate rendezvous.

A couple are flying a kite from the hill while, in a multi-coloured rainbow van with a pop-up roof, eggs and bacon are being fried and the smell drifts over. I pass a wizened man with a beard, who had stripped to the waist, showing off his tattoos. Hunkered down on the step of a caravan beside his half-breed lurcher, he tells me many of the vans have been parked up for a few nights and have 'settled in nicely'. We are far enough away from the traditional solstice trouble-spots for the Wiltshire Constabulary not to put in an appearance, and there is a good atmosphere building between the temporary inhabitants.

The only flashpoints are the dogs. I've noticed before that travellers take pride in giving their dogs considerable liberties; many a conversation between travellers exchanging astrological titbits or benign platitudes is rudely interrupted by their dogs having a go at each other.

As I stroll by one van, a bulldog of some mixed and mutinous disposition has a go at me with a snap at my legs that thankfully doesn't quite connect. His purple-haired owner is apologetic: 'Sorry love, Marley never normally does that. He's a good dog really.' It's a line I suspect she uses often.

Eating my sandwiches and some of Mike's boiled eggs, I overhear one family having a long discussion as to whether they should go to Stonehenge or Avebury for the solstice; where the police presence will be most oppressive or intrusive; and how to camp near by, given that so many restrictions are in place (English Heritage guidelines to attending the solstice at Stonehenge run to ten pages of detailed and petty rules).

'You know what?' says the man. 'I think I really can't be bothered to go anywhere! Why don't we just stay here instead? It's a beautiful spot, we've got the tent up and I can't be arsed to take it down.'

'You mean, not go anywhere else?' asks his young son, tautologically, in the way of children.

'Yeah.'

'Great!'

*

Is there any finer approach in England than along the 'Avenue' to Avebury?

The red grass-heads catch the light in the meadows through which it leads, a meandering row of megalithic stones drawing the walker from Overton Hill to the largest stone circle in England.

Certainly the Saxons seemed to think so. They were drawn here and established a settlement among the stones that has created a problem ever since, for the village spills over and around the circle in a way that muddies the picture of what should be a crisp and clean prehistoric triumph.

I've been to Avebury before, but never quite like this, after walking so many miles. I had stopped at the Sanctuary, a sad little spot just where the Icknield Way crosses the busy A4: a row of concrete markers is all that remains of what was once its own proud stone circle; at least one can see why they built it here, in one of those curious spots that, while not high, commands a view in many directions.

Opposite on Overton Hill lay three long barrows, echoes of the even larger Kennett East Barrow to the south. I thought of the long-held and poetic myth of the sleeping men inside, not least because stretched out along Overton Hill were the potential revellers for the solstice festival, looking like extras from *Mad Max*. Many were already reclined in poses of post-alcoholic and pre-match stupor, made all the more impressive by the constant thump of techno through which they were sleeping. The techno was coming from a van that looked like a mobile tattooist's outfit, guarded by shaved and combat-jacketed heavies who would have been a shoo-in for the Gewisse West Saxon army.

Coming into Avebury, I experienced my usual disorientation. It was as if a theme park had managed to build two sites on top of each other: the 'perfect English village' (rose-covered cottages, pub, church and extremely grand manor) dropped over the wild, prehistoric site. It's always been an uneasy mix: in medieval times, the villagers tried to bury many of the prehistoric stones to rid themselves of these reminders of 'devil worship'.

One villager got himself buried in the process. When his

skeleton was found under a stone in 1938, it was thought that the monument had toppled over him as he tried to remove it: coins, scissors and an iron medical probe found by the body suggested that he was 'a medieval barber surgeon' and the story was satisfyingly complete. Except that later examination of that same skeleton has shown that he was already dead before being buried, so that the tale of 'the stone's revenge' is more illuminating for the avidity with which it was grasped than any historical truth.

But it illustrates the complexity of Avebury. Two large stone circles with two smaller stone circles set within them; a figure of eight. What could and should be simpler?

For a start, only twenty-seven or so of the original ninety-six stones survive. Many of those not buried by the medieval villagers were used by later eighteenth-century builders as source materials for all those model cottages. Nor do they have the simple and satisfying astronomical alignments of Stonehenge, although that hasn't stopped people trying to find them. The great advantage of a circle is that with stones facing in so many directions, some are bound to hit astronomically determined points if you try hard enough.

The museum was named after the benefactor of Avebury, Alexander Keiller, 'the marmalade king' who made a fortune from his Dundee factory and poured that fortune into preserving the site in the 1930s. Like many a modern archaeological museum, it proved unsatisfying, trying so hard to be accessible and open that there was nothing to see: several pop-up displays and timeline charts showed what was happening in Egypt at the same time.

Dispirited, I had a cup of tea and wandered around the circle. From the east and the lane leading to Herne Way, which had been blocked off to all traffic by police, a stream of wild-looking travellers were arriving. The last time I had seen so many rasta-locked pilgrims had been at the Kumbh Mela Festival in Haridwar, on the edge of the Himalaya. There weren't any ash-smeared, naked *naga saddhus*; but there were many who looked as if they had been on the road a long time and, more to the point, as if they 'couldn't give a fuck' if anybody got in their way. One or two nervous-looking community policeman were giving them a wide berth.

Intrigued, I headed out along the lane from which they were coming – a route I wanted to take anyway, as Herne Way was an ancient track that fed into the Icknield Way back on the Downs. I passed a tall and imposing figure, his face beaten dark by the sun despite his leather hat, and wearing a cloak and multicoloured trousers.

'Uh, where have you come from?' I asked, hesitantly.

'Rainbow.'

I wasn't quite sure how to take this, but presumed it was both metaphorical and unanswerable, so pressed on, past another trio of rasta-locked travellers who were clutching their bottles of Special Brew.

They were greeted effusively by a man in a purple suit who was heading up the hill behind me. 'Brothers, it's good to see you again.'

When he caught up with me, I asked his name.

'Neptune.'

Neptune was easier to talk to than the earlier dark stranger. It's hard to be intimidated by someone who is wearing a purple suit and looks a bit like Fat Boy Slim. I asked him where he was heading.

'To the Rainbow Circle. It's somewhere up beyond the hill. In the trees. I've only just arrived. I'm late.'

I couldn't help thinking of the White Rabbit. Neptune had a shaved head and sandy, rather worried features. He was walking fast, despite a large pack and some Sainsbury's carrier bags; I struggled to keep up with him.

As it happened, I had heard of the Rainbow Circle many years before, but didn't know that it still existed: I knew that its very occasional gatherings were supposed to be secret and spontaneous events.

Neptune explained that if we followed little scraps of coloured cloth tied as discreet markers along the way, we would find the gathering. To help us further, young couples lying beside the path hailed Neptune with a 'welcome home', hugged us both and pointed in the right direction.

I had already walked many miles that day and thought of Avebury as my final destination, but there was something about this unexpected deviation that drew me on, and Neptune was walking so fast that I didn't have much chance to think.

Neptune told me a little bit about his life: he had spent some time in an ashram and lived in Spain. He was now carrying all his possessions on his back and in the carrier bags. Tentatively, I asked him how he had got involved with the Rainbow.

'*Involved!*' he exclaimed. '*Involved!* I've never really thought of it as being *involved.* You don't really get *involved* with the Rainbow Circle. It either draws you in or it doesn't.' Neptune stopped to stare at me, with the questioning look of someone who has been asked to explain jazz, then started fast up the hill again.

Careful not to commit another social solecism, I thought the least I could do was help Neptune and carry his purple jacket and carrier bags, given that I had left all my own stuff in Avebury.

The gesture seemed appreciated. 'You can come and join us if you want,' said Neptune, a little diffidently. 'There'll probably be a cup of tea.'

✶

I'm not sure quite what I had expected, but it wasn't this. I had imagined a raggle-taggle of tents and vans rather like the ones I had seen earlier at Overton Hill. But that was not what awaited us.

Neptune and I arrived at a beautiful small grove of beech trees beside a sunny meadow in which a white horse stood. The sound of voices called us inside the grove. A child was swinging from a branch on a home-made wooden sling. In the centre of the grove was a clearing, with one enormous beech tree reaching up and forming almost a cathedral spire; around it was a great circle of other beeches.

In the clearing that they made were the members of the Rainbow Circle, who one by one greeted and embraced us: 'Welcome home.' There must have been some fifty of them, of all ages. Beyond the beeches there were ramshackle tents stretching away into the rest of the small wood.

I felt a moment of great release. We all have some prelapsarian image of how life should be if the shackles were loosened and we were not in perpetual debt to the company store. Mine has always been of a woodland community – of the sort of carefree childhood that swinging from the trees in the sun represented.

As always when you arrive in any gathering it took a moment to sort the wood from the trees and the individuals from the group. A quiet concentration seemed to have brought people here – a concern for individual and spiritual harmony, but also for living in a temporary community of like-minded souls. A cooking tent had been set up to one side, as had a 'shamanic teepee' and a 'chai tent' just out of the woods in the sun.

The child finished on the swing and I took his place. A great cry went up from the clearing: 'Food Circle!' Nothing happened. Neptune came by, anxiously searching for a place to put up his tent. 'I want to walk right round the wood before I decide,' he told me. I asked him what Food Circle was. He explained that it was the communal meal, but that they would probably have to call Food Circle for at least three times before anyone actually came. I was welcome to join them 'if I put something into the hat': a quaint expression, I thought.

As I was swinging, I overheard a conversation between an older, red-haired woman called Lyn and a young novitiate girl who, like me, had just arrived:

'The highest point of creativity is at 12.30 tomorrow, on the solstice itself,' Lyn pronounced, without additional explanation.

'Is that astrologically?'

Lyn paused and gave the younger girl a look that was of almost professorial severity: 'No, *astronomically*. So yes, it's at exactly 12.30 tomorrow. If we get ready thirty seconds before that and all focus, I mean *really focus*, then we will be celebrating at the actual highest moment of creativity.'

'The one thing I'm worried about is where we're going to do it. Being in the middle of the wood isn't a very good place for a solar ceremony.'

The 'food circle' was called for a third and final time. From out of the woods and trees a surprising amount of people congregated, many barefoot, in hippie skirts, shirts, beads and anything from the Indian subcontinent.

As the large group held hands in the clearing, I realised I was the only one wearing a watch. A guitarist was playing. The group started to sway in time to the music. The songs were simple ones, in praise of living in the present, of experiencing the elements, of treating each other with warmth. Various waves and impulses were set up: kissing the hand or cheek of the person next to you, and 'passing it on' to the next person. By (happy) chance I was between two attractive women – an impulse I tried to suppress – but there was an appealing innocence in the way men, women and children were holding hands in a large circle.

Lyn called for volunteers to walk around the circle with the food, a large vat of brown-rice mix that tasted better than it looked. I didn't have a bowl or spoon with me, so ate scooping the rice up with my fingers, as I've done when staying in Moroccan villages. The girl who had just arrived, like me, and had asked Lyn about the solstice, looked a bit puzzled – 'Oh, is that how we're supposed to do it?' she asked.

Elia was a slight girl in a fringed moccasin jacket and had startlingly blue eyes. She told me that she had been to only one Rainbow Circle before – in Israel. She beamed beatifically. In her early twenties, she had been born when the sixties were just a distant memory, as had most of the people around the circle.

When the meal ended, a floppy felt hat was brought round for the donations that I realise Neptune had been referring to. Everyone put into the hat what they could afford.

✻

The sun has gone down and I'm starting to get cold. I head back into Avebury fast, falling in with a couple who've parked on the hill above — but only after a series of run-ins with the police who've tried to stop Brian from driving up there: 'The policeman told me to fuck off. That's what he actually said: "Fuck off." I was shocked. But I know there's a legal right of way so there was nothing he could do to stop me. In fact that's probably exactly why he told me to fuck off.'

Brian is a delivery driver for Sainsbury Online, which is why he knows the local routes (although I can't quite believe he makes deliveries up the ancient trackway of Overton Hill; that the Rainbow Circle in their beech wood 'order in'). It's true that the police have an odd attitude to the solstice festivities: unable to stop them, they have adopted a tone of grudging and surly acquiescence, much in the way they did at the Notting Hill Carnival in the early days.

There is a large sign up by the pub in Avebury declaring that dogs will be used to search suspects. And there are plenty of likely suspects sprawled around the stones to the south, many of whom have settled in for hours. As I arrive, a samba band starts up among the stones, and the accompanying dancers twirl blazing flame-throwers around their heads. 'Now that's some tricky shit,' says a teenage girl next to me in a strong Wiltshire accent.

The atmosphere is like a raucous bonfire night, with added Druids: a man with a bearskin mask passes among the crowds;

the accessory of choice for many is a tall wooden staff on which to lean while watching samba dancers or patrolling police. The revellers keep clear of the wild-looking travellers' dogs that are eying up all the exposed human flesh. After a day's sunning, it must look as plump and tempting to them as barbecued sausage.

I retrieve my bags and manage to get some sleep before 4.30 and the early dawn. Rather than join those who've been partying all night around the stones to the south, I wander to a much quieter area in the north-east. A few people have gathered by the big stones that were once, when upright, set as a triptych and may have been orientated towards the rising sun. Loud snores are coming from a sleeping-bagged bundle at the bottom of the largest stone, where it looks as if someone is going to sleep through this year's dawn solstice.

I talk to a tall man in a grey cloak with a staff, who lives in Malmesbury. He has the languid, tired manners of an Anglican vicar.

'Are you a Pagan?' he asks, as if it were the most natural question in the world.

I mumble the sort of non-committal generalities I usually do if someone asks if I'm a Christian. My hesitancy is reinforced when he then asks if I'm a Christian and I have to give a similar response.

'Paganism,' he explains patiently, 'is tied to a sense of place, of being rooted in a landscape. If you're drawn to a place like Avebury, then you're probably a Pagan.'

I nod politely.

'Not that it's easy being a Pagan,' he sighs, and leans on his staff to peer moodily at the ground. 'The problem about Paganism is that because it's all local, and about local places, we don't organise ourselves on a national basis very well.' For a moment he sounds like a Liberal Democrat. 'What matters to a Pagan in Malmesbury is completely different to what matters to a Pagan in' — and he casts around for an exotic example — 'to a Pagan in, say, Devizes.' He pauses. 'Or for that matter in Aylesbury. There are a surprising amount of Pagans in Aylesbury.

'Trying to organise Pagans is like trying to herd cats,' he says, with bitterness. 'It's solstice day, the most sacred day of the year, and most of them have gone to the wrong part of the circle to celebrate!'

It is true that it is surprisingly empty. I gravitate to the most comfortable stone in the triptych group and lean against the rock to eat the fruit I have in my pack, some strawberries and blueberries that have chilled during the night and taste delicious.

From my vantage point, the clear, early dawn light of the sun picks out the stones with a far greater clarity than they normally have for me. I ask myself a basic question: why is Avebury in a circle (or for that matter, why are most prehistoric monuments in Britain)? Which is, after all, more difficult to construct than a square.

A circle is what children form when they hold hands. It is what adults would like to do and like to have — a community of equals: a round table. But it rarely happens. It is aspirational. It's what for a moment I did with the Rainbow Circle in the trees. It is making yourself whole with others. It is the shape of the sun.

I lean back against the rock of the megalith and close my eyes. Far off I can hear the sound of the samba players in the other meadow, beating up a storm.

*

I am naturally drawn back to the beech wood. It's later in the morning and even the bacon butty from the temporary stall set up outside Avebury's pub hasn't helped dispel that sense of sleeping in your clothes and having been up most of the night. I've remembered Lyn's words about a 12.30 focus of energy, and I'm curious.

I find the Rainbow Circle thinking about having a late breakfast. Mark is hunched over the fire, looking cold. He tells me they've been playing drums to the full moon all the previous night, which is why everyone is so tired. Mark had intrigued me the evening before when we'd circled around the fire, an older man with a face that suggested he had lived through some difficult times; a gypsy look, with an old hat worn over a silk scarf draped across his shoulders. He speaks with a Liverpudlian Irish brogue. He has plenty of half-finished and home-made tattoos, and tells me he learned *tai chi* as part of a drug rehabilitation programme; he shows me a few simple exercises.

As we peer at the embers of the fire, he tells me a story that has become a fable among the group: that the wood had been found by a Lithuanian traveller who had for several years lived there on and off, sleeping near by in an old shepherd's shed and clearing the grove of wild ground cover. The Lithuanian had told a man, who had told a woman, who had told a man about it – in good Irish style – and that man had been a member of Rainbow Circle and had led them all there. It has the satisfying ring of myth, and Mark tells the story well, peering at the fire as he does so.

Others slowly join us for coffee and breakfast. I hand out some fruit and bags of nuts I've brought from the small village store in Avebury.

When the full group is assembled, Lyn announces that we need to focus. A blond rasta-haired man called Blue, who has been playing the pan pipes and has a calm, contemplative face, suggests we form ourselves as circles, an inner one facing out, and an outer one facing in, so that we all are partnered and looking in someone's eyes. The idea is to hold the gaze of the person opposite 'until you make a connection'.

Under normal circumstances this would be excruciating. In the sunshine that comes through the trees (quieting Lyn's fear that the wood was no place for a solstice ceremony), with the drums beating and in a hypoxic state after a night half awake, it feels perfectly natural.

We circle around each other, then bend down to touch the ground, still gazing at the other person. If this is paganism, it makes a certain amount of elemental sense – a direct connection with the sun and earth, with no mediating deities or theology.

That said, I find looking directly into someone's eyes, a stranger's eyes, problematic. It's a reminder that the way we establish intimacy – or friendship – is not by a long continual stare (which in the animal world would be mistaken for hostility), but by glancing away and then back at people; real intimacy and connection are made when those glances coincide, when both look back at each other at the same time. I remember that admonition of E M Forster's to 'only connect', and how difficult that is.

Holding someone's gaze for minutes on end is hard work. I quickly learn the way out: to give a little sigh, or the Indian greeting of *Namaste*, as if you've mentally embraced each other, and then move on. And while I'm not sure I make any real connections, looking frankly and fearlessly in people's faces is better than the common English practice of avoiding the other's eyes.

Holding your partner's gaze becomes more important (or difficult, depending on the partner) as several of the participants slip off all their clothes to be 'skyclad'. The music builds in intensity. We start dancing free-form, like teenagers at a disco where you are neither quite dancing alone nor with a specific partner. Just about everyone has stripped at least to the waist.

A young woman from Bristol with an alert, enthusiastic face who, if she were not topless, would be a dead ringer for a primary-school teacher, leads us all in a chanting workshop. She divides us up into sopranos, altos and tenors, and coaxes a surprisingly good performance out of her improvised choir. Our voices build, lift and harmonise. The sunshine coming down through the trees is blinding.

*

There is a ghost present for me at this feast and his name is Jeremy Sandford. A leonine, craggy presence, in his coat of uncured goatskin.

I first met Jeremy in the late 1980s, when the tide had been against him for some time and was only just beginning to turn. Jeremy had stayed resolutely committed to the ideals of the 1960s long after they had become unfashionable and even derided: not just free love and plenty of cannabis — although he subscribed to both — but, above all, free housing or at least some easing of the belt on the constraints of a system that allowed thousands of homes to stay empty and neglected while elsewhere landlords charged extortionate rates for crude bed-and-breakfast.

His script for *Cathy Come Home*, with which he made his name, had done more to raise public consciousness of the housing issue than just about anything else and led to the forming of the charity Shelter. It had been one of the most watched and controversial BBC dramas ever made. But that had been in 1966. Twenty-five years later, in 1991, a decade of Thatcherism had hardened attitudes. Together we made a film sequel, called *Cathy Where Are You Now*, which revisited those same problems of housing and showed that the situation for many people had if anything got worse, not better.

It was Jeremy who first told me about the Rainbow Circle camps, and how elusive they were to find. He had known many of the organisers, like Sid Rawle, the so-called 'king of the hippies', who had set up 'Tipi Valley' in Wales; Jeremy had hosted some of their early gatherings at his home, Hatfield Court, on the Welsh borders.

The Rainbow Circle traced their lineage back to the Windsor Free Festival of 1972, the first illegal parties at Stonehenge and the sixties counter-culture that, by the time I met Jeremy, had been as superseded as the Druids they revered. To a soundtrack of Hawkwind, Motorhead and the Incredible String Band, the last of the hippies lived on in exile around the Welsh borders or

Glastonbury, searching for magic mushrooms and an alternative society. They were harassed by police who at one point, the infamous 'battle of the Beanfield' in 1985, intercepted a convoy on its way to a Stonehenge Free Festival and set about the travellers' families with batons in a way that was universally condemned.

For years Jeremy had taken up the cudgels in their defence and we discussed the predicament of travellers in the film we were trying to make. Not that working with Jeremy was easy. He was of the sixties persuasion that any decision was 'closure' and so should not be taken until after the last possible moment. At one point I asked him, in desperation, if he would ever finish the script before filming began. It was already months overdue. 'Don't worry, Hugh,' he told me, puffing on a joint like a Zeppelin: 'I'm working on it in my dream-life.'

He brought an agreeable amount of anarchy to the staid corridors of the BBC, down which he trailed the whiff of that uncured goatskin coat. To the consternation of my fastidious executive producer, Jeremy used his BBC desk as a recycling point for any timber or plastic he found lying in the streets of Bristol. We went in search of the travelling communities who were squatting in lay-bys and under the A4 flyover by the docks. He opened my eyes to the hardships they endured.

Jeremy could also be mischievous and funny, as befitted a man who had once roamed Mexico looking for magic mushrooms. It was he who first told me about the bitter rivalry between Rainbow Circle and the larger, more established group they had seceded from, Dragon Order.

Dragon Order was a more settled organisation, with regular publicised camps and set fees to join. At some point around 1987, a group of rebels had decided this was all too organised and split off to form Rainbow Circle, with a more happy-go-lucky, anarchic ethos. I discovered that Lyn Lovell, the woman who had been trying to arrange the solstice celebration in the wood, had been one of the original founders of 'The Rainbow'.

According to Jeremy — who like any dramatist loved a good conflict — Dragon Order regarded Rainbow Circle as irresponsible hooligans just out to party, with too much Special Brew and constant techno. Meanwhile Rainbow Circle thought that Dragon Order were middle-class weekenders, not really 'living the life' or hard-core enough; one had complained to Jeremy, in disgust, that 'at Dragon Order camps they have washing-up rotas!'

Now Jeremy was dead. At his funeral near Leominster, travellers had descended from all over the country to play at his wake. He would have been in his element here.

In a way, the endless splits and visions of the counter-culture world still mirrored the original problems at the heart of the sixties dream: on the one hand, the idealism of a spiritual community closer to the earth, with home schooling and a self-sufficient lifestyle; on the other, the reality of trying to make this work, of decision-making 'closure' in an occasionally hostile world.

Just over the few days I spent with the Rainbow Circle camp, which always last a lunar month from full moon to full moon, some of the highs and lows of the sixties could be seen. The very free-form nature of the camp caused problems — people came and went in an easygoing way, but that also meant no one knew who everyone was. I noticed Neptune continually forgetting names; he told me that it was a bit like an ashram — you had moments of intense highs and then days of more domestic mediocrity, sorting tents, washing and food. The danger was that the longer you stayed, the more the ratio inclined to the dull day-to-day.

From the intensity of first moments like the solstice celebration in the woods, I wound down later to a more measured Circle gathering that was held beside the fire. A 'vision-stick' was passed around from participant to participant. Whoever held it voiced their concerns.

The gentle blond rasta-headed Blue, who had led the solstice dancing, took the vision stick and spoke of his fear that the gatherings might attract those who wanted more to 'party with ganja' than use it as an occasional release. The rubric given to newcomers attending the Rainbow Circle was careful about this, perhaps mindful of the old criticisms that Dragon Order had made about them:

> Come and experience a truly healthy and happy way of being. Switch off the computer NOW, and come and meet your family, a family of living light. Remember the essentials – cup, bowl and spoon and adequate clothing, bedding and shelter. Please do not bring alcohol, synthetic drugs, electric items or dogs.

On my last night a posse of drummers and guitarists arrived: one had an unusual 'travelling guitar', like a balalaika. I went to sleep in my tent among the trees with the sound of drums and massed guitars in my ears.

Next morning I slipped away quietly with a few goodbyes to the last men and women standing. Many were asleep on the bare earth: Mark was muttering a little incoherently about a girl who had sung so beautifully the night before that he had fallen in love with her: 'She's absolutely *gorgeous*. But troubled – look at her there, she's sleeping on the ground.'

As I left, I passed a dark, intense-looking man who was observing the proceedings and smoking a thin gold-tipped ciga-rette. I asked him who he was. 'I am Ilim, the Lithuanian,' he said. 'I lived here for years. And I cleared the place. I always hoped that something like this would happen – that people would join me here, in the wood that I found.'

In dreams begin responsibilities.

✳

They stand in a clear line along the Wiltshire Downs facing north: facing an enemy we do not know. The remarkable hill-forts of the Downs that I now start to come to – first Barbury, then Liddington, and Uffington in the distance with its white horse – may have been begun in the Bronze Age, but it was in the Iron Age of the first millennium BC that they reached their apogee.

Their purpose seems clear, defensively sited as they are on the northern slopes of the Downs, the better to aim their slingshots at any approaching enemy, and with such a large space inside them that an entire community could shelter for protection. Their great ditches and double ramparts are still impressive. Yet these days they are visited more by sheep than people – even forts like Barbury, which can lay claim to being one of the most historic sites in Britain. And it is far from clear that they were primarily military: some, just as at Maiden Castle earlier, are too large and may also have been places of congregation and prestige.

Long after its use or not as a prehistoric fort, Barbury crops up as the location of one of the most significant and forgotten battles in British history. In AD 556 Cynric, the leader of the West Saxons, fought a decisive engagement with the Britons at and below Barbury Castle. The Britons were defeated. The Saxons went on to create Wessex; many of the remaining Britons became slaves.

It is almost too cinematic to be true, given that the hill-fort had probably been built a good thousand years before the battle took place – as if a climactic episode of the Second World War had taken place at Agincourt, or there had been a pitched machine-gun battle inside the Colosseum in Rome.

I arrive on a beautiful but crisp spring morning. The trackway from Avebury has been lined with cranesbill and elderflower, and curls around the escarpment of the Marlborough Downs. There is a wind in the trees. I feel invigorated by my time with the Rainbow Circle; not because I share their views, but because it has been time spent in a different mindset from my own.

No one else visits the fort when I'm there. Just walking round the earthworks takes a while – they enclose some thirteen acres. I remember a comment made by a naturalist, Anthony Bulfield, who once came this way: that if you walk around the ramparts of Barbury Castle, you have walked around England. The line of the Downs turns here from the north towards the east and in doing so opens up views in every direction; Barbury Castle is on the precise point of the turn.

I become conscious of the incessant calling of the rooks from the stand of trees beside the castle. Iron Age man was obsessed with these birds. At the hill-forts and later Romano-British settlements like Dorchester, rooks and also ravens, the largest of the corvids, were often buried alongside humans.

What is it about ravens and rooks that made them so fascinating? To the casual passer-by they can be sinister – their harsh cawing coming from high stands on bare trees. A rookery is an austere place leading to madness. Tennyson's heroes deliver their neurotic and mad monologues to the sound of rooks screeching in the Lincolnshire background.

The raven has always been a creature of myth, for its intelligence, longevity (at twenty-five to forty years, Tennyson's 'many-winter'd crow' had at least the life expectancy of an Iron Age man) and capacity to mimic or follow human behaviour. But not necessarily for its loyalty. A raven is not like a dog. Corvids are cunning with their intelligence, able to steal from an Iron Age camp.

In the ancient European world, from Greece to Celtic Britain, raven calls were thought to be messages sent from the underworld to the living. One can see how. That 'caw' has the rasp of death to it. And prophecy. Apollo is said to have listened to the utterances of a raven. The Celtic raven-god, Lugh, the god of war, was told by his fellow ravens when enemies approached. In Celtic mythology, ravens were one of the animals thought to be used by shape-shifters, themselves often old women dressed in black rags, the Mor Regan or witch-harridans.

Some ravens may have been domesticated by their Druid

handlers, like the tame ravens at the Tower of London today. It would make for an arresting image – the priest with a large raven perched on his shoulder, for they are large birds, bigger than buzzards; and such an image has been found, at Moux in France, as a Gallo-Roman stone relief.

The Celts practised what modern Parsees call 'sky burials' and archaeologists more ponderously 'excarnation': the exposure of a corpse on a platform or hill so that the bones can be picked clean by scavenging birds, of which the raven would be the largest and most predominant. Only then would the bones be buried, sometimes together with some of the birds. There has been academic speculation that at the time of death the Druids may even have summoned the ravens to come with a special call, much as vultures are summoned by Parsee priests to similar modern sky burials in India.

The practice of burying ravens with humans continued well past the Celtic Iron Age and into the Romano-British period. But then it stopped. Not a single Anglo-Saxon grave has been found with corvid remains. It is just one more reminder that life in Britain changed more with the Anglo-Saxons than with the Romans.

There was a small country lane that led up to Barbury from the plain below and some friends had kindly used it to bring my mountain bike. Much as I enjoyed the walking, I wanted to do this next section at speed – and the descent along the broad green swathes of turf into the village of Ogbourne St George below was fabulous.

As my children liked to point out, mine was not an up-to-date mountain bike. Made twenty-five years ago, when they were still a novelty, it had no suspension and what they used to call a 'tight frame', so that the rider felt every last jolt on the track. Going across a furrowed field was like using a pneumatic drill.

But on the turf, and with the wind and sun behind me, I felt I was flying down the slope. The cries of the rooks died off and I started to hear the wood pigeons in the wooded valleys below.

If the rooks and crows were emblematic of the Iron Age hill-forts, then surely the wood pigeon was the bird of the Saxon villages that replaced them.

At the bottom of the hill lay Ogbourne St George ('Ogbourne' comes from Anglo-Saxon and means 'the source of the River Og' – the 'bourn' suffix often referring to places where rivers flow off the chalk, like Eastbourne below the Sussex Downs). By an accident of land management, it had retained the nucleus of the late Anglo-Saxon village intact: a manor house right next to the church, surrounded by fields. The rest of the village had grown up a little distance away.

As I thundered down the slope I could feel the ground underneath the wheels changing from the high chalk and grazing land of the Downs to the arable clay of the river valley below. Fields of green, early wheat were coming up to meet me.

In one short ride I was dropping down out of history by a millennium, from the Celtic world of hill-forts and high cattle grazing to the Saxon world of villages and farms. This was a generalisation – of course there were some Celtic farmers and Saxon shepherds. But it was broadly true. And when you're travelling at speed down a grassy slope, it's not the moment for finesse or the slightest wobble, or you'll come off your bike.

The village had daffodils growing by one of the small ponds the River Og leaves in its wake as it flows through: at first I noticed them because of the King Alfred daffodils – almost too obvious a symbol of the village's Saxon provenance. But in among the plain yellow of the King Alfreds, someone had carefully planted the far rarer (and more expensive) *cyclamineus* daffodils with their flared-back wings, like startled horses. Good as the mountain bike had been, it made me wish that I'd galloped down that fabulous green swathe of turf into the village.

✳

I don't like keeping to paths. The original Icknield Way was anyhow hardly route-mapped in the modern style with signposts. It diverged in many places. Better to think of it as a route with tendrils. Those travelling with large numbers of cattle or horses would have needed different routes from those travelling on foot alone, just as happens today in the Andes or any developing part of the world.

Past Ogbourne St George and on one of my small digressions from the main Icknield Way as it ran along the Downs, I stumbled on a small cottage in a valley that fell away to the north. It reminded me instantly of the gamekeeper's home that Richard Jefferies once described in his book of the same name – a little down at heel (for the valleys facing Swindon did not have the upmarket value of the Cotswolds or the Marlborough Downs), a little battered and worn at the sides, like Jefferies' gamekeeper's jacket where he continually rested his gun. Although this, admittedly, did not have the vermin hanging from the rafters that also caught Jefferies' attention.

Richard Jefferies was born near here in 1848 and made the Wiltshire countryside his own. As a boy he would roam over these same Iron Age forts, particularly the one at Liddington Hill which I was approaching. He too had noticed the rooks that haunt these hills, without sentimentality: the gamekeeper he describes in his first and most memorable book, *The Gamekeeper at Home*, organised rook shoots in the spring at which a 'rook-shooting party from the grand house' were invited to take pot-shots at them with rifles and even crossbows.

As a writer, he has the rare patience to wait, and observe, and record the details that a more casual visitor to the countryside might miss. He knows precisely how the poacher sets a trap for a hare – the exact height and shape of the loop for a snare, the difference a few inches can make to capture or escape; and has sympathy for the poor hare, whose foot is often stripped of flesh but held, subjecting the animal to a slow and painful death. He knows how the gamekeeper strips down his gun; how a ferret seeks the warmth of its owner's pocket, 'nuzzling down with a little hay'; how a jay patrolling a hedge pretends 'an utter indifference' to the small birds it is intent on eating.

Like the best natural history writing, his simple observational prose seems to come to him as naturally as the water down one of his rills. But it didn't. Despite having lived and breathed the Wiltshire countryside on a small struggling farm, for many years he tried to write something completely different — romantic novels of high society that never took off because, in the view of one of his later editors, they were unnatural: 'What he knew of men and women was largely confined to his acquaintanceship with farmers and their wives.' It took him years to accept that he was best at writing about what he knew and to abandon his novel-writing ambitions. The stream of fifteen books that he then, 'like an unleashed whippet', produced in the last illness-plagued decade of his life were proof of how fluent his talent was.

His sheer prolixity means that if he is now read today, it is in edited selections — which is a shame, as the original slim books are just the size to slip into a poacher's pocket. My copy of *The Gamekeeper at Home* with its dove-grey and ochre sleeve, from the uniform edition produced in 1948 for the centenary of Jefferies' birth, has been one of my favourite books ever since I first read it thirty years ago.

In the past, Jefferies has been patronised for the plainness of his style (that same earlier editor again: 'He is lacking as a grammarian and as a stylist he is by no means in the first rank') but it is precisely that unadorned, natural approach that I like. There are no purple patches of prose waiting like a swamp to sink the unwary reader. He affects the directness of his first hero, the gamekeeper, whose thoughts are 'not always flattering or very delicately expressed; and his view is not forgotten'.

My own experience of gamekeepers has been less rosy. On one occasion not far from here, I was walking with a dog along a public footpath through the woods when a keeper bounded up and threatened to throw me off the land. With luck, as I was a little way from home, I had an Ordnance Survey map in my pocket which showed the footpath. Moreover, the dog was on a lead. 'Well,' blasted the keeper, a raw-boned, tall man, 'it's only a public footpath when the pheasants are not being reared.' I wasn't sure whether to laugh or unleash the dog on him.

Jefferies was not just interested in gamekeepers for their obviously close contact with the land. As the son of a struggling farmer, he was always aware of the small divisions of rank and status in the countryside. The gamekeeper had an interestingly ambivalent status, in the confidence of his master and respected by him – indeed depended on by him – for the provision of shooting and country knowledge. One of Jefferies' cleverest passages is where he describes how a gamekeeper can subtly, or unscrupulously, influence a landowner's opinion of his tenant farmers:

> Passing across the turnips, the landlord, who perhaps never sees his farms save when thus crossing them with a gun, remarks that they look clean and free from weeds; whereupon the keeper, walking respectfully a little in the rear, replies that so-and-so, the tenant, is a capital farmer, a preserver of foxes and game, but has suffered from the floods – a reply that leads to enquiries, and perhaps a welcome reduction of rents. On the other hand, the owner's attention is thus often called to abuses.

There is no sentimentality. One object Jefferies describes beside his gamekeeper's cottage is an old, disused mantrap: 'The jaws of this iron wolf are horrible to contemplate – rows of serrated projections, which fit into each other when closed, alternating with spikes a couple of inches long, like tusks . . . They seem to snap together with a vicious energy, powerful enough to break the bone of the leg; and assuredly no man ever got free whose foot was once caught by these terrible teeth.' Jefferies tells the story of one old man, a mole catcher, who had been caught in the trap when a young boy and had gone lame in one foot as a consequence. It is the last detail he adds that has always stayed with me: 'The trap could be chained to its place if desired; but, as a matter of fact, the chain was unnecessary, for no man could possibly drag this torturing clog along.'

Jefferies was constantly aware of how the countryside was changing. Within his lifetime, from 1848 to 1887, Swindon was transformed from a small market town to a railway metropolis, and the building of the railways brought labourers and itinerants to the nearby woodlands. Jefferies used the neologism 'tramps' in quotation marks to show how recent the term was. When not actually poaching, these newcomers caused plenty of irritation for the gamekeeper, whether cutting down young saplings to sell as walking sticks (those with a spiral groove curving up from the growth of a honeysuckle vine were the most valuable), gathering hazelnuts and pulling off branches in the process, or, worst of all, lighting fires in the hollow of trees 'just for the sport'.

In some ways, Jefferies shares much in common with D H Lawrence – and not just an interest in gamekeepers. Both had a view of nature that was driven by loss and by the illness that was consuming them, and so made every moment wrested from life more precious. Jefferies was tubercular. For the last ten years of life, when he was writing the countryside books, he was forced to leave the Wiltshire he loved for London, to seek a scrappy literary living. He and his young family were desperately poor. His father's farm had gone bankrupt.

The almost hallucinatory tone of his extraordinary autobiography, *The Story of My Heart*, in which he imagines himself on Liddington Hill dissolving into time, is testament to a man who wanted to lose, not find himself, in nature: 'Listening to the sighing of the grass I felt immortality.' Lying close to the man who he imagines has been buried for 2,000 years in a tumulus a few feet away, his thoughts 'slip back the twenty centuries in a moment to the forest-days when he hurled the spear, or shot with the bow, hunting the deer, and could return again swiftly to this moment, so his spirit could endure from then till now, and the time was nothing'.

Jefferies' last years were not happy ones. He wrote about the countryside that was most accessible from London, around the fringes of Surrey. His novel *After London* (1885) was a post-apocalyptic view of what would happen if that city was overwhelmed, submerged, returned to nature: a vision he relished. Despite increasing illness, he managed still to summon up vistas of the old countryside: a lane where clematis grew below Worthing, and memories of the Icknield Way, which for him had always remained a talismanic route to the sea and freedom over the Downs, even as his own horizons darkened:

A broad green track runs for many a long, long mile across the Downs, now following the ridges, now winding past at the foot of a grassy slope, then stretching away through cornfield and fallow.

Plough and harrow press hard on the ancient track, and yet dare not encroach upon it. With varying width, from twenty to fifty yards, it runs like a green riband through the sea of corn — a width that allows a flock of sheep to travel easily side by side, spread abroad, and snatch a bite as they pass.

The track winds away yet further, over hill after hill;

but a summer's day is not long enough to trace it to the end.

Jefferies died impoverished in 1887, just thirty-eight years old. I thought of him as I biked up to Liddington. From the ramparts of the Iron Age hill-fort, I looked down to see Coate Farm, where he was born, and its nearby reservoir, now almost completely subsumed by Swindon: the fastest-growing city in the country with its hospital and car plant and high-tech matchbox factories lining the railroad and the M4. He wrote about the lake and waterbanks in *Bevis: The Story of a Boy*, a book that was later to influence Kenneth Grahame's *The Wind in the Willows*.

Jefferies came up here endlessly as a boy, and not just to empathise with the bodies below the turf. From here he could survey his kingdom, both Swindon below and more importantly the Downs stretching away to either side:

There is a hill to which I used to resort . . . The labour of walking three miles to it, all the while gradually ascending, seemed to clear my blood of the heaviness accumulated at home. On a warm summer day the slow continued rise required continual effort, which carried away the sense of oppression. The familiar everyday scene was soon out of sight; I came to other trees, meadows, and fields; I began to breathe a new air and to have a fresher aspiration . . . Moving up the sweet short turf, at every step my heart seemed to obtain a wider horizon of feeling; with every inhalation of rich pure air, a deeper desire. The very light of the sun was whiter and more brilliant here. By the time I had reached the summit I had entirely forgotten the petty circumstances and the annoyances of existence. I felt myself, myself.

As soon as I arrived, I could hear skylarks everywhere. The point about a skylark's song is not its sheer beauty, although considerable: it is the way that the acoustic is constantly changing as the skylark is on the move, the music first seeming to come out of the earth and the grass, then rocketing upwards in a cascade of notes and still spluttering high up in the sky, like the end of a firework, when it seems impossible that one should still hear it. Like Jefferies' voice. I remember suddenly his phrase, 'the lark's song is like a waterfall in the sky'.

Liddington camp is a place of dreams. It lies a little off the main track – there is no footpath across to it, so some satisfying trespassing is involved – which makes it a more private place than the other Iron Age forts.

One can almost believe the old story that King Arthur fought the momentous battle of Mount Badon here, which halted the advancing Saxons in the early sixth century and kept Britain Celtic for another half-century. One can believe but without a huge amount of evidence: we know that 'a battle of Mount Badon' was successfully won by the Romano-British around AD 500; we don't know where that was and we don't know with any certainty who led them. But in the absence of fact, Arthur, if he existed, makes a fine symbolic victor. And given that Barbury Castle is still visible behind me in the distance, where the Britons were later decisively beaten themselves by Cynric and the West Saxons in AD 556, Liddington Hill makes a fine place to have held back the inevitable.

*

And I'm away. Leaving Jefferies behind and coming out of the Wiltshire hills as I swoop down towards the M4. The map marks an enticing pub just across the motorway and before the ascent up Fox Hill into the Berkshire Downs beyond. The thought gives me wings as I hit a brief stretch of tarmac road and get the speedometer up to thirty miles an hour, which is nothing in a car but feels good on a mountain bike. I swoop over the M4 on a high bridge that leaves me feeling like the angel of the West, as I stretch out my arms from the handlebars and look down on the stream of traffic below. The metal of the car roofs glints in the sun and looks glorious.

Who needs a caravanserai carrying jet from Yorkshire, amber from the Baltic and blue faience beads from Egypt, as they had in the Bronze Age along the Icknield Way, when you can have the turquoise, silver and red of the modern car streaming past in an endless display of wealth and speed? No amount of walking will stop me from loving the sound and sight of a motor car. Like Mr Toad, the far-off poop-pooping of a vehicle coming down a country lane excites in me more admiration than condemnation. I would rather be buried in an Alfa Romeo, like an Anglo-Saxon king in his longboat, than with my boots and walking stick, however many miles across the Andes, Himalaya and now England they might have taken me.

The wind is spilled out of my sails when I reach the promised pub. It has been turned into an Indian restaurant, like so many in the villages of southern England. I enjoy a curry as much as the next man, but not when I've got a hill to climb.

Maybe it's the lack of liquid intake or the fact that I've been on the move for some time, but I feel a little hypoxic when I reach Wayland's Smithy, with its long barrow tomb. My legs are shaking as I leave the bike by the stile and wander down from the Icknield Way towards the Smithy. It is a place I've been to before, but many, many years ago – enough decades for me to remember only the approach into the trees, but not the actual tomb.

Three things take me aback: the scale of the barrow — it is almost 200 feet long; the incredible antiquity — at around 3500 BC, it is even older than Stonehenge and Avebury; and the glade of encircling beech trees around it, which remind me of the Rainbow Circle camp back near Overton Hill.

I also remember when I last came here before, thirty years ago. I had not long moved from London to the country and like many a neophyte was far more enthusiastic for its pleasures than most of the other teenage residents, who were desperate to get to the bright lights of Oxford and Reading.

My family came for a picnic along this stretch of the Icknield Way, a walk that had to adapt to the slower pace of my grandmother and younger sisters, so did not extend very far. But it did reach the Smithy. There is an old photo of us having a picnic, with my brother Ben and his recently acquired girl-friend, Kari, an exotic foreign girl whom he had picked up on a train to the general surprise and admiration of the rest of the family. And there is another photo of me walking the path wearing an old tweed jacket, an act of deliberate and absurd affectation given that I would not have been seen dead in one in London. I started to read *The Countryman*, a pocket-book-sized magazine like *The Reader's Digest*, with articles on burning rural issues of the day like the controversial introduction of oilseed rape. If able to get away with it, I would have smoked a pipe.

Just a mile or two further on from Wayland's Smithy was a far better-known landmark, the White Horse of Uffington. The best way to see it has always been from the train travelling westward between London and Bristol, a route I must have taken hundreds of times. Glance up at the right moment, somewhere between the dreariness of Didcot and Swindon, and there is the White Horse running across its hill, a memory of a wild time, but in your same direction of travel.

There are other white horses scattered across the Downs: at Marlborough, at Pewsey, at Hackpen Hill and the one I had stopped at on Old Adam Hill; some nine in all. But these others are later imitations, all cut into the turf since the eighteenth century.

The horse at Uffington is the progenitor, and an ancient one. Optical Stimulated Luminescence (OSL) dating shows it to have been made in the Bronze Age around 1000 BC; so confirming the aesthetic dating first made by a local vicar back in 1740, writing under the wonderful name 'Philalethes Rusticus', who pointed out the similarity between Uffington and the representation of horses on Bronze Age coins.

It is the delicacy of the White Horse that you notice when walking close to it. The startled eye. The gapped legs. The fluidity that has made some mistake it for a greyhound. It is hard to think of more delicate tracery on the landscape, as it lies askance the slope, with the mound of Dragon Hill below. The later white horses are all chunkier, more obvious affairs, though many have great charm; but they are shire horses to Uffington's sleek racing breed.

I find it remarkable to think how long the horse has been

preserved; without regular scouring of the chalk, the grass would grow over it again, although its position on a steep slope may inhibit the speed of that growth. As Thomas Baskerville put it in 1677, 'some that dwell hereabouts have an obligation upon their hands to repair and cleanse this landmark, or else in time it may turn green like the rest of the hill, and be forgotten.'

The likely reason for its survival is that the scouring of the horse provided a good excuse for a party. In 1738, the Revd Francis Wise, an Oxford don who did much to publicise the White Horse and other chalk figures, described how people came from all the villages around every seven years to do the cleaning, with an accompanying two-day fair that had a reputation for disorder and debauchery. It was paid for by the local Lord of the Manor as one of the conditions on which he held his land. There is nothing an Englishman likes so much as a free drink, particularly if it's paid for by his boss, and the fair became a popular tradition.

Thomas Hughes, of *Tom Brown's Schooldays*, gave a full description of a later fair in his 1857 novel *The Scouring of the White Horse*. It was held within the banks of the Uffington Iron Age fort and was

> decked out with nuts and apples and gingerbread, and all sorts of sucks and food, and children's toys, and cheap ribbons, knives, braces, straps and all manner of gaudy looking articles . . . an acrobat was swinging backwards and forwards on the slack rope, and turning head over heels at the end of each swing . . . The whole space was filled with all sorts of people, from ladies looking as if they had just come from Kensington Gardens, down to the ragged little gypsy children.

They had considerable difficulty getting the elephants' van up onto the Downs for the circus. Hughes mentions, with disapproval, an earlier fair at which a female smoking marathon was held; a gallon of gin was awarded to the woman who smoked the most tobacco in an hour.

The scourings continued, if not quite at regular seven-year intervals, in a more English way whenever the White Horse fell into such a state of decay that there was a public outcry. Although in a good condition in 1940, the horse had to be turfed over for concealment from the German bombers, as they used it as a landmark. Since then it has been cleaned and cared for by English Heritage and the National Trust.

Far more interesting than its preservation over the last few centuries is its preservation over 3,000 years. It stands as a remarkable emblem of continuity: a Bronze Age horse that was scoured later by Celts, the Romano-British and the Saxons, let alone Normans, Tudors and Stuarts.

*

For a long time, until the arrival of Optical Stimulated Luminescence as an archaeological technique, it was thought the White Horse commemorated Alfred the Great's defeat of the Vikings, an idea that was particularly strong in the nineteenth century. The Victorians liked to aggrandise Alfred wherever possible. He was the spitting image of their own Prince Albert: studious, energetic, pious and of Germanic origin. The statues they put up to Alfred in Wantage and Winchester show him as a solid, bearded Victorian sage, albeit one who has dressed up with a sword and shield for a pageant. Contemporary Anglo-Saxon coinage shows that Alfred was actually clean-shaven and gaunt, as you might expect from a man who suffered from constant pains in the abdomen.

Alfred's place as the only king to be afforded the piquant soubriquet 'the Great' was assured by his own efforts. As Churchill said, 'History will be kind to me, for I intend to write it.' Alfred's court cleric, Bishop Asser, assigned the duty of writing 'the authorised biography' while the king was still alive, kept to the brief. While just shy of hagiography, Alfred is a prodigy who aged four already outshines his older brothers; later, he battles with both Danes and illness courageously, and single-handedly founds the English navy and legal system. In vain have later historians pointed out that the foundations of a Saxon legal system were already well in place and that Sutton Hoo is but one reminder of how earlier Saxon kings had built many long-boats, not least to arrive in England in the first place. Asser's 'official version' has sunk deep into the national psyche.

That the White Horse was thought to commemorate a victory by Alfred is revealing, as is the way an Iron Age hill-fort near by has become known as 'Alfred's Castle'. He fought many of his key battles against the Vikings along the same ridge of Iron Age hill-forts that I had passed along my journey; just as many other key battles of the first millennium had also taken place along this line of the Berkshire and Wiltshire Downs: the Romano-British defeat of the Saxons at Mount Badon, either at Liddington or just further south at Baydon, and the Saxon defeat of the British below Barbury Castle.

The reason is simple and strategic. Once an invading army, be they Romans, Saxons, or Vikings, had landed in the South-East, at some stage they would try to push up the Thames and head west, passing through the narrow Goring Gap where the river cuts between the hills.

The strategy for any 'home guard' was to lure them away from the Thames and then attack from the commanding heights of the Berkshire Downs – from forts like Uffington, Liddington, Barbury, defensive positions all connected by the Icknield Way. The Downs were the fortified centre of southern England; take them and you commanded Wessex. Far from being just 'Iron Age forts', the hill-forts may have been established far earlier, in the Bronze Age, to resist the Celtic invaders who brought the Iron Age to Britain; then fortified yet further by those Celts to resist the Romans, whose descendants the Romano-British were likewise to resist the Saxons, who in turn fought their battles with the Vikings along the same heights. A lot of blood had been spilled along the Vale of the White Horse. On the slopes near by, the remains of hastily buried men have been found, some with Saxon, some with Romano-British artefacts.

If England had a heart to defend, it was this. No wonder that as late as the Second World War, a row of concrete pillboxes was built along the River Thames as it cuts through the Goring Gap. Some can still be seen today, mouldering at the bottom of river lawns and used as latrines by hikers along the Thames Path.

The Home Guard built the pillboxes to defend the envisaged Nazi advance out of London, in case the German 9th Army planned to take the same route – the Goering Gap? – as had all previous invaders if they wanted to dominate southern England after 'Operation Sea Lion'. British military command envisaged a scenario where Nazi troop-boats rolled up the Thames, navigating locks with German efficiency; although surely the likelihood was that their tanks would have used the nearby roads?

At Dorchester-on-Thames, one abandoned Second World War pillbox sits directly at the end of the Dyke Hills, the twin long barrows that formed the impressive centre of an Iron Age and later Saxon settlement. Any Home Guard soldier manning the pillbox would have faced his attackers down this row of prehistoric barrows.

Perhaps some deep historical memory had been triggered, and the British High Command had contingency plans to retreat in the face of the German advance to the Berkshire Downs as a last line of defence; to look down from those hills that even a Panzer division couldn't climb, with their military base set back towards the Marlborough Downs at the rear and with their camps on Salisbury Plain? Would the forts of Banbury, Liddington and Uffington have been used for one last time?

*

I passed several gallops after leaving the White Horse and crossing the high country heading east towards the River Thames. It was curious how rarely anyone made the obvious point that the White Horse was galloping across some of the firmest going in the country for racecourse training. The map is speckled with places associated with the racing world: Lambourn Downs, East Ilsey and Lockinge.

We have always been a nation of riders. When Caesar arrived, he was impressed by the dexterity of our horsemen as they wheeled their chariots on the shore. That this was 'the land of the horse' can be seen by Bronze Age coins, which used the same galloping iconography as at Uffington.

Yet sometimes it can appear that we have forgotten our equine past: that riding has become a minority pursuit for those rich enough to pursue it, attended by a complicated rite of passage from gymkhana to showjumping, constricted in a formal dress of jodhpurs and black leather, with a compulsory riding hat.

As a boy, I never learned to ride in England. It didn't seem like a world I wanted to join: riding schools where you had to parade around in tight circles and be shouted at by bossy, brisk women.

I only learned later, when I went to Latin America: first in Mexico at a cattle ranch; then leading expeditions into the Andes in Peru, where the muleteers usually had a few horses to go with the mules. This was riding of a more satisfying sort. Just get on a horse and go. No concerns about deportment, tack or wearing a hat, and where you could ride with a loose rein, western-style.

Only weeks before beginning this walk across England, I had been to a small village in the Andes called Huancacalle. It was a place I had visited many times over the previous thirty years. The locals used horses to carry goods over the mountain passes and down towards the Amazon, which lay beyond. They were natural and superb horsemen.

A fiesta was taking place for their patron saint and to celebrate, the locals had organised a race up the village street. This was horse racing at its most primal. The village street was unpaved and no wider than a country lane, running alongside houses and shops. The riders went bareback, careering down the street against each other and past the villagers, who whooped them on. Being an Andean festival, most of the revellers had already drunk a great deal; some of the riders also looked far from sober. The technique was to ride your opponent off the track, using your outstretched hands if necessary to impede his horse.

That spirit of pure horsemanship can still sometimes be found in England, but you have to look for it. The point-to-point held each Easter at Lockinge, not far from here on the Icknield Way, was a fine example. The jockeys might not be allowed to ride each other off the course – nor were they riding bareback – but there was a fine spirit of amateur competition, helped by the geography of the place: the spectators massed on a hill, with the racecourse spread out below them and rolling around the fields with a natural gait. In the Easter sunshine, with the jockeys in their colours, and the women in theirs, it was a splendid sight.

I enjoyed it even more because it was the only place in England where I regularly won my bets.

I remembered Cobbett's enthusiasm for horses, not just as a way of getting about the country for his *Rural Rides*, but because he considered that when it came to horses, 'the English so far surpass all the rest of the world that there is no room for comparison'. The sound he most liked when travelling was the hammering of horses' hooves on a flint road.

✲

Before descending from the Downs to the River Thames, I came to a place of almost mesmeric attraction. It is the site of one of the most momentous battles in British history. But what also intrigued me was that I must have passed or driven by it hundreds of times before without ever so much as giving the place a glance. The site lies just off a particularly bad junction, where four roads meet at the rise of a hill, and there is a blind dip before they do so.

Kingstanding Hill must be one of the most neglected battlegrounds in England, the setting for a historic victory over the Vikings: a victory that prefigured their eventual expulsion from Wessex. It was where Alfred the Great made his name and arguably proved his right to be king.

I dropped down onto it along the ancient Fair Mile track, wide enough for prehistoric man to have herded cattle down to the various fords over the Thames below. Kingstanding Hill made immediate sense as a defensive position. It guarded the flanks of the Downs, where they turned the corner, heading north from Reading and then west into Wessex.

So it was not surprising that King Ethelred and his younger brother Alfred, yet to become either ' Great' or king, chose this position to mount a crucial defence of Wessex. Their Viking opponents were led by the savage Lothbrok brothers, sons of the legendary Ragnar Lothbrok. The brothers had come to avenge their father's earlier death in England.

By 871, Viking raids had turned from being an occasional catastrophe – like the sack of Lindisfarne in 793 – to a sustained assault by the Danes. Their 'Great Army' had conquered the other large Anglo-Saxon kingdoms of England, Mercia and Northumbria. They had also just conquered East Anglia – killing King Edmund of the East Angles in the process – and then marched on Reading, coming down the Icknield Way from Thetford in Suffolk.

Only Wessex was left. The Vikings took and held Reading, emerging from its fort like 'savage wolves', according to *The Anglo-Saxon Chronicle*, to beat back Ethelred and Alfred, killing their most loyal henchman, ealdorman Æthelwulf, in the process.

The Saxon brothers had managed to regroup – but if they were not able to hold Kingstanding Hill, then the Vikings would swing around into Wessex and the stronghold of the Downs, using both the Thames and the undefended Icknield Way for access; worse still, they had reinforcements on the way.

One glance at the land was enough to show how cleverly the Saxons had chosen their defensive position. There were two parallel spurs running out from the Downs towards the Thames: Kingstanding Hill and Moulsford Common. These were divided by a deep valley, which now contained the inappropriately named Starveall Farm, a prosperous-looking place of paddocks and pheasant shooting; but there was no disguising the steepness of the gorge between the two opposing hills. The Saxons occupied Kingstanding Hill, inviting the Vikings to occupy the other.

Alfred was still in his early twenties, the youngest by some way of five brothers (he seems to have been a late afterthought, when his mother was in her forties); even given Saxon mortality rates, no one expected him to be king. But the other brothers died early, whether from battle wounds or the attrition of defending the now last Saxon kingdom left in England. Alfred, trained more to be a clerical scholar than a warrior, had to buckle on his shield.

His loyal biographer Asser stresses, with revealing overemphasis, that Alfred was the 'heir apparent' and even that he could have been king already, so popular was he; but his older brother King Ethelred had two sons, the rightful heirs – and Alfred had yet to show any military prowess.

The battle of Ashdown that now ensued was to make his name. In a curious incident, King Ethelred was late in coming to the battlefield because he insisted on going to mass; it is unclear from Asser's account, never reliable, whether he regards this as piety or cowardice. Whatever the reason, Alfred had to lead the charge 'like a wild boar', according to Asser, drawing the flank of the Vikings where the hill dipped towards the river. Once the Norsemen had broken formation, Ethelred, arriving late on the scene, made a more frontal charge across the valley. Between the brothers, they scattered the Viking army. Asser reports with relish that two of the Norsemen kings and four earls were killed, along with 'thousands' of their men.

As I arrived, two red kites were searching ponderously over the field, the first I had seen on my journey. It was a scorching summer's day, so clear that I could see a woman feeding the horses down in Starveall Farm below in the valley, and the sheep dotted on the far hillside.

But the battle of Ashdown was fought in the depths of winter, on 8 January 871. The Vikings liked to attack the Saxons around the feasts of Christmas – some years later, in 878, they would almost defeat and capture Alfred, now King Alfred, at Chippenham when they attacked on Twelfth Night – both because they could exploit the Christian festivities and were accustomed to fighting in the cold; England in winter must have been a spring dip for those used to the Baltic.

Therein lies much of the reason for Ethelred's and Alfred's success. To get from Reading to Kingstanding Hill would have taken the Vikings the best part of four hours' hard marching. They would have arrived to find a rested and prepared English army. And the defeated Vikings then had to return to Reading in the dark of a short winter's day, while harassed by their Saxon opponents.

So Ethelred and Alfred had successfully lured the Vikings too far from their base. Overconfident, the Vikings had taken the bait, perhaps scornful of Saxon fighting ability. If so, the worm turned.

The battle was not decisive – the Vikings regrouped with reinforcements from King Guthrum, who was to prove Alfred's most long-lasting Viking opponent, and Alfred was to endure many vicissitudes before finally defeating Guthrum at Eddington in 878. But Ashdown was a turning point psychologically. It showed the Vikings – and the Saxons themselves – that the invaders could be defeated.

When Ethelred died not long afterwards, worn out by the ceaseless incursions of the Vikings, Alfred was a shoo-in for the succession, despite not being the natural 'heir apparent'.

Of the images we have inherited of Alfred – the wise full-bearded sage of Victorian legend, the henpecked minder of the 'cakes' – I far preferred the image I now had of him at Ashdown: the headstrong young prince, charging over a frosted field towards the Viking host who had shown the temerity to invade Wessex and kill his most trusted ealdorman – of Alfred as a wild boar.

Of course there was nothing here now to show any of this: a little smoke moving across the valley bottom; the scavenger red kites hovering; and a few off-road bikes gunning up along the Ridgeway.

✢

Many will tell you that the Icknield Way (or Ridgeway as it is known locally for this section) descended towards the river at Goring on Thames. Walkers are funnelled in that direction for the 'convenient amenities'. But that was not the route I wanted to take.

There were several reasons for this. Goring is a plush resort, popular in Edwardian boating days, with large hotels and substantial pubs. The default drink is gin and tonic. Oscar Wilde rented a large house there for a season with Lord Alfred 'Bosie' Douglas; it was Bosie's demand that this be an expensive riverside house that pushed Oscar into a financial crisis and the spiral of disastrous events that led to his downfall. Both George Michael and Geri Halliwell have houses near by. The Indian restaurant does baked sea bass.

Instead I wanted to cross the Thames a few miles further north, from Cholsey to Little Stoke. There were good historical reasons for choosing this ford. Scholars agree that the Icknield Way diverges here into a number of crossings of the river; which one prehistoric man chose might have depended on how many cattle he needed to take across. The fields on either side of the ancient ford at Little Stoke are littered with Iron Age artefacts. It is rare not to see the metal detectors out at a weekend. And this is where Edward Thomas chose to cross for his book on the Icknield Way a century ago.

It was Edward Thomas's book that had partly inspired me to do this journey in the first place. I had been reading it carefully as I travelled; with some frustration, as he took the journey in reverse, from Norfolk towards Dorset, and so I was having to read his account backwards; and with some surprise, as it was not quite the book I had imagined it might be.

One might expect *The Icknield Way*, which he published in 1913, to be Thomas at his most poetic, even though at this stage of his life he was still writing prose. He turned to poetry only shortly afterwards for his last few years, at Robert Frost's suggestion, before being killed in the First World War on Easter Monday, 1917. And yes, there are wildflowers in the hedgerows and the mystic sense of the road as 'a shining serpent in the wet'. But there is also an underlying darkness, a gloom, that leads him off in other directions.

Edward Thomas's reputation as a poet has grown exponentially during the century since his death. His adaptation of Frost's plain-speaking verse to an English setting was greatly influential on Auden; more recent poets like Glyn Maxwell and Matthew Hollis sing his praises. Yet I suspect that if Thomas had not become so fine a poet, his earlier prose books would be far less admired: many are journeyman works, written at speed and under pressure, as he complained at the time. There is the odd flash of genius and much makeweight material. His book on *The Icknield Way* is a case in point. He had suggested several other topics before the publishers pointed him in this direction. After a brilliant dedicatory preface, the book gets bogged down in a minute description of exactly where the route went.

Letters show that at the time he was suffering from a bleak depression, the black dog trotting along at his side. He wistfully quotes Leslie Stephen, who had remarked that walking was a panacea for writers that could have cured Samuel Johnson. There is the sense of a man glad to have no company with him. He talks to no one.

A row of red-brick houses at Cleeve remind him of all the unimaginative, lumpen buildings for labourers, far from the wisteria-clad Georgian rectories that Edwardian England congratulated itself upon, just as *Country Life* England still does. In his poem 'Wind and Mist' he talked of one such red-brick house with a garden where 'the flint was the one crop that never failed. The clay first broke my heart and then my back.'

The preface contains some wonderful, mystical lines: 'I could not find a beginning or an ending to the Icknield Way. It is thus a symbol of mortal things with their beginnings and ends always in immortal darkness.' And it was difficult to resist this clarion call to follow in his footsteps: 'there is nothing beyond the furthest of far ridges except a signpost to unknown places.'

When Thomas arrived at Little Stoke and the Thames from Norfolk, he was halfway through his journey, so I was meeting him at midpoint in the route, so to speak, coming the other way, as I took the Ferry Road down from Cholsea.

In his day there was still a ferry in operation across the Thames – and there is still the old ferryman's cottage just up the bank – but now there was only one way to cross, short of a five-mile walk around the nearest bridge. I folded up my clothes in the backpack, left the bike under some bushes, and swam.

After days of travel on the hills, the shock of cold water was both welcome and extreme. The sun was out and by the time I was halfway across, the edge had been taken off that first cold shock. On the other side of the bank, the flowering horse chestnuts were casting deep pools of shadow along the bank. There was a lane directly ahead and I could see up the trees to a familiar house at the far end.

For there was a final and less scholarly reason for wanting to make this my Icknield Way crossing of the Thames, and reach Little Stoke on the other bank. It was where I lived.

Chapter 3

Homecoming

'Now it passes on and I begin to lose it,' Rat said presently.
O Mole! the beauty of it! The merry bubble and joy, the thin,
clear, happy call of the distant piping! Such music I never dreamed
of, and the call in it is stronger even than the music is sweet!
Row on, Mole, row! For the music and the call must be for us.'
   The Mole, greatly wondering, obeyed. 'I hear nothing myself,'
he said, 'but the wind playing in the reeds and rushes and osiers.'
                    Kenneth Grahame, *The Wind in the Willows*

My family had lived at Little Stoke for over thirty years.
Which is not to say I always had. It was my parents' house.
I had lived here as a boy and then travelled away, both to Latin
America for books, films and expeditions, and also to Bristol
where I had a house of my own for many years, and married.
But Little Stoke had always played a central part in my life, partly
because I had first come here as a city boy from London, aged
sixteen, and the shock of arriving in the country had been both
deep and pleasant; it was perhaps because the countryside had
once been foreign for me, not familiar, that it still held such
appeal. And in recent years I had returned there as a refuge after
a painful divorce and exile from Bristol, as a natural place to
retreat to, to rebuild. My parents had since moved on from their
house, and I remained, renting out a thatched barn near by.

   Little Stoke is a small hamlet of just a few houses, between
the two larger villages of North Stoke and South Stoke, which
also lie on the river. There is a big Manor Farm, to which most
of the surrounding land belongs, some cottages up on the first
outlying hill that rises towards the Chilterns, and the old ferryman

and dairyman's cottages. And the house that we had lived in, a white house with green shutters that faced down a willow-lined lawn to the river, with an adjoining old barn.

There was a small orchard and a rambling walled garden which we planted with vegetables when we first arrived, my mother being determined to lead the Good Life in as self-sufficient a way as possible; we kept chickens in a movable coop that we wheeled around the lawn, leaving scorched squares of acrid grass from the chicken excrement. My sisters kept a pony in the paddock.

When I was young I used to sit under the willows along the backwater to read, or take a small motorbike up into the hills, or follow the traditional English pastime of messing around on the river in small boats.

Over the years, I had swum the river many times. But this was different. This was after a long journey and some time away, a coming home. It was early evening by the time I crossed and the usual traffic of small crafts and barges had more or less disappeared, although I kept an eye open for the almost silent rowing skiffs sculling down from the Oxford University boathouses upriver: lethal, sharp bows, and a helmsman looking backwards made these potential assassins in the water, particularly as the last thing they expected to find in the Thames was a lone and silent swimmer.

Although perhaps they should. For in the last few years, swimmers, like the freshwater fish, have started to come back to the upper Thames. Where once I saw another swimmer perhaps every other year, now there were far more in a week.

I can date it back to a single summer's day a few years before. I was sitting with my boys in the barn when we saw four swimmers in wetsuits crunching their way down the gravel of the lane. Some of them were large and well cushioned, as is the way with long-distance swimmers. Their more svelte leader turned out to be Kate Rew, whose book *Wild Swim* had done much to popularise the idea, and who had founded the Outdoor Swimming Society; she lived close by and sometimes came here to swim with a group down to South Stoke. We joined them.

Particularly in the evening I loved to float downstream, with the odd curious cow looking down from the banks of the fields, and to see the coots, moorhens, and crested grebes up close as they glided out from the overhanging branches of the tall horse chestnut trees. Sometimes I startled a kingfisher, which would startle me back even more with its small rocket propulsion away from the bank, a shot of turquoise and gold like an Italian firecracker going off.

So to swim back home after my long journey from the coast made emotional as well as practical sense. After dealing with some of those practicalities – like rowing a dingy back across the river to retrieve my clothes, pack and bicycle – I lay on the ferryman's old jetty and let the setting sun fall on me. The flambeaus of the horse chestnut trees were lit up by the last rays of light, like lanterns for a river regatta.

It was a disorientating homecoming in some ways – as if Little Stoke, which I had known all my adult life, was somehow repositioned in my mind. I had always thought of it as just the place my family happened to live: its central position on the Icknield Way had never registered more than as an abstract fact; nor that this was such a heartland for the Anglo-Saxons.

By following the Icknield Way up from the Dorset coast, I had been going with the historical weather behind me, so to speak, as a good walker should: I had come from the earliest prehistoric beginnings of England and through its Celtic and Iron Age development; now I was in the centre of the Saxon world, of the so-called 'Dark Ages' after the Romans departed Britain. And ahead lay the Viking invasions on the coast of East Anglia that brought that world to an end.

I had shied away from the Anglo-Saxons at school, and for that matter at university, where my English Literature course started late enough, with Chaucer, to avoid their study. Looking at the history books again, I realised why. The long complicated genealogical tables of kings' names – Æthelbald, Æthelberht, Æthelred – with little detail to distinguish the reigns of most of them, aside from Alfred the Great, and the battles between the rival kingdoms of Wessex, Mercia and Northumbria, had left me cold.

What I had now begun to appreciate far more was the Anglo-Saxon culture not of the courts but of the fields: the farms, homesteads and hunting lodges that had established a pattern of village life which had endured for over a millennium; being back at home for a while would enable me to re-examine that village life with the shock of familiarity.

✻

There is nothing like sleeping in clean sheets after travelling rough. The comforts of home. Even listening to the electric kettle boil gave me pleasure. One of the principal reasons to camp, surely, is to help you appreciate domestic mundanities. I went to bed with a cup of tea and a book.

At 4.30 in the morning I was woken in those clean sheets by a frantic knocking on my door. Feeling like Badger, I went to see who had got lost in the night. It was my Czech girlfriend Irena, who lived on the London fringes of Kent, some way distant. I could tell she had not come out of a feverish desire to see me; it was the middle of the working week and she commuted into London. Her face was tear-stained and dishevelled.

'It's the chickens.'

This had been a disaster waiting to happen. Like many Londoners, Irena craved the countryside, and yet couldn't move out easily because of work and school commitments. So she had bought chickens for her suburban garden: three, named in the traditional way after American states and Fleetwood Mac songs – Utah, Amber, and Green Manalishi.

This was fine in principle. But her area of leafy south London was like a town in a western before Gary Cooper or Jimmy Stewart arrived: foxes lounged on street corners, watching passers-by with nonchalant insolence; their cubs gambled in the laurel hedges; when I wrote at her house, a vixen stalked past the garden windows on regular, hourly patrol.

Like a good homesteader, Irena had put in thorough defences: the coop was underwired; the perimeter defended with trip-wire searchlights and sonic alarms; but still they came.

Amber had already been taken, in broad daylight. Now presumably Utah and Green Manalishi had gone the way of all fowl.

'They didn't get Utah.'

From the BMW behind her, I could hear the faint clucking of an alarmed hen. Irena looked at me. I had just become a chicken rescue home.

I gave her tea and breakfast and she caught the first dawn train to London and her job. Utah looked around my barn, which had comforting rafters and thatch, like an extended coop. She gave a contented gurgle. I knew exactly what she was thinking: 'This is a place where I could lay my eggs.'

Before she discovered the delights of my duvet, I rang my sister, who lived not so far away and kept chickens; one more to add to the flock.

*

This area of South Oxfordshire was still surprisingly empty and agricultural for a place within striking distance of London, although farming had changed greatly during my lifetime.

'It's the London boroughs. They round up the urban foxes, put them on trains and release them off the embankment at Goring. First real bit of countryside they reach out of London. We never used to get foxes here. It's not fox country.'

Sarah Phipps was looking mournfully at her chickens, which had suffered recent fox depredations. We were sitting on the back lawn of her Old Vicarage Farm in nearby South Stoke, a cheerful jumble of fields and vegetable gardens stretching down to the river, with the odd cow ambling across the meadows. But now only the odd cow. Time was, when Sarah and her husband John first started farming here over half a century ago, they had a herd of sixty Jersey cattle; their friend Tony Knowles worked with them as a dairyman and had always lived in the house, together with a cheerful assortment of lodgers, waifs and strays whom Sarah had mothered down the years I had known them.

Which had been some time. Almost my first memory of meeting them was at the celebrations for the Queen's Silver Jubilee in 1977, when a float paraded around the village packed with neighbourhood dignitaries in Roman togas and cod armour, and John and

Sarah had an open party on the meadows. Another local farmer filmed it all on Super-8; the reel had often been played at village hall events since, so had become part of local folklore.

'Even then, the village was mainly a farming one,' Sarah added as we were reminiscing about the Jubilee. 'When John first came to the village in 1948, there were hardly any tractors. Everything was horse-drawn. When he bought the farm in 1956, it was about the only private property in the village; the rest were owned by one of the Oxford colleges and rented out to agricultural labourers. We had three shops, a school and a post office. Everything had to be here as the wives didn't have cars. Now there's hardly a farmworker left – or for that matter a horse. Let alone shops or a post office. The pub is hanging on by a thread. The work all gets contracted out. Some big farms around here don't have a single worker of their own. And they've all had to diversify.'

Sarah and John's herd had contracted over the years, not least through the difficulties of dealing with milk quotas ('Ours was set during a bad year,' said Sarah darkly, 'so artificially low and completely unfair') and their determination to have characterful Jerseys rather than the usual dull, black-and-white Friesians, a breed whose popularity only exploded to monoculture and monochrome proportions in the 1970s. To make up the income, they had leased out many of the surrounding outhouses to businesses, including one that renovated old cars, a business very much after John and Tony's own hearts.

John was aged eighty, a gentleman farmer of the old school who chain-smoked and wore a panama hat. Tony, their old friend and dairyman, was now eighty-three and getting frailer. When I was a boy, I remember him as a tall, tremendously strong man who winched boats out of the river when no one else could. He shared John's passion for cars and had a 1934 MG NA Magnet, even if, as he said, it usually stayed in one of their garages, under repair.

Sarah had come here from Wales where she had grown up near Abergavenny and had a countrywoman's relish for the down-to-earth. Later, over dinner with John and Tony and assorted offspring, she expanded on the foxes that were being dumped in verdant South Oxfordshire by unscrupulous London boroughs.

'Someone saw them doing it,' she said.

I murmured that perhaps it was just one of those myths that people wanted to believe.

'We live by myth,' pronounced John wisely, holding an unlit cigarette as a temporary sublimation activity. The dining room was full of family portraits and fine furniture, covered with old farming magazines and the homely clutter that had grown over half a century of living in the house.

I asked politely about the red kites that had started to appear in numbers over this part of Oxfordshire ever since being reintroduced on the Getty estate, which lies inland from the Thames on the Chilterns. One of the most characteristic sights at Little Stoke over the last few years had been to see their forked-tail figures swoop down over the fields as they searched for carrion.

Sarah reacted strongly. 'Well for a start, they are *not* just carrion birds. People say they are, but they're not. They'll take small chicks. I've seen them try to get among the chickens — although if a hen got hold of one, they'd get a kicking, as kites aren't big birds, only about four and a half pounds at best. And they take songbird chicks. I know they do, because they take them into our pine trees to eat them, and the bits drip down.'

She paused dramatically to announce this last detail; her seven-year-old grandson Josh looked momentarily disconcerted, but then turned his attention back to the Yorkshire pudding. He was being brought up to country ways — just before dinner he reported that the dog was regurgitating whatever it was she had just caught in the hedgerow. Sarah told him that it was the one breed that had learned to regurgitate food for its pups, the Hungarian Vizsla.

Sarah had always been full of arcane and intriguing country lore. She had a keen interest in ley lines and was disappointed that I had not been following them more closely as I tracked across the country from the south-west. I shared the scepticism of archaeologist Richard Atkinson, who had once demonstrated that if you drew lines between all the telephone boxes in a county, you would get enough boxes lying on the same axis to prove the existence of 'telephone box ley lines', just as you can with ancient monuments.

But Sarah was a strong advocate: 'Glastonbury, Avebury, Stonehenge – they are all places where the Michael ley line crosses with the Mary ley line, the masculine and feminine energies combining.' She made a cross with her fingers. 'Whereas Crowmarsh [a village just upriver] is way off them. That's why it was a leper colony.'

Everyone looked surprised.

'Were there leper colonies in England?' asked Tony.

'Absolutely. They had to put them somewhere,' said Sarah firmly. 'A friend of mine invited me over to a cottage she had bought in Crowmarsh. I couldn't stay in it for more than twenty minutes. Gave me the heebie-jeebies. Gave her the creeps as well. She sold it after six months. When she dug over the garden for vegetables, she found a row of skulls.'

I had a quiet beer with Tony later in the evening. He told me he was still upset about the time when his herd was down to a dozen cows, and half had to be slaughtered and incinerated. 'I made sure I wasn't around that day.' Almost all the rest had been due to go just a few months before we met, but there was a last-minute 'reprieve' and he was able to keep the remaining four. He still got up each dawn to let the cows out of their sheds and take them down to the river. 'It's easy in the evenings because they find their own way back to the sheds.' Jerseys are smaller, more delicate cattle than the robust Friesians (one reason for increasing Friesian supremacy in the battle of the cows) and Tony felt protective about them. He still cut their hay from the meadows in late summer, but where once he used to cut 5,000 bales, now he cut just 200.

Over the road at the Perch and Pike, I had a nightcap at the bar and bumped into Paul, one of the last farmworkers still living in the village. He was about my age.

'Don't listen to what all the farmers tell you. Business is booming. It's incredibly profitable. We're only early summer and most of the crops on the fields round here have been pre-sold already for harvesting. There's a lot of demand out there. And not just wheat. Oilseed rape is booming and some of these speciality crops, like poppies, do very well.'

I had seen the fields of poppies coming right up to my barn, the mauve ones that are cultivated for medicinal morphine (and, so local anecdote had it, were monitored carefully around harvesting time to make sure no one got the wrong idea and treated them as an Afghan-style drugs crop). Together with the yellow of the oilseed rape fields, this part of the country was beginning to look like an oriental rug.

Paul told me how the farms along the old Icknield Way had been forced to pool their resources. A modern combine harvester could cost around £200,000. As agribusinesses, the arable farms at least were flourishing.

'Not that much of the money gets down to the workers!' Paul added. Wages were still low. He depended on overtime: twelve- to fourteen-hour shifts a day.

The change in the character of the village meant that there was much less sympathy for farming. At times, Paul encountered outright hostility, particularly when he was spraying the fields, and local drivers went by shielding their faces ostentatiously and gesturing. Or they complained if he was harvesting late at night because of the noise and the lights. The police had been sent out to talk to him.

I had been aware of this myself. The lanes around Little Stoke had been awash with slurry manure for a week when they were dressing the fields, and the lorries had slopped their loads around. It didn't matter much with my old car – when I had been able to drive it – but some of my neighbours in upmarket BMWs and 4x4s were not happy at looking as if they had just run a rally through a mudbath.

'Still, you get all sorts here now,' said Paul. He told me of an American couple who complained on moving to the village about the loud bell-ringing from the local church. There was amusement at the subsequent Parish Council meeting when the motion was debated and had to be paused several times because of the noise made by the twenty high-speed trains that pass through the centre of the village each hour.

The bridge and cutting that the railway creates as it carves its way through South Stoke is a cause of social division. There is a sense that you are either on the right or wrong side of the tracks: down towards the river and the meadows and the pub, with their more spacious detached dwellings, at the leafy end of the village; or in the shadow of the railway, in one of the old terraced labourers' cottages, with the trains thundering overhead.

*

If Dorset at the start of my journey had been Hardy country, then this was Kenneth Grahame's. Every house along the river laid claim to be the inspiration for Toad Hall, every island to be where Pan played his pipes 'at the Gates of Dawn'. The Wild Woods behind me in the Chilterns; the railway along which Toad made his escape from jail; the ring of Downs to the south, Ratty's 'Mountains of the Moon, beyond which was the Wide World'; and of course the riverbank itself: all were near by.

Kenneth Grahame was a figure I found fascinating, a traveller who had returned to his childhood home. His early years had been spent on the Thames at Cookham. Then, after decades working in London at the Bank of England and journeys abroad, he returned to Cookham in his forties, now married and with a son, and wrote

The Wind in the Willows in 1908. Later, he lived in a succession of homes along the river from me, at Blewbury and Pangbourne.

An admirer of Richard Jefferies, he tramped for miles along the Icknield Way and some of his first essays were on the pleasures of walking:

> Join [the Icknield Way] at the point where it crosses the Thames; at once it strikes you out and away from the habitable world in a splendid, purposeful manner, running along the highest ridge of the Downs a broad green ribbon of turf, with but a shade of difference from the neighbouring grass, yet distinct for all that. No villages nor homesteads tempt it aside or modify its course for a yard; should you lose the track where it is blended with the bordering turf or merged in and obliterated by criss-cross paths, you have only to walk straight on, taking heed of no alternative to right or left; and in a minute 'tis with you again – arisen out of the earth as it were.

Like Jefferies, Grahame was fascinated by his own childhood as a period of receptivity, of openness to nature, and he drew inspiration for *The Wind in the Willows* from Jefferies' novel *Bevis, the Story of a Boy*, set along the waterbank.

When *The Wind in the Willows* appeared, the anonymous *Times* reviewer dismissed it with what must be one of the worst and funniest judgement calls in the history of literary criticism: 'As a contribution to natural history, this work is negligible.' It needed Arnold Bennett, in *Punch*, to see that 'the book is an urbane exercise in irony at the expense of the English character and of mankind. It is entirely successful.'

And the well-loved characters are archetypes of the different sorts of English male: shy bachelor Mole, worldly Ratty, boastful Toad and strong, silent Badger. What prevents them from being stuffed animals is that along with the most comfortable of English characteristics – a fondness for picnics, messing around in boats and eating tea in their slippers – is some strikingly neurotic behaviour: the sort of deep disturbance that often lies beneath the English skin.

Toad is the most extreme manifestation of this: his glazed 'poop-pooping', the self-delusional addiction for boats, caravans and then finally – his hard drug – for cars, which leaves him in 'violent paroxysms'. Mole cries frequently and has equally violent paroxysms of grief at the thought of the home he has abandoned; while Ratty at one point has to be physically restrained from absconding to the warm South for a life of unspecified Mediterranean pleasures. As for Badger, he already has a reputation for latent violence – even the Wild Wooders are afraid of him – before we see him laying about with his ash cudgel.

There are hardly any female characters in *The Wind in the Willows* – not even a boyish Tinkerbell figure, let alone a Mrs Mole (although an early draft suggested one). Their absence allows Grahame to focus on a different component of the Englishman's character. What drives his creatures is not romance but an obsession with 'home', a word that is repeated almost a hundred times throughout the book.

The story begins with Mole leaving Mole End and finishes with Toad, helped by his friends, regaining Toad Hall. Throughout, 'homesickness' is an emotion so strong it almost incapacitates its victims. Yet there is a constant oscillation between the need to create a home and the need to escape it: the tension between the allure of 'The Open Road', as Grahame calls his chapter introducing the car, and the retreat to the womb-like home, of which Mole's is the most emblematic. At one point poor Mole, when he's been away for some time, gets a whiff of the smell of his own burrow on the breeze and the effect is almost electric:

Home! That was what they meant, those caressing appeals, those soft touches wafted through the air, those invisible little hands pulling and tugging, all one way!

The English love of the home goes with an overwhelming protectiveness. I was used on my travels in South America to the near-universal concept of *mi casa es su casa*, 'my home is yours', the welcome given to almost complete strangers – often by those who can least afford it. To give someone a bed for the night, or to share the family's meal with them, is instinctive.

The English equivalent was 'my home is not yours but very much mine, although I might invite you to stay if I like you a great deal.' We don't have shotguns loaded, in the way of the American West, to see off the unwanted; but we have cold indifference and 'Beware of the Dog'. The first sight Mole has of Toad Hall is a noticeboard saying: 'Private. No Landing Allowed.' The only reason Mole and Ratty dare to knock on Badger's door is because they are lost in the Wild Wood at night: 'I've never even ventured to call on him at his own home myself, though I know him so well,' says Ratty.

Badger's reaction is as English as it comes: an initial gruff crossness that anyone has dared knock on his door; then a warm welcome and, when he takes Mole aside for a private tour, the perfect summary of why an Englishman's home is his castle: 'You know exactly where you are. Nothing can happen to you, and nothing can get at you. You're entirely your own master.' The unstated subtext, from confirmed bachelor to confirmed bachelor, is 'as long as you don't get married'.

Badger's warren is more substantial than might have been expected for, in a fine flight of fancy, Grahame gives him the ruins of a Roman city as a sett with, Mole notes in comical wonder, masonry, pillars, arches and pavements: '"How on earth, Badger," he said at last, "did you ever find time and strength to do all this? It's astonishing!"'

Just as Jefferies wrote his post-apocalyptical account of London after the fall, when nature had again taken over the city, so Grahame relishes Badger's explanation of how, while the creators 'built to last, for they thought their city would last forever', it now lies subsumed beneath the Wild Wood, forgotten by everyone.

Grahame was unhappy when he wrote *The Wind in the Willows*. His marriage had been a disaster. His only son, Alastair, had fits of bad behaviour that were the model for Toad's. His own health was failing and he was soon to lose his job at the Bank of England.

The return to the Thames was an attempt to re-create a golden summer that was beginning, by 1908, to be overshadowed by war and social change as the Edwardian era ended. The ferrets, weasels and foxes of the Wild Wood prefigure the anarchists and social-ists who would assault Toad Halls all over Europe.

The most intense of all the chapters is the one in which Mole and Ratty hear Pan playing his pipes on some islands just upstream. The ostensible, tenuous link to the plot is that Otter has lost his son, so Mole and Ratty go looking for 'young Portly'. Most abridgements of the book for children, let alone plays and films, lose this section.

But the epiphany that Mole and Ratty experience upstream is intense; it is the place of Ratty's song-dream, the place 'the music played to me':

> In midmost of the stream, embraced in the weir's shim-mering arm-spread, a small island lay anchored, fringed close with willow and silver birch and alder. Reserved, shy, but full of significance, it hid whatever it might hold behind a veil, keeping it till the hour should come, and, with the hour, those who were called and chosen.
>
> ('The Piper at the Gates of Dawn')

The epiphany is short. The animals experience a glimpse of Pan for just a few seconds before dawn. When the sun rises, they forget what they have seen — his gift to them, so they are not left with a sense of endless regret. Is Grahame here writing about his own childhood? That, if he had not remembered it so intensely, he would not forever be trying to re-create its fugitive happiness, like his contemporary J M Barrie and the Lost Boys?

But there is a happier aspect to *The Wind in the Willows*. No novel so celebrates idleness. Grahame claimed to be congenitally lazy – he left his bank early each day and took long holidays. Like Toad, he liked to stay in bed in the mornings. The whole book is a paean to sloth.

He saw life on the waterbank as essentially for slackers. *The Wind in the Willows* makes clear that oarsmen who try too hard, like Toad and Mole, fall in the river. Rat has the right attitude: 'Believe me, my young friend, there is NOTHING – absolutely nothing – half so much worth doing as simply messing about in boats.' Grahame had written an essay, 'Loafing', in which he extolled the joys of doing just that on the riverbank, preferably after a full breakfast, while serious, early-start oarsmen exhausted themselves on the water.

He experienced the same sense of satisfaction at seeing a cyclist labouring past him on a hill, 'dusty, sweating, a piteous thing to look upon'. Even better than walking, he liked the feeling at the end of the day when he could relapse into a pub for 'unnumbered chops with country ale' and when

the hard facts of life begin to swim in a golden mist. You are isled from accustomed cares and worries – you are set in a peculiar nook of rest. Then old failures seem partial successes, then old loves come back in their fairest form, but this time with never a shadow of regret, then old jokes renew their youth and flavour. You ask nothing of the gods above, nothing of men below – not even their company. To-morrow you shall begin life again: shall write your book, make your fortune, do anything; meanwhile you sit, and the jolly world swings round, and you seem to hear it circle to the music of the spheres.

It was in his heroic declaration of laziness that Grahame was at his most appealing. He would have been a fabulous companion for a walk or a picnic, like Ratty.

I sometimes took my boys down by canoe to some small islands that lay close by on the river. They were deserted, scraggy islands of willow and brush, not far from the railway bridge Brunel built to take his Great Western line to Bristol, but they had the charm of wild abandoned places that no one visited.

We liked floating down there in winter. Mole, when he entered the Wild Wood, 'thought that he had never seen so far and so intimately into the insides of things as on that winter day when Nature was deep in her annual slumber and seemed to have kicked the clothes off'. Along the river there was then no cover for the herons who all summer had hidden in the shallows under the low branches of trees. Now they stood sentinel, as if by being still no one could see the flash of their yellow beaks against the bare branches. Dylan Thomas described herons, with their lugubrious solemnity, as priests. We glided right up to them on the riverbank in the canoe; when the awkward pretence that they were invisible could no longer be sustained, they flew ponderously across our bows.

There were plenty of moorhens, grebes and the odd kingfisher; an invasion of Canada geese; and terns. But despite being almost ideal territory for otters – a jumble of undisturbed brush willow and alder, with shallow waterways between the different islands – there were none for Pan to rescue.

Even when Grahame wrote, his otters were anachronistic. Richard Jefferies had already complained in the late nineteenth century that the Thames had become too polluted and hunted for otters to survive. Of all the river creatures, they are the best indicator of water purity, as I knew from the Amazon where the far larger and more savage giant river otters – sometimes called river wolves – are one of the best signs of ecological health.

But otters are slowly coming back to the Thames. There have been a few sightings, near the source at Lechlade, although none as yet near here. Still, every time we canoed down, particularly at dusk, for otters love the night, the boys and I would float as quietly as possible past the islands in the hope that a velvety and sleek body might slither into the water.

✷

My own home was isolated, a barn on the edge of the Little Stoke hamlet and looking out over the fields of what locals called 'the prairie'. I had started renting it from the new owners when my parents sold the main house some two years before.

It was small – one room in which to cook, live and work, with two bedrooms off – but it suited me perfectly. Not only was Little Stoke the place to which I had been returning all my adult life, but for a writer living on his own, it provided peace as well as roots, and a place where my children were able to run free – or dive into the river – when they were with me.

The attached plot of land around the barn was wild enough not to be a garden. There was a copse of young silver birches, rowan trees and beech, which I thinned, with a hammock strung between two trees to lie in as a displacement activity when not writing. A long hedge of brambles separated me from the fields, with a view over them to the Chilterns beyond. The rabbits had pockmarked the ground and dug many of their holes at the edge of the brambles, so that their burrows were protected from above.

There was a great concentration of wood pigeons at Little Stoke. Their constant cooing was like a hubble-bubble of pots on a stove. My other favourite birds were the green woodpeckers which scavenged for ants outside the big, wide window of my bedroom, with their insistent and total absorption in the job at hand; and the charm of goldfinches, which came to glean the heads of the teasels and thistles, which I left long to encourage them. I spent hours watching them out of the window. My abiding fondness for birds comes from a sense that in England the many migratory species are both foreign and familiar, resident aliens.

I had been a friend of Roger Deakin before his sad death in 2006, and greatly admired his books like *Wildwood*, which had inspired a renaissance of natural history writing. But Roger inspired me most with his sheds. I once took my children to meet him at his home on the edge of a Suffolk common. He made a point of first showing them his many writing sheds, which included an old railwaymen's carriage half buried in saplings and a gypsy wooden caravan. Each had a bed made up, so that he could sleep in any one at any time, as the mood took him. My children were enchanted; and then disappointed when he revealed that he did have a house as well.

I had three sheds, if not as well formed as Roger's: one down by the river, another at the end of the grass meadow and one by the barn itself. Only this last was for the proper purpose of a shed, to store things in. The other two were for writing, either looking out over the Thames with its chestnut-lined banks, or over the fields to the Chilterns. I had set up camp beds in each of them. By sleeping in different sheds each night, I could pretend I was still on the move, even though I was patently resting up for a while before heading on.

✳

There is a kestrel over the skyline, hovering just a fraction above the horizon so that its wings are parallel with it. And then we rise higher up the hill and it is lost against the grasses.

I'm climbing Wittenham Clumps with my old friend Robin Buxton. As we get higher, I begin to feel like a kestrel myself. The view is breathtaking. From these two hills beside the Thames, one can see back towards the Uffington White Horse in one direction and on up the Icknield Way towards the ridge line of the Chilterns the other. Directly below, the Thames winds from Wallingford around the old West Saxon centre of Dorchester, with its barrows and abbey.

No surprise that one of the twin hills that make up Wittenham Clumps should have been another Iron Age hill-fort, the latest in the line that I've been tracing from the west, now meeting its natural barrier at the Thames. In the eighteenth century the hilltops were wooded over, for picturesque effect: an effect that was still admired in the early twentieth century, when Paul Nash returned here frequently for a series of landscape portraits. The two prominent hills above the river are a landmark for miles, along with Didcot Power Station. From some angles in Oxfordshire, the sites seem to mimic each other; the cooling towers of Didcot are likewise grouped into two sectors. Looking down from the Clumps, the power station seems so close you could roll a pebble down the slopes and hit the concrete walls.

The last time Robin and I climbed anything together it was Mount Kilimanjaro, some 20,000 feet rather than 500. Robin came with me on a filming expedition to investigate the endemic flora – the giant senecio and lobelia – isolated on the 'island in the sky' with its shrinking glaciers. We were given permission by the authorities to spend two punishing nights on the summit; normally you have to descend immediately and cannot put up a camp.

Under the best of circumstances, this would have been a challenge. But for Robin it was additionally hard. As a small child in the 1950s, he was brought up within sight of Kilimanjaro, on the Kenyan plains. The family was hit by a local polio epidemic. His father died and Robin was left polio-disabled. He walks with a stick. To climb the Western Breach, the hardest route up the mountain, was a challenge he had set himself because the wildlife of Kilimanjaro had always fascinated him and, like many with a disability, he was determined not to let it impede him.

With us, we had Kenton Cool as a guide, one of the finest mountaineers of his generation, and a mixed British and Tanzanian crew. Ironically, given that part of our research was to show how the glaciers had diminished, our ascent up the Western Breach was badly hampered by snow. This meant that Robin was unable to make the last 3,000 feet to the very top, to his considerable sadness; he asked his younger Tanzanian colleague, Michael Ngatoluwa, to take the measurements he wanted.

I had been impressed then by Robin's courage and determination and by the way he could share his knowledge of natural history with the ease of someone who had a total command of his subject. Now he was equally quick to explain the delicate ecosystem of Wittenham Clumps; for many years he had helped run the Trust that administered the nature reserve.

They had been trying to reseed the meadows below the Clumps with wildflowers for some time, without success. As anyone who's ever tried to do the same on their lawn knows, 'You can't buy a meadow in a seedbag,' as Robin put it. Grass is much more resilient than most wildflowers, particularly if the soil is rich, so they won't take.

The breakthrough on Robin's meadows came with the introduction of yellow rattle in the wildflower mix, which weakened the grass to allow other wildflowers through – typically long-headed daisies, but also goat's beard and Loddon lilies, which are like snowdrops on steroids. Now there were fifty hectares of wildflower meadow around the Clumps, and Hereford beef cattle to graze them.

Earth Trust, the nature conservancy charity established by Robin's family, took over the Clumps in 1984. Since then, they had used no fertiliser, planted 10,000 oaks and converted an old barn as an ecology centre for the community. This was true stewardship of the land. An intriguing division was used by the Ministry of Agriculture to allocate set-aside grants: there were 'entry-level stewards', farmers who might maintain hedgerows and do a certain amount of ecological management; and there were 'high-level stewards', like Robin's Earth Trust, who dedicated themselves to such land management for the ecology rather than profit.

I had heard plenty of anecdotal evidence in local pubs, from farmworkers talking out of turn and into their drinks, that farmers had welcomed the 'entry-level stewardship', pocketed the subsidy, and then planted out meadows and maintained copses in a way that uniquely benefited – pheasants. 'Funny that,' one farmworker added with a smile. 'Nothing to do with renting out their land for shooting. Of course.' (Pause for reflective sip of Brakspeer.) 'The thing about estate managers is that the bastards will always get the right angle on every scheme going. And pot the red in the pocket.'

The view we had enjoyed from Mount Kilimanjaro, at almost 20,000 feet, was both extraordinary and celebrated: nearby Mount Meru, the plains stretching away, the glaciers in the foreground. The view from Wittenham Clumps, at less than 1,000 feet, could hardly compare. But scale is everything. I remember George Band, the youngest member of the 1953 Everest team, telling me that when they left Snowdonia after practising for the Himalaya, some were sorry to leave. The British Lake District is a pocket hand-kerchief compared to the Patagonian lakes, yet I would rather be walking down from Helvellyn than Bariloche.

One thing Kilimanjaro has in common with Wittenham Clumps – a sense of origin. It is difficult to be anywhere near the plains of East Africa or the Rift Valley without reflecting on how *Homo sapiens* fanned out from there across Africa, and north to the Middle East and beyond.

To look down at the placid plain around Dorchester is to see where the West Saxons first established themselves, before spreading further west to create the heartland for what later became England. You can see the appeal for the Anglo-Saxons: the river close by, the fertile soil and the sense of previous occupation. Just as later at Avebury, they were drawn to sites that had a sense of history, perhaps to mark their own ownership of the land, like many colonising tribes. One can see it from their place names, many of which incorporate references to ancient monuments.

Looking south towards Wallingford, I remembered a charming comment by the Irish naturalist and bohemian Robert Gibbings when he came here, that many woodpeckers nested in the trees, but none faced due south: 'like many other birds, the woodpeckers do not care for the sun in their eyes when nesting.'

Robert Gibbings' *Sweet Thames Run Softly* is a forgotten classic. In 1939, the fifty-year-old Gibbings decided to build a small punt and float lazily down the Thames, looking at the wildlife through a glass-bottomed box that he held over the side. He examined dragonflies, moths and the long-held belief that pike will always attack other fish 'broadside-on', seizing them by the flank. He slept on his boat by covering it with a tarpaulin.

The opening attacks the reader broadside-on:

> Having travelled more than 50,000 miles over salt water, and having visited the five continents of the world, it occurred to me that it might be fun to explore the River Thames, in whose valley I had lived for 15 years. It seemed to me that it would be a neat and compact little journey within clearly defined limits. It would be restful, too, for I plan to float downstream at the river's own pace, and to look for nothing but what I might see as I moved along, consigning all guidebooks to the devil, and offering the same hospitality to insistent and obtuse advisers.

The book is an escapist retreat from the approaching war. It is also funny, with an Irish eye for a story in a bar and a pretty girl, of whom Gibbings seems to meet a disproportionate amount, many of them swimming nymph-like in the Thames: 'I wonder why it is that girls in the water seem so much more attractive than they do on the land . . . It may be some strange harking back to the primitive. Have not our ancestors all emerged from the sea?' At one point he lifts his tarpaulin cover in a dawn shower to see the naked form of the local bargirl slipping along the bank and into the river when the weather has kept everyone else away, 'a naiad shining all over with the rain'; he solicitously invites her aboard for an innocent cup of tea.

Despite years of canoeing up and down the same stretch of river, I've yet to meet a naked bargirl, but many of the other delights that Gibbings describes are still there: the way a kingfisher blends in so finely with the willows that only the keenest eye can pick them out – some children in particular have the knack; the long ducking of the moorhen below the water so that their re-appearance seems both improbable and a surprise; the shimmer of huge, dark-blue dragonflies, a reminder of their Pleistocene ancestor whose wingspan measured twenty-seven inches.

I have at least seen far more of the great crested grebe than he ever did, as they have now colonised the upper Thames. He failed to find a single one despite searching them out for their exotic courtship dance: the birds approach each other, raise their necks and exotic crested ruffs until they are face to face and then shake their heads violently from side to side, before settling into a slow motion: 'the beak and head of each bird were swung slowly from side to side as if the bird was searching the horizon for it knew not what.'

After leaving Wittenham Clumps, Robin and I paddle downriver towards Dorchester in his old Canadian canoe. I feel for an odd moment as if I'm on the Amazon, not the Thames, perhaps because that was the last place I floated along a river with a naturalist – but also because the river from here to Oxford feels remarkably empty for an area not so far from London. The stretch beside Dorchester is covered with thick trees on both banks. I have biked here with my boys and then swum out from under the overhanging trees into the sun-filled centre channel, a wonderful moment like swimming out of a tunnel. As evening falls on us, there are hardly any boats or traffic, and not a house to be seen. Instead, the only movement is from the clouds of turquoise dragonflies that hang close to Robin and me on the water.

There are two remarkable long barrows we can see over the riverbank known as the Dyke Hills, constructed in Neolithic times and later used as burial grounds by the Saxons (and then for that pillbox in the Second World War). The tombs of a fifth-century man and woman have been excavated from the Dyke

Hills; their grave goods can be seen at the Ashmolean in Oxford. Saxon remains from such an early period are rare and have prompted much academic debate on the intermingling of Romano-British and Saxon culture after the Romans left. There are belts, buckles, bracelets and an early cruciform brooch. However, what caught my attention was an object that has prompted no academic interest whatsoever – a key that was buried with the woman. To take anything to the grave implies a secret, but a key is a double secret.

The key is also a provocation. What is it that had been locked? A door, a casket, a chest?

One of the saddest exhibits I have seen in recent years was a collection of first-century keys that Jewish refugees from the Roman occupation of Galilee had taken with them to the caves of the holy land, keys of the houses to which they would never return; just as Palestinian refugees still hold the keys to their old houses in Israel today.

This key is chunky, the equivalent of a mortise lock. It is the key to something that mattered; something that, like so much else about the early Anglo-Saxons, we do not know.

To visit Dorchester is to remember both how little we know about our past and how badly we have treated its monuments. But the very neglect has a potency. Jerome K Jerome broke off from his usual charming round of light riverside anecdotes when he passed: 'Dorchester is very old, and it was very strong and great once. Now it sits aside from the stirring world, and nods and dreams.' (*Three Men in a Boat.*)

*

There's something mesmeric about the way a bird of prey alights on your arm. It's to do with both the tremendous speed of approach and the stalling when it lands, an almost filmic effect of fast and slow motion. It is also, for the first couple of times, alarming. You are being jumped on by the straining talons of a predator.

To understand the Anglo-Saxons I needed to understand their obsessions. Studying village settlement patterns is all very well, but how much would you know of twenty-first-century man from council tax registers? Better to spend five minutes playing an Xbox.

The Anglo-Saxons were obsessed with hawking. As one academic put it, 'In modern sociological terms falconry was an almost perfect example of conspicuous consumption: it was expensive, time-consuming, and useless.' No wonder that by the eleventh century and the end of the Anglo-Saxon occupation, it had become an essential part of any noble's education.

At the battle of Maldon in 991, great play is made of the fact that a follower of the Anglo-Saxon leader Earl Byrhtnoth lets his beloved hawk fly from his hand to the wood before facing the Viking hordes:

Loosed he from his hands his darling to fly,
His hawk to the wood, and to the battle strode.
From that one could tell that the chieftain would never
Weaken in the warfare.
(*The Battle of Maldon*, translated by Wilfrid Berridge)

Earl Byrhtnoth has already asked his warriors to send their horses far off from the battle; the equivalent of Cortes's later actions in Mexico when he broke up the boats in which the conquistadores had landed. But a horse is easily reclaimed. Not so a hawk. To free your hawk was a symbol of total commitment to both your cause and most likely death, the fate that awaited Earl Byrhtnoth himself.

As a romantic and desperate gesture, it could not have come at a more significant battle. For Maldon signalled the beginning of the end for the Anglo-Saxons. By 991, there had been no Viking raids for well-nigh a century, since the time of Alfred the Great. The young Ethelred the Unready was on the throne. Earl Byrhtnoth was his most senior noble, a tall man in his sixties who commanded respect. So when a large Viking fleet appeared off the coast of Suffolk in the summer of that year, and sacked Ipswich, he was the man sent to confront them when they reached Essex, his own dominions. He stood on the shoreline and told the arrogant Viking messenger who was demanding payment that 'This was Ethelred's land.' Or, to use a phrase that was only just becoming current, 'Englalond'.

The Battle of Maldon, the poem that commemorates the battle – or what is left of it, as the manuscript was partially burned – is as moving an English war poem as any written before the First World War, and an elegy for the turning of tides and of a civilisation. In the poem, ravens circle overhead waiting for the carrion corpses to present themselves. The young chieftain will never reclaim his hawk.

The raids that followed on for the half-century after Maldon created the turmoil that led to the Norman invasion of 1066. At Maldon, the Anglo-Saxon 'shield-wall' collapsed against the Vikings, just as it was later to collapse at the battle of Hastings to those Viking cousins, the Normans.

There were Anglo-Saxon hunting lodges all over Oxfordshire: a large one at Blenheim, just north of Oxford; and another in the Chiltern woods at the old settlement of Swyncombe. And there were still some active falconers.

I track down one called David Hughes, who lives just a mile or so from my barn. David is about forty-seven ('I think,' he says engagingly) and a countryman of the most reassuring sort. He wears a Viyella shirt, green breeches and yellow shooting socks. During the course of the day he lets slip a beguiling and unexpected past: his first job came about because he saw a vacancy for 'Assistant Lion Trainer' in Yorkshire, where he grew up. He spent eight years as a lion-tamer for Gandey's Circus, where he met his wife Tracy, who was looking after the horses. Some years later, they moved south to rural Oxfordshire. David turned to falconry. His experience with lions and other animals (the job at the circus had expanded to include both bears and elephants) was an ideal preparation for creatures that if anything are even less biddable.

And there is a considerable element of showmanship of the most enjoyable sort to what David does now. To teach me, he uses dead chicks as bait, so that the birds fly between us and I can be eyeballed up close by each raptor. Having a hunter's eye staring at you out of a feral ball of fluff just a foot away from your own vulnerable face is unnerving: it feels like a game of dare where you are not allowed to blink.

During a brief training session before we set off, he reminds me to keep my gauntleted forearm held high and pointing upwards, as the bird will land on the highest available part of any 'perch', in this case your body. If your arm is down, this will be your exposed shoulder, and painful.

A great deal of the charm of the day I spend with David lies in his conversation. Keeping a bird to the right 'hunting weight' is an obsession of his, and for good reason: the bird needs to be kept healthy but with enough appetite to return to be fed. Otherwise no amount of imprinting or bonding with its social peer group will stop it from just taking off and away, 'and that can be thousands of pounds flying over the horizon'. While the hawks (and David's ferrets) are tagged with radio receivers for retrieval, a lot of time can be spent trying to get them back, particularly as they are no respecter of natural boundaries like rivers or fences. There is an old, unwritten convention that a falconer can enter someone else's land to retrieve a bird, although not any prey it might have illegally killed.

Over his cup of tea and morning cigarillo, David talks about the changes he has seen in the countryside. He thinks it's too easy to make the usual assumptions about how 'it's all commuters now and the heart has gone out of the villages'. That needs to be qualified by 'some villages', as I've noticed myself.

'You get places where the church is now open only one day a month, the pub has to be run by agency management, if it's open at all, and despite a perfectly good primary in the village, the locals send their children to private schools outside.'

And yet, as David points out, the next door village may have a thriving pub, allotments, cricket team, well-attended school and that ultimate rosette for the community-minded, a small shop run by local volunteers. The difference can be minimal – a few energetic and strong-minded individuals, a village layout that is more than just a strip alongside a road and something more intangible, which if I were less agnostic I would describe as its soul.

As for the farmers and their continual complaints, David, who at times has lived in tied cottages on their land, takes a blunt view: 'At the end of the day, you never see a poor farmer. Do you?'

After the initial training at his falconry, I head over with David and two of the Harris hawks to a twenty-acre bank that comes down from the Berkshire Downs towards the Thames. Given that pheasant is ideal prey for any self-respecting raptor, gamekeepers don't welcome David to their estates where there is shooting, so he chooses his hunting ground carefully. This bank is combed with rabbit holes and has some light scrub as cover. As countryside, it's not prepossessing, but an attractive aspect of falconry is that the birds lead you to parts of the country you might otherwise ignore.

During the hours we spend hunting I begin to understand the Anglo-Saxon obsession. It's precisely because the birds are only partly biddable. You can suggest but they will lead. The popular notion that the bird flies off, attacks prey and then lands again on an outstretched regal arm is laughable. I spend far more time even with an expert like David chasing the birds than using the birds to chase.

The hawks will take you either deep into the wood or across the water. For the Anglo-Saxon aristocracy – and the Norman kings that followed them – the appeal was not only of the hunt but also of the fierce independence the birds showed them, far more than any subject or vassal dared. These are not animals that you can command.

They provided as well an opportunity to display your place in the pecking order. According to the medieval *Book of St Albans*, only kings were allowed peregrine falcons, barons could have buzzards, while humble yeomen aspired to a kestrel; priests could use sparrowhawks; while women were assigned the small but effective merlin falcon. The cost, time and apparatus – the cages, called 'mews', the hoods, jesses, bells and lures – made it a rich person's sport, or at least an aspirational one for the lower orders.

David has plenty of hunting birds to choose from: a peregrine-saker hybrid, which combines the speed of the peregrine – up to 180 mph on the stoop – with the strength of the saker, so esteemed by the Arab world; or the goshawk ('a psychopath of a bird'), much used by cooks in medieval times as a cheap but effective killing machine. The birds that he has brought this time, two Harris hawks, can hunt mercilessly for hours.

Harris hawks have been imported from their native America since the late 1970s and are much valued by British falconers for their ability, in David's words, 'to twist and turn in the air like running dogs as they chase a rabbit down'. They are also relatively cheap: hundreds rather than thousands of pounds, compared to sakers or gyr falcons. In captivity they can live for twenty years.

A wild buzzard and a kestrel are already patrolling the skies, so we know we're in good company. David has ferrets and dogs to help flush the rabbits.

He quickly points out that any 'throwing' of the bird is strictly for the movies – you don't cast your hawk off with a princely command: it chooses when it flies and if there is a glimmer of prey, that will be faster than any possible human reaction. Quite often the Harris hawks choose to perch on hawthorn shrubs to get a better vantage point as the dogs and ferrets go about their business below. But my bird sometimes returns to my arm, a feeling I find reassuring: an extension of a more primeval element of yourself. There's no illusion that it is a tame bird – more like an ally that for reasons of mutual convenience is choosing to work with you.

The rabbits are smart enough to head upwind when pursued and know the intricate lair of their burrows like the back of their paws, so the chase is by no means one-sided: most get away. When a hawk does hit a rabbit the impact is bone crunching. But David is not doing it for the kill. There is an honesty and directness about a relationship with a hunting bird that is unlike any other in the animal kingdom. It is that which so attracted the Anglo-Saxons.

✻

The Saxons were also obsessive law-makers. This might seem axiomatic. Of course they were. Wasn't everybody?

Well, no. Elsewhere in Europe at the time, there was little other law-making 'west of Byzantium', according to the expert on the subject, Patrick Wormald. The English were unusual in having an evolving legal system.

Despite Alfred's self-appointed billing as the creator of that law, the Anglo-Saxons had developed and refined a judicial code for centuries and continued to do so after his death. Moreover, after their conversion to Christianity, the law was developed in parallel with Mosaic law. Wormald suggests that 'the logic of the evident parallels between Israelite and English custom was that the English could *and should* themselves be a Holy People, answerable for their shortcomings to God.'

The law centred around the notion of *wergild*, 'man-payment', the value set upon a person's life and extracted if they were killed in a feud. As these values were laid down in a hierarchical way, depending on the victim's status, we can tell much about how those hierarchies changed over time.

In early seventh-century laws, when the Anglo-Saxons were still 'a band of brothers' who had travelled across the seas to a hostile country, the *wergild* of a nobleman was roughly only three times that of a freeman, a relatively equitable ratio. Over the ensuing centuries, as society became more stratified, the ratio increased to about 6:1 and the *wergild* became payable not just to kinsmen but to the Crown. It also became the basis for fines of other sorts, from theft to military desertion, acting as a form of 'tax banding'.

By the eleventh century and the time of the Norman invasion, there was a lot you could be fined for. Sexual ethics were particularly severe. It was one of the only periods in our history – the other was Cromwell's Commonwealth – when adultery was a civil as well as a religious offence. So was marrying a widow within a year of her husband's death, particularly if you had killed him yourself.

One revelation in particular fascinated me — that by the end of
the Anglo-Saxon period, so narrow was canonical law that you were
forbidden from marrying any relative closer than a fourth cousin.
I would be hard pressed to name any fourth cousin; the risk of
marrying one by accident must have been as constant a concern as
the risks of premarital sex. 'Do we share the same great-great-great-
grandfather?' It must have promoted social mobility and a sharing
of the gene pool; young men needed to travel away from their
village to find a wife who wasn't a distant relation.

Just to complicate matters further, a woman's *wergild* was determined not by the man she married, but by the class into which
she was born. This must have given rise to some nice judgements
of social distinction that would have delighted Jane Austen.
Today's English class-system is just that — an English one, with
its roots in the Anglo-Saxon world. After all, given your place
in the hierarchy was a monetary one based on the value placed
on your dead body, and tax, status and marriage prospects all
stemmed from that, then you were naturally as obsessed with
class in the ninth century as in the nineteenth, or for that matter
in the twenty-first.

*

If my home at Little Stoke had been Mole's down by the riverbank, then lying on the slopes of the Chilterns above was the
Wild Wood. This was where I had wandered at the start of my
journey, near Berins Hill, with its beech trees as wild as the
Amazon and old West Saxon history.

And at the heart of the Ipsden woods, Norman Cox was the
spitting image of Badger.

He had been abrasive on the phone, when I had asked for
directions to reach his house in the notoriously confusing

network of small lanes that laced the woods and adjoining valleys together.

'Are you stupid? Can't you take directions properly! I said not Braziers Lane, but the next left.'

But he didn't cuff me when we met, and came down to the gate to let me in. The 'man from the Council' who had visited him recently had received much shorter shrift.

'He wanted me to plant a hedge to screen the house from the lane. A hedge. I told him, "I'm not planting a hedge." He said, "You are." I said, "I'm far too busy to plant and keep trimming a hedge. I've got a business to run. I'm not sitting on my fucking arse like you lot in the Council." He wasn't very happy with me.'

This was said with some satisfaction. Norman was now eighty. He had left school at fourteen – 'I never graded on to the grammar school in Henley' – and had worked in the woods ever since: first for some of the local estates and then setting up his own timber and scrap business, clearing out the forest for firewood that the estates didn't have the time or manpower to do themselves.

He was acknowledged as the most experienced gamekeeper in the area, an impression he liked to reinforce himself, having managed the shooting for several estates before he retired. He gave a wry shake of the head as he reflected on how poorly some of the estates were now run: 'They're only getting some 10 per cent of the pheasants and partridges they put down. They don't know how to manage them.' Another gamekeeper, now long dead, he described as 'a twisted bastard' who used to pretend to his estate manager that he had put down far more birds than he had.

Both his scrap and firewood business had brought him into contact with some of the gypsy families along the Chilterns. 'In the old days, the gypsies could burn my cars down for the scrap – not any more.' For Norman, regulations had been squeezing the life and enjoyment out of the countryside. 'I used to keep pigs out at the back — Gloucester Old Spot. But then it got too complicated selling them. At least we can still eat muntjac liver. Now that's lovely fried on a bit of toast.'

Gamekeeping suited Norman for other reasons. He was a phenomenally good shot and not shy of telling me so. A typical Norman story involved birds flying over, but not past, him at a shoot (forty-one pheasants falling from his forty-two shots), and the titled sportsman further down the line looking disgruntled but congratulating Norman.

I asked him cautiously about poachers, without mentioning that I had talked to Simon, who had given me so much advice on my initial return to England from South America. Norman became a little circumspect. 'Well, let's just say that the local policeman gave me some advice when I started gamekeeping. He told me that if I got wind of anyone about near the breeding pens, "to put on a mask, take a pick handle and have a go at them — and then just walk away".'

Despite his gruffness, most of Norman's stories were about kindness: about farmers who let him live on their margins, or gave him good deals in return for the odd brace of pheasant or a day's shooting. He talked of an old gentleman farmer we both knew, a gentleman in every sense, Stephen Hart, who said to Norman that he could borrow any of his farming equipment at any time, as long as Stephen was able to do the same with his — 'knowing full well that I didn't have anything he could possibly want. It was his way of making it easy for me.' In the end, Stephen had sadly lost his own farm; as a tenant farmer, he could no longer afford the rent increases, so it reverted to the owners.

As a gamekeeper, Norman had rented a cottage from a more benevolent landlord, Michael Reade — the Reades being an old Ipsden family — who had charged him a peppercorn rent of just £1 a week. 'He was a lovely man. I'd do anything for him. He would have done anything for me.'

It's the end of our conversation. Norman's anger and energy have wound down. The shadows have crept along from the Ipsden woods and into the valley.

*

I recognised that I was staying too long at home before moving on. I should have been following the advice of the old Ray Charles song: 'Hit the road, Jack / and don't you come back / no more, no more, no more.' The rest of the Icknield Way was awaiting me.

But the old thatched barn was such a comforting presence. It had a long room open to the rafters in which I could write. I enjoyed waking up and seeing the woodpeckers and those gold-finches and the blue tits from my bedroom window, or sleeping out in the sheds. My hammock was swinging between its two silver birches. I was swimming in the river each day. It was the height of summer. The glory days in England do not last long and need to be taken.

My only excuse – a lame one – was that travellers on the Icknield Way doubtless stopped here in earlier days. The Thames was a natural crossroads, from which they could strike south-east downriver along the Goring Gap, one of the few passageways through the hills that surround what is now London, or follow the river upstream to Oxford and the north country beyond. It was a natural meeting and market place from Neolithic to Anglo-Saxon times.

In the distance, the Chilterns rose up as the route I should be taking towards the North Sea and distant Norfolk. But I felt a continuing reluctance. I've often had it in the middle of a journey. A moment when you wonder if the restlessness of travelling could be commuted into the savouring of one place

– in this case my home. And again I'm Mole, when he comes back to his home after adventures in the Wild Wood and is suddenly struck by his desertion:

> He let his eyes wander round his old room . . . He saw clearly how plain and simple – how narrow, even – it all was; but clearly, too, how much it all meant to him, and the special value of some such anchorage in one's existence . . . He knew he must return to the larger stage. But it was good to think he had this to come back to; this place which was all his own, these things which were so glad to see him again and could always be counted upon for the same simple welcome.

Any such sentimentality/*heimatliebe* was rudely awakened early one morning when I was having breakfast. It was a beautiful day. I was eating a bacon sandwich and the sun was shining. My landlord rang.

'Hugh, you know we said that it was fine for you to stay in the barn for the next few years and the foreseeable future?'

'Yes.'

'Well, we've changed our minds. You need to leave by September.'

I had the rest of the summer to find a new home.

I found it difficult to absorb. I went to each of my writing sheds in turn and tried to write about it in my diary. Nothing came. I stared out of the window at the circle of fourteen silver birches we had planted by the river, one for each of my parents' grandchildren; at the shadows lengthening under the chestnut boughs along the riverbank. Then I swam as far upriver as I could and let the current drift me back.

No summer looks as beautiful as the last one you spend in a place. The cow parsley was higher and with a whiter intensity than I could ever remember; the dog roses in the hedges more prolific; in the dark shadows under the chestnuts, old hosta plants spread their silvery blue leaves, as big as saucers.

Leaving somewhere that you've known all your adult life as a home is both hard and easy. Hard in that I'd known it longer than I had been writing books, or making films, or been married, or had children, so that I had decades of identity pinned to the place. Easy, I tried to tell myself, because wherever I now went, I would still always be carrying the essence of Little Stoke within me. A Quechua woman in Peru called Nilda Callañaupa once told me that the reason to make pilgrimages was that 'it makes you more comfortable as a human being to have different parts of the landscape within you'. It is possible to absorb a place.

At the best of times travel can be a sublimation of whatever troubles may be brewing at home. Now, more than ever, I wanted to follow the Icknield Way up the coast to Norfolk, to get to the other side of the country, in every sense. A journey that had begun out of curiosity about England — what sort of a country it was becoming, what sort of a country it had been right from its early prehistory — was now a more urgent search. If I was shortly to become homeless, I needed to know what it was I wanted; what were the essential ingredients of the England I was looking for? And where, more practically, did I now want to live myself?

*

George Orwell's grave lay a few miles away from me, at Sutton Courtenay, where his plain tombstone says 'Here lies Eric Arthur Blair, born 25 June 1903, died 21 January 1950'. People associate him with East Anglia, because of the adopted name he took from the Suffolk river and the virulence with which he wrote about Southwold, where the family later moved; but his earlier formative years were all in the Thames Valley.

In *Nineteen Eighty-Four*, when Winston and Julia escape to the countryside for an illicit rendezvous, the image of 'the Golden Country' may draw on Orwell's own childhood experiences of Shiplake beside the Thames:

> They were standing in the shade of hazel bushes. The sunlight, filtering through innumerable leaves, was still hot on their faces. Winston looked out into the field beyond, and underwent a curious, slow shock of recognition. He knew it by sight. An old, close-bitten pasture, with a foot-path wandering across it and a molehill here and there. In the ragged hedge on the opposite side the boughs of the elm trees swayed just perceptibly in the breeze, and their leaves stirred faintly in dense masses like women's hair. Surely somewhere nearby, but out of sight, there must be a stream with green pools where dace were swimming?
>
> 'Isn't there a stream somewhere near here?' he whispered.
>
> 'That's right, there is a stream. It's at the edge of the next field, actually. There are fish in it, great big ones. You can watch them lying in the pools under the willow trees, waving their tails.'
>
> 'It's the Golden Country – almost,' he murmured.
>
> 'The Golden Country?'
>
> 'It's nothing, really. A landscape I've seen sometimes in a dream.'

Recent revisionist biographies have questioned the old image of Orwell as the conscientious man of the left who fought in Spain and believed in austere Tribune values. They have suggested instead a man with a tougher, womanising side, quite often brutal in his treatment of people. But for me he was still a hero, who had not allowed the constraints of class to blinker him, and who had taken the road to Wigan Pier with his eyes wide open.

What would Orwell have made of Britain today? The Britain in which inequalities of wealth were if anything as pronounced as in the 1930s? There might not be the same bone-crunching malnutrition and absolute poverty – although there were more people who fell through the gap than was often acknowledged – but there was still an almost obscene disparity between the few 'Masters of the Universe' operating out of a gilded circle in London, the bankers, technocrats and media lords on six-figure salaries, and the families I saw counting the pennies in the village Co-ops.

He would have been appalled, above all, by the way his 'Newspeak' had been adopted, the blandness of policy directives, the talk of 'moving on', 'planning initiatives', of anaemic politicians whose leaders could be told apart only by the colour of their ties.

The country was changing and many of the people I had met on my journey were disenfranchised, stuck in jobs and places they didn't want to be. With the privilege of a traveller, I could pass through and observe. But at some stage I would have to face up to my own reckoning.

Chapter 4

Homeleaving

'You think you're so clever and classless and free
but you're still fucking peasants as far as I can see.'
John Lennon, 'Working Class Hero'

I packed my sleeping bag and kit, and finally headed on up the Icknield Way and towards the Chilterns.

Did the colours look fresher, the green after the rain more succulent, the dark lanes into the beech trees more inviting, now that I was leaving my home not just for a journey but for good? Thirty years before, I had motorbiked through these lanes at dawn, on my way to college, the steam rising from the tarmac filtering and softening even further the colours of the leaves.

The names on the signposts as I headed inland from the river were like a roll-call from different eras of my life: South Stoke where one of my sisters had got married; Checkendon where my other sister had; Catsbrain Hill; Stoke Row; the road up Berins Hill past an old eccentric zoo that was kept at Wellplace Farm, now long closed, and up into Ipsden and the heart of the woods.

I went to see Elizabeth Chatwin, who had continued living at her house at Homer End since her husband, the writer Bruce Chatwin, died in 1989. Elizabeth had been kind to me since I moved back to Oxfordshire after my separation; she had invited me, among other things, to several Thanksgiving meals, which, as an expatriate American, she celebrated with due pomp, ceremony and cranberry sauce.

As I came up the drive to her house, I surprised a muntjac

deer, which bolted away into the woods; muntjac had proliferated over the past few years, helped by their fertility cycle. They can breed all year, unlike other animals restricted to set seasons. Some landowners disliked them as pests; I enjoyed the beauty of their startled, exaggerated high kicks, like cheerleaders.

Elizabeth had a direct countrywoman's approach, which I valued. She was a good person to see when you needed cheering up. It was clear why she had always been such a good traveller – to Afghanistan, with Bruce and Peter Levi, and to India with Penelope Betjeman: her resilience was infectious. Now in her late seventies and suffering from arthritis, she still undertook arduous journeys.

There were some dead pheasants outside the door waiting to be plucked. On one of my first visits, a neighbour had dropped by with some rabbits which she had asked me to help skin – if not quite as a test, then certainly as a rite of passage.

But the animals that Elizabeth most favoured were sheep. On coming to Homer End in 1981, she had brought ten of them from the Chatwins' previous house near Stow on the Wold.

Growing up in America, Elizabeth had been surrounded by animals and she had once wanted to be a vet. In the Cotswolds, she had helped neighbours with their flocks, and they had presented her with a few ewes in return. Over the years at Homer End, she had grown the herd to some thirty ewes, and borrowed a ram from a neighbour each year to produce more.

While the sheep 'rooted her', as she put it, and gave her purpose, she complained that the new rules concerning abattoirs made it hard for sheep farmers. Once, local butchers used local abattoirs. Now the five local butchers in the nearby market town had closed, and the supermarkets' domination of the business had centralised abattoirs at just a few locations in the country, meaning that livestock had to travel an inhumane – and uneconomic – distance to be slaughtered.

For a while, Elizabeth had employed a licensed slaughterer to come to her own premises.

'Then that was stopped for health and safety reasons. Worse still, when I used one abattoir, I wasn't sure if the shrink-wrapped cuts I got back at the end were from my own sheep. The whole point is that you want to sell – and eat – your own animals.'

Hygiene regulations now prevented sheep farmers from being present when their sheep were slaughtered. The layman might think this a blessing, but as farmers point out, if you've brought sheep into the world, you want to see with your own eyes that they have been despatched as humanely as possible.

Sheep were one of the few subjects on which I had ever heard Elizabeth get emotional. She had stuck with the black Welsh mountain breed that she had started with in Stow, although it was clear her fancy had sometimes strayed elsewhere. 'I fell in love with Gotland ewes in Scotland. Cloud grey with glossy curly wool, for sheepskin coats. So polite and aristocratic – compared to my grumpy black Welsh sheep who growl and grind their teeth.' She demonstrated.

I told her that she sounded like one of those men who could

have any girl they wanted, but settled for the plain one rather than the gorgeous blonde. 'Well, it is a bit like that.'

The sheep had been a solitary passion. Bruce had often been away travelling and was anyway not much interested. 'He didn't like to touch the sheep. But he would let himself be used as a post. So he stood stock-still in a field and let the sheep be herded round him.'

'Michael Ignatieff used to come and stay, and I made him help as well. So that once he complained that all he ever did when he saw us was "sheep business".'

Ignatieff gave a live and impromptu elegy for Chatwin on the day of his death in the cold January of 1989, on *The Late Show*. It was a bravura and moving bit of television, not now accessible on YouTube or the Internet, but I remember it vividly at the time of transmission. He described how he had visited the Chatwins several times in Bruce's last months, when he was dying from AIDS and being nursed by Elizabeth. How Chatwin had lain down outside on the grass wearing a pair of Vuarnet glacier sunglasses with side pieces to stop reflected glare, and the sky and clouds had been mirrored in them. It was an image I had always remembered, and thought of whenever I came back to the house and garden.

Ignatieff had also written perceptively about his friend. His claim, in *The New York Review of Books*, that 'his own character was one of his greatest inventions', is often repeated. Less well known is how he ended that same sentence: that he was 'at the same time the most restlessly cosmopolitan English writer of his generation'.

Chatwin died in 1989 just when the world was changing: the Iron Curtain coming down; the Internet beginning. He wrote when there were still secrets to be found in libraries – when knowledge could be more compartmentalised, hidden, like the rare artefacts he collected; Elizabeth had showed me the Peruvian pre-Columbian cloak of hummingbird feathers they had always kept above their bed.

Knowledge had now become more democratic. It was all 'out there', somewhere, on a server. The more arcane settings of *Utz* in communist Prague, or the isolation of Patagonia, let alone of the Black Hill on the Welsh borders, had passed. We were all connected now. But perhaps, as a result, we had lost his furious urge to talk.

✳

'Aewelm' means 'the spring or well source' in Anglo-Saxon. Ewelme lay just off the Icknield Way a few miles on from Elizabeth, a perfectly formed small village in a dip between the Thames and the Chilterns that had retained much of its ancient Saxon and medieval shape. The chalk stream that flowed through it – and attracted the Saxons, who loved clear water rising – once made the village prosperous from trout and watercress. The watercress beds had been recently restored, although much to local frustration the perfectly good cress could not be sold, due to EU regulations.

The village was small and out of the way, protected in its dip; perhaps the reason that Cromwell's men failed to rip apart the church in the way they did the rest of royalist Oxfordshire. It was the extraordinarily well preserved flint and stone church I had come back to see, as I had many times in the past.

I am not a great churchgoer or indeed church visitor. But there was something about Ewelme church that would lure in even a devout apostate like Philip Larkin. It sits by a medieval almshouse and the oldest occupied school in the country, a medieval complex made homely by the wood and the scale. Even so, the richness of the interior belies the plain front. In the fifteenth century the church enjoyed aristocratic patronage by the powerful Dukes of Suffolk, the de la Poles, one of whom married Chaucer's grand-daughter, Alice.

Her tomb is quite remarkable. On top, the marble effigy lies in repose, clothed in the habit of a vowess (a widow who has taken a vow not to remarry), a ring on the third finger of her right hand, her hands clasped in prayer in a conventional way. Less commonly, she has the order of the Garter tied around her left arm; Alice was an influential woman for her time, thrice married (so her final vow wasn't that hard to make), owner of the estates of those three dead husbands and deeply enmeshed in the Wars of the Roses.

Around the tomb's canopy and on the ceiling of the chapel to the side are multiple angels: some of the earliest wooden carvings in the country and similar in style to those in Suffolk churches like Blythburgh, as you would expect for the Duchess of Suffolk. Attendant angels hold heraldic shields along the side of the tomb. More sinuous angels, like lizards, cling to the marble pillow on which Alice lies, their wings folded back to meet its curves.

But it is what lies beneath her tomb that always draws me back. Bend down to the floor, look through the marble grille and there is a second effigy, directly parallel to the one above. Again it is the Duchess. But this time Alice has been carved in the rictus of death, naked in a winding sheet, in direct parallel to the calm poise of the statue above. Her back is bent up, arched in pain, her teeth bared, her ribs protruding. It is a shocking image.

Moreover, it is an image commissioned by her son, John, the next Duke of Suffolk. What strange mixture of filial piety and horror at his mother's death prompted him? He had experienced a disturbed childhood. The de la Poles were regarded as upstarts by the nobility, merchant stock who were derided for adding the Norman affectation of 'de la' to the plebeian name of Pole. His father William, Alice's third husband, had been on the wrong side in the Wars of the Roses, supporting Henry VI and alienating the Yorkist clique who arranged for him to be exiled. When he boarded a ship to escape, he was seized, beheaded and left as a corpse on the beach at Dover. Before he died, William was just able to write a moving letter to his son hoping that he would 'pass all the great tempests and troubles of this wretched world'. Yet on reaching his majority, John himself became a strong supporter of those rival Yorkists and Richard III — and then of Henry VII when he triumphed over the House of York at Bosworth; no wonder that John was known as 'the trimmer Duke'. His mother Alice had similarly twisted and turned between factions in the Wars of the Roses.

Such 'cadaver tombs' were not unknown across Europe in the fifteenth century when John had this one of his mother carved after her death in 1475. Similar tombs had been erected for Henry II of France by his wife Catherine de Medici, and for various clerics in England. Masaccio had illustrated one in Florence in his celebrated *Trinity* of 1428, the first painting that many visitors see when they arrive at the city, as it stands in Santa Maria Novella just opposite the railway station. Beneath the fresco of the *Trinity* lies a painted corpse with a stark message: 'I once was what now you are and what I am, you shall yet be.'

But this tomb for Alice, Duchess of Suffolk, is unusual and far more than just a *memento mori*. For a start, it is one of the very few known of a single woman; her son John could hardly have carved a tomb to his father as well, given that he had married into the assassins' family. The sculpted skeleton too is brutally lifelike: the toes curling up, the ribs pressing through the skin, the arms emaciated as one would expect in an old woman of seventy.

There are few other places in England that bring home so well the psychotic disturbance of the Wars of the Roses, a period that has always fascinated me: perhaps Tewkesbury Abbey, where the Yorkists barricaded in the last of the Lancastrians before butchering them; Towton, where 28,000 people died on the battlefield, more casualties in a single day than in any other battle fought on British soil; or the walls of York where the heads of Richard Plantagenet and his son Edmund were skewered.

But Alice's tomb has a peculiar horror all of its own. It is the Munch *Scream* of the fifteenth century. It belies the placid face of England as smooth in repose as the marble effigy on top of the tomb; underneath, buried by the weight of centuries, is a twisting and turning effigy that will not rest.

✳

I carried on up the outlying hills of the Chilterns. As many as nine red kites were wheeling overhead and searching the skies – or rather searching from the sky, as they peered down for dead prey. It was near here on the Getty estate, in 1989, that the species were reintroduced to England after their extinction. At first welcomed as a triumph, locals were now murmuring that the release programme had been all too successful. Both the local countryside and towns were patrolled by fleets of the birds, their distinctive pronged tail and slightly heavy flight making them instantly identifiable even by the worst birdwatcher.

Kites are primarily scavengers, although if I had a fiver for every countryman or woman like Sarah Phipps who had told me they had lost livestock to them, I could stand a round of drinks at a farmers' market. I wasn't too worried about the tales of guinea pigs snatched from village gardens, or chicks for that matter — but I did find their cry oppressive: a thin shriek that died away on the wind. With the nine circling above me as I climbed the hill — and with a certain amount of the weight of the world on my shoulders after my eviction — I felt for a moment like Frodo in *Lord of the Rings,* with the Nazgul circling in for the kill, an idea so laughable that I instantly felt better.

The kites would have been a familiar sight back in Ewelme during the Wars of the Roses. Medieval towns encouraged them as unpaid street cleaners, although they were not much loved, any more than vultures in India: Shakespeare was still using 'you kite' as an insult, or the more satisfying nickname for them, 'you puttock'. Hollinshed includes them as 'fowls which we repute unclean' along with ravens, crows and choughs.

Perhaps their unpopularity was as much to do with the battle-field. Kites would have competed with crows to strip the flesh from the dead after the battles of the Wars of the Roses.

I thought of Malory again and his attempt to create a lost Arthurian world to put against what must have seemed the complete anarchy of that time. A recent biography suggests that he visited Ewelme and Alice, Duchess of Suffolk. She was precisely the sort of powerful yet pious woman who figures in his chronicle.

Malory's work has stayed so centrally in the English imagi-nation because it tells of loss. There is an undercurrent of regret running through our history. What could have been. The unicorn disappearing into the trees. The loss of Roman Britain. The loss of Albion. The loss of Empire. We are forever constructing narratives in which a golden sunlit time — the Pax Romana, the Elizabethan golden age, that Edwardian summer before the First

World War, a brief moment in the mid-sixties with the Beatles – prefigure anarchy and decay.

I remembered how as a teenager in the 1970s, there was a sense of disappointment: that this was a failed decade, the hangover after the sixties dream. The Beatles had split up. Altamont had driven a nail into the idea of free festivals and peace 'n love. Terrorism was rife from the Munich Olympics to Northern Ireland. Industrial dispute had led to bitter winters of strikes and discontent. England was a tribal place of factions and class with divisions hammered out as surely as the wall put up between the Falls and Shankill roads in Belfast. I wished then that I had been born ten years earlier.

In retrospect, the seventies were a fabulous decade that produced far better music, film and attitude than the sixties ever had. Punk was an ethos of self-invention and do-it-yourself, and openness to the unexpected, that has always stayed with me. But I'm not sure I realised that at the time.

Are we bad at living in the present? Always yearning for a past peace that is more perceived than real, wanting to turn the clock back as well as forward. Or is it because the future is always so uncertain? The pace of change in England has often been so ferocious that we cling on to the past, like shipwrecked sailors to a plank of wood.

*

The light is coming low through the trees when I turn the corner and see Danny sitting up ahead beside his caravan. He is tall, with shaved hair, heavily tattooed, maybe in his thirties. His four large shire horses are grazing along the verges of the Icknield Way, and in the field beyond the fence. Danny is on a mobile phone (a gift, it occurs to me, to travellers), while the most beautiful wooden caravan stands on the path, a saucepan of coffee still smoking on a fire near by.

We ease into conversation – it's too beautiful a caravan to pass without saying something – and it emerges that Danny built it with his wife in Norfolk a few years back and is now very slowly winding his way towards the west, perhaps branching up to Herefordshire – so, rather like Edward Thomas, is doing the same journey that I am, but in reverse. It may take him years rather than months to complete, as he tries to get work as he goes.

I ask him if everyone is friendly when he meets them; he is cautious in his reply. 'Well, only some. When we were travelling through Suffolk, which was hard, we found that they liked us to stay for one night only, on the village green, because it looks good with the caravan. Any more and they're not interested. They start getting worried. And if you're going to work, you need to stay for more than a night.'

He's been travelling since he was a teenager, but does not come from a travelling family. He was adopted in Newbury ('by a kind couple who are now dead'), and brought up there but felt he had failed at school and left at sixteen for the open road – 'and I haven't looked back'. He too had known Jeremy Sandford, and had read his book about the horse fairs of Yorkshire.

The caravan is a throwback, a conscious and artificial homage to a previous travelling age. In many places the old drovers' tracks no longer serve their original function – they can be too rutted to travel along or, worse, some local councils have put up bollards, more to stop four-wheel-drive vehicles than caravans, although few councils welcome travellers of any sort.

This is borne out later that evening when a farmer in the local pub overhears me talking about Danny's caravan on the Ridgeway.

'Fucking pikeys,' he says. 'I hate them. That guy's horses have been eating my grass. They'll take anything if it isn't nailed down, and then some.'

'Tractors are the worst. They'll take them in the middle of the night, drive them up onto a container vehicle and be in Felixstowe by dawn before you know anything has happened. Then ship them to Poland. There are a lot of shiny new British tractors in Poland.'

His face darkens. He is already well tanned after what transpires has been a fortnight's skiing in Courchevel. He is in his fifties, lean and saturnine.

Someone else asks him what he'd do if he caught any thieves or poachers. 'Ram the vehicle,' he says unhesitatingly. 'And if any pikeys were trying to get out at the time, so much the better. The police won't do a thing against them. Particularly if there's any colour involved. Just don't want to go there. A lot of those pikey camps are "no-go zones",' he snorts. 'No-fucking-go zones. What's that about?'

It doesn't seem the right time to mention my appreciation of Danny's hand-tooled wooden caravan, or his magnificent shire horses.

'I'm getting some concrete blocks put on the drovers' road. That'll stop the bastards.'

And sure enough, concrete posts appear shortly afterwards on the Watlington stretch of the Icknield Way. I remember when bollards started appearing around Bristol in the 1980s to stop travellers parking up under flyovers or on lay-bys. Now you get them around even motorway service stations.

Like the good burghers of Suffolk, we like the idea that there are still some romantic souls travelling the highways and byways of old England in the traditional manner. We just don't want them to come our way.

*

When I was eighteen, I used to ride a motorbike across this stretch of southern Oxfordshire to Henley Sixth Form College where I was briefly a student.

The Sex Pistols were at full throttle around then. One day I made the mistake of listening to *Never Mind the Bollocks* before getting on my motorbike and was more hyped up than I should have been, with Steve Jones's incendiary guitar riffs running through me like too much coffee or amphetamine. This would not have mattered — I knew the route like the back of my leather glove — if a farmer hadn't decided to put loose gravel down on the corner of a country lane that had done perfectly well without it for the previous year.

The bike skidded and I landed in the corner of a nearby field. The bike came off worse than I did, with bent forks. A farmworker was leaning over a gate, watching me. He had a drawl so slow you could play an entire punk song by the time he had finished one of his sentences.

'Sorry about that . . . I only jus' put that gravel down.'

I was too winded by the fall to say anything. As so often in life, a suitable riposte came to me only in retrospect. Nor was it something *The Archers* could have broadcast.

It was a cold winter and I got in the habit of stopping off for a 'whisky mac' (ginger wine and cheap whisky) at one of the many small country pubs that still lay along the old coaching route from London to Oxford. At one, the Crooked Billet in Stoke Row, there was no beer pump at the bar. The elderly landlord went down to the cellar for each pint, drawn directly from the barrel. The only food was a packet of pork scratchings. A dog was in permanent occupation of a battered old sofa in front of the fire. There were two rooms, or 'snugs', both so small and close together that you could hear every conversation in the pub. Most of the time there was just one group conversation going on anyway.

Today the Crooked Billet is a gastro-pub of the fanciest sort:

tuna carpaccio; seared diver-caught scallops; Moroccan spiced rump of local lamb, harissa, chargrilled Mediterranean vegetables and barley couscous. No ploughman's lunch, but there is always the 'sticky-glazed pink-carved duck breast with foie gras mash'.

A large conservatory extension has been built out from the bar, in which candles are lit at each table for dinner. Worst of all, there is no bar.

Not far away on the Thames, the Leatherne Bottel has suffered a similar fate. This was once a favourite for boating folk messing around on the river; it was where the 'Three Men in a Boat' stopped to hear the famous fishing story in which every visitor to the pub – and the barman – claimed to have caught the large perch stuffed and hanging over the bar, only for it to turn out to be plaster of Paris.

The whole pub is now made out of plaster of Paris. The interior has been gutted and replaced with Los Angeles faux gilt and naked cherubs. The waitresses wear black. There is a maître d'. On a recent visit I made by boat, when there was no alternative place to stop, we found that the chef and some of his staff had thrown 'a hissy fit', as they say in Pinewood, and trashed the toilets in true rock-star fashion, before leaving.

But deep in the woods between the two, I now came to a pub that had changed not at all. At the Black Horse near Checkendon, the beer was still fetched from kegs. For food the choice was between a pickled egg or a pickled onion. When I asked the pub landlady if she could describe the difference between the bitters they stocked, she said, briskly: 'Well, it's all beer.' Then she went back to watch the television in the kitchen. In the old days, Norman had told me, he usually paid for his pint here with a brace of pheasants.

Higher up on the Chilterns, I ended the day at another pub I liked, the Fox and Hounds at Christmas Common. The landlord there had occasional music nights when locals turned up and busked – a group of Irish musicians or, the night that I arrived, a lad called Alex in a woolly hat singing 'Cocaine Blues' and then the Stones' 'You Can't Always Get What You Want'. His voice had the right rasp to it, as if he were still smoking in the now smoke-free pub – a change, incidentally, that no amount of nostalgia for the old pubs causes me any regret. Under the bar lay the landlord's enormous grey Irish wolfhound, the noblest of dogs, and one with a fine Celtic pedigree – the Celts used them to attack the Ancient Greeks at Delphi. I always trust a pub with a dog.

Alex started up on a cover of the Kings of Leon's 'Sex on Fire', and the man at the bar beside me told me he used to hear the song being played at Basra on British Services Radio when he was in the army. He said it reminded him of driving out into the Iraqi streets in the sunlight, when you didn't quite know what was going to happen next.

*

The next morning, I made a small detour to St Peter's at Easington. Compared to Ewelme, it would have been hard to find a plainer, more bare medieval church, or a more out of the way one, down a tiny lane in a hamlet of just a few houses. I later discovered that many inhabitants of nearby Watlington were unaware of its existence. A rare historical report of the fourteenth-century church described it as 'very ordinary', but it was the austerity that attracted me: there was no steeple, it backed onto a farmyard and looked like a barn; inside, there was a plain, battered Norman font and whitewashed walls. It was the sort of chapel to which Malory sent his Grail knights.

The church had a record of one Roger Quartermaine, who in 1683 'desired to be buried in Easington churchyard. I bequeath to my son, Roger, my wearing apparel and my Bible; to my daughter, Martha Shepherd, my table and form, my brass porridge pot, and my little brass kettle.' That detail about the porridge pot caught my eye; if you don't have much, it matters to whom you bequeath your few possessions.

The reason for searching out the old church was a fine painting by John Piper, which had piqued my curiosity; he had used the long grass in the overgrown cemetery to make St Peter's look even more as if it were in the middle of a meadow.

The Pipers had lived not far from here, in Fawley Bottom. John Piper worked with another local, John Betjeman, to produce *The Shell Guide to Oxfordshire*, as well as to other counties. His 'romantic modernist' sensibility had helped bring landscape painting back into the fold of modern art in England when abstract work was sweeping all before it: Piper's early studies of prehistoric monuments, which he, like Paul Nash, appreciated, were followed by paintings of old churches, washed in bleak, monochrome colours to preserve them from any charge of sentimentality.

I admired John Piper greatly. But it was his son Edward, also an artist, whom I had known and whom I thought of as I walked on from the church along the high lanes, with the wide curl of the Chilterns ahead revealed by the slight ridge I was traversing and the sunshine that had accompanied me for most of my journey.

Many ghosts had already joined me on my walk. You can't get to fifty without having a fair amount of friends who have died. Jeremy Sandford, Roger Deakin, and my old mentor from film school, George Brandt, all had jostled around my thoughts. I had met most of them when they were themselves in their fifties, and I was younger. Now I was their contemporary, so to speak.

But of those who had died, Edward was perhaps the one for whom I felt the most affinity. I had got to know him in the late 1980s. His art was selling well both here and in the States; his dealer wanted to commission a film about him, as none had ever been made. Knowing that I admired his work, and had been unable to afford to buy any, he approached me with an offer made attractive because I would be part-paid in paintings.

I went to see Edward at his studio in Somerset. He began by saying that he was hopelessly shy and reticent, particularly when discussing his art. Then he never stopped talking.

Edward had grown up in the shadow of the reputation of his father John, to whom he was close, but he reacted in the best possible way — by taking the essence of his father's work and steering it in a completely new direction. While John's English landscapes were drenched in a subdued drizzle, Edward's looked as if they might have been painted in the South of France. He brought the colour and light back into English landscape. A child of the 'Here Comes the Sun' sixties — a child growing up in these same Oxfordshire hills — he took the saturated colours of Pop Art, a movement he briefly dallied with, and poured them over his landscapes.

His pictures reminded me of how long England had been under the clouds artistically. From Turner through to John Piper and Lowry, painters had loved to portray the country as one of clouds, mists and rain, with a brooding black sky behind. No wonder the English had become so convinced that we had such bad weather, as our artists were always telling us so – fallaciously. If my travels abroad had taught me anything, it was that we had a fabulous climate: temperate and mild, with a surprising amount of sunshine. Five minutes in the Andes, or the barren plateau of Tibet, or India before the monsoon – let alone Washington's humid summer – would have had most of the moaners in bus shelters throughout the country scurrying back to this 'green and pleasant land', as Blake described it just before the artistic weather-front closed in.

With the odd exception – like Eric Ravilious, whose clear planes of colour needed light, or foreign visitors like Raoul Dufy – you had to go back to Constable to find much sunshine around in English artistic skies. And it was Constable who started the move to grey. His cloud studies persuaded fellow artists that bad weather was more interesting.

As I looked at the hills where Edward had grown up, bathed in sunlight, I thought that he was well suited temperamentally to flood the colour back. As I got to know him during the intensity of filming, I found him both energetic and vital. He had inherited the striking looks of his father, who even in his eighties was described as one of Britain's most handsome men: they both had deep-set, piercing eyes, a high domed forehead and sculpted cheekbones. But whereas this look suited John's more melancholy temperament, it didn't quite match Edward's more extrovert character. His face didn't fit him, somehow; perhaps why he didn't like to be photographed or filmed.

He engaged with life: with jazz, which he played constantly, either himself or on record; with the fireworks show he organised annually for the Chelsea Arts Club; with his art, of course; but above all with women, or rather the female form. While I liked his landscapes for their colour and vibrancy, it was his nudes for which he was best known. Perhaps because his father had not really 'gone there', and certainly because of his own sexual energy, Edward was obsessively drawn to paint nudes.

There were a lot of them. All round his studio were paintings of nude women in mirrors, in stockings, in washes of purple and green like Matisse (whom Edward admired, with a twist: his *Red Knickers* was a sixties tribute to the master's *Red Studio*). We filmed him in the studio drawing a model called Diane, with my cousin Rachel Bell as a female camera operator so that it would not feel voyeuristic or intrusive; Edward himself often undressed when he painted his models.

Diane was unusual in that Edward had got to know her when she bought some of his paintings. Edward engaged all of his models with a light banter, a mixture of running commentary on his work — 'That line's wrong, I'm bored with that — let's start again' — and discussions about how they might want to rearrange themselves on a chair or sofa. His wife and first model, Prue, had taught him, he said, to make the model feel that she was the subject and not the object of any painting.

His nude women were very English — pale skinned, either brunettes or with flames of auburn hair. One was the mother of some children at the same school as his own. Edward told me how nervous he had been, going round to her house, knocking on the door and asking her to pose — to which, like most of the women he asked, she agreed.

Anyone who ever thought that Englishwomen might be less inherently sensual than their European counterparts should take a crash course in Edward's nudes. He encouraged his models, as one of them put it, to be relaxed with their own sexuality, and they were. This was not nudity of a classical purity but of a bedroom directness, in which genitalia were displayed and celebrated (Edward complained that while classical art taught the student much about ways of painting a nose, or an eye, there were few antecedents for how to paint a vulva). The poses were often chosen by the models themselves.

Another reason that models liked Edward was that he worked incredibly fast. At art school he had hated the Slade's insistence on meticulous observation and draughtsmanship, going instead for the quick, intuitive line. Edward had given up Pop Art because he couldn't be bothered to spend so much time filling in the big, solid blocks of colour that the style required. As he had grown into his mature period, his drawing got faster and faster, like one of the straightahead, hard-bop Art Blakey standards he listened to while working. I watched him do one painting where the ink was still wet on the first line he'd drawn as he came to the last.

This approach ran a high risk of failure and the paintings could jack-knife. But when his line ran true, there was a fluidity to his nudes and portraits that I found entrancing.

Edward was restless with his disciplines too, picking up photography along with the painting. He journeyed from Dartmoor to the Orkneys to photograph *Rings of Stone: The Prehistoric Circles of Britain and Ireland*, written by Aubrey Burl and still the standard gazetteer on the subject. He photographed Stonehenge under snow and intuitively showed how stone circles reflected the landscape around them, as at Balquhain, in north-eastern Scotland, which Keats described as 'a dismal cirque of Druids' stones, upon a forlorn moor'. It was seeing Edward's pictures of the circles around the country that had first got me interested in the Neolithic culture that produced them.

Like his father, he travelled England for the Shell Guides, covering some thirty counties at great speed. Being Edward, he took the opportunity to photograph not only the landscapes but also plenty of nudes in the landscape, often treating their flesh very texturally, as Bill Brandt did.

Needless to say, the nudes didn't get into the Shell Guides and have rarely been seen. Edward showed them to me in portfolio. One was of a nude woman lying face down among seaweed, so the curves and texture of her back contrasted with the black, sinuous folds of the water and the plants. At about the only ever exhibition of his photos – in the Fox Talbot Museum at Lacock – the National Trust thought some prints too explicit and asked that they be withdrawn.

The process of filming together was intense because Edward was an intense person. But it acquired a further urgency. The exhibition Edward was preparing, and at which the film was to be shown, had already been billed as 'Edward Piper: The First 50 Years'. Halfway through the filming, Edward discovered that he had terminal cancer. Understandably, he told no one but his close family. What I thought of as a film marking a staging post in Edward's evolving career – his father John was still alive and very much working at eighty-five – was suddenly, for him, a final testament and the only film of him painting that would ever be made; but I did not know that.

I struggled to contain and absorb everything that he poured into the documentary, and could not understand his exigency. As well as filming him at work in the studio – a joy, because he worked so fast – we followed as he rushed around Bristol at equally great speed to complete a landscape painting, and then back home drew one of his favourite models, Christine, sitting in the garden with a blaze of flowers around her auburn hair.

Edward might have worked at great speed but there was always a moment when he would pause and appraise, whether a model or a landscape or his work. One thing he often talked about was how to stop and look, particularly at landscape; how easy it was to walk through a place without truly seeing it, and how the painter's gaze could isolate the important detail and compress.

I was in my twenties, starting a fledgling film career and at first nervous of the considerable Piper charisma; Edward treated me like one of his models to put me at my ease, by talking non-stop on everything from jazz to Matisse. He had the gift of talking to everyone, young or old, as if they were equals.

Kenneth Clark had described his parents John and Myfanwy as 'two of the most completely humanised people I have ever known'; Edward inherited that. The studio house that he and Prue converted in Somerset, with a print of Picasso's *New Year* on the kitchen door, was filled with light and music and very good cooking; Prue, as well as being a skilled ceramicist, was a cookery writer.

I admired Edward for bringing the Mediterranean to England; for his love of colour and women and good food; and for the sense of an ancient culture rippling under the landscape. He was never apologetic about the country, in the way that so many artists and intellectuals feel they have to be.

And then he was gone. So quickly. I only discovered his full name in the obituaries: Edward Blake Christmas Piper. His father John was devastated and died shortly afterwards.

I had a few of Edward's paintings as a result of the filming – a magical woman's head against the trees, like an English dryad, and some of the nudes. What should have been a friend-ship that continued for another twenty years had been cut short. But I could hear his light, high voice inside my head as I headed towards the Chilterns, telling me that he wasn't sure if Eric Dolphy's *Out to Lunch* was as good a jazz record as everyone said it was.

*

I reached Watlington, the town just under the Chilterns that marks the start of the Icknield Way's long traverse across those hills. Several nearby farms and houses are called Icknield, as is the secondary school.

Watlington was an attractive market town that I already knew, as my sister Katie and her family lived there, with a fine medieval

Town Hall at its central crossroads; lying on the Oxford coaching road from London, it used to have even more pubs than elsewhere in the county – a dozen at least. Then late in the nineteenth century, a Methodist spoilsport called George Wilkinson bought six just to close them down.

Edward Thomas passed through here not long afterwards, describing it as 'all of a piece and rustic, but urban in its compression of house against house'. To escape the noise of a 'pleasure fair' that was passing through, he went into one of the surviving taprooms, 'where the music did not penetrate and the weary were at rest. It was a most beautiful evening, and the swifts were shrieking low down along the deserted streets at nine o'clock. I should like to see them crowded with sheep from Ilsley, and the old drover wearing a thistle in his cap, or with Welsh ponies going to Stokenchurch Fair over the Chilterns.'

Like me, Thomas measured out his progress in this part of the world by pubs, from the Plough at Britwell Salome to the Shakespeare at Wallingford, and preferred the taprooms where there were 'men, politics, crops and beer' to the private bars where he found nothing but polished tables and trapped flies buzzing around – and nothing to smell. He had a lovely phrase for the Chilterns that lay ahead of me, 'wooded on their crests and in the hollows, not very high, but shapely'.

There was a fair taking place in Watlington on the day I passed through. The local morris men were dancing.

Morris dancers can make real countrymen uneasy. In Jez Butterworth's play *Jerusalem*, set in a Wiltshire village, there is much mockery of the local man who dresses up in his garters and bells for the visitors on the village green.

I felt ambivalent, but also sorry for the dancers in the heat. The narrow streets of Watlington were trapping the summer sun. They were dancing in front of a barbecue on the pavement outside the local butchers, and their faces had taken on the livid hue of the roasting sausages as they hit their batons and twirled their handkerchiefs; how they must have itched to use those same handkerchiefs on their perspiring brows.

The troupe were from nearby Towersey and followed a pattern I've observed right around the country: all were old men except one; the older ones were built more like rugby fans than rugby players, so their white shirts were pulled tight over substantial girths that swayed ponderously as they swung around each other; the only young man was, as always, lean enough to emphasise the contrast in stomach size.

The local women were looking on more out of the historical reverence that afflicts the English than from any particular lust or admiration. Only a musician playing the squeezebox, with a jauntily tilted hat and less need to sweat, exuded the air of nomadic restlessness and allure that the morris men once brought with them: for they are no more English than the white wisteria which so gracefully adorns the more upmarket cottage walls along the High Street.

Nor is the dance quite as old as is sometimes thought. Rather than the medieval tradition people assume it must be, like a mummers' play, the term 'morris dancing' derives from 'moorish dance' and originated in Spain in the fifteenth century, with the dancers using swords rather than sticks to tap each other as they swirled. Brought over to England at the time of Henry VII, when the costumed Spanish dancers gave an energetic presentation before the king in the Christmas celebrations of 1494, it proved a popular success.

A century later, in 1600, Shakespearean actor Will Kemp performed 'a morris dance' all the way from Norwich to London as a publicity stunt, although by then the dance had lost much of its Spanish associations – not surprisingly, given the hostility to Spain shown by the Tudors throughout the late sixteenth century.

Its popularity was ensured when Oliver Cromwell and the

Puritans banned the dance; its subsequent re-establishment by Charles II could be seen as a return to a 'Merrie England' of ales and dancing on the village green, although in fact it was about as authentically English as a paella.

*

One of the onlookers at the morris dancing told me about a funeral that had recently been held in Watlington for Nathan Buckland, the patriarch of the local travelling showmen community. A horse-drawn cortège had gone down the high street and 600 people had packed the church.

His widow Julie told me what had made her husband so remarkable and well loved. Any hesitancy about intruding on her grief, after a forty-two-year marriage, she removed by reassuring me that, far from it, she wanted to talk both about him and about the secretive showmen community. Secretive because over the years they have often experienced prejudice. Villages that quite like the excitement of an annual fair are often less enthusiastic about the travelling showmen who accompany them, with their caravans and supposed 'loose morals'. They get tarred with the same brush as other travelling communities.

'Some people put showmen down as gypsies — and there's good and bad in them, like all of us,' said Julie.

I was impressed that Watlington, which Edward Thomas remembered as hosting a pleasure fair when he passed, had always gone out of its way to offer the travelling showmen 'winter quarters', a plot where more than twenty large families put up their mobile homes in the months when traditionally they rested. Nathan, born in 1945 to one of those families, had grown up in these winter quarters and at the local school, Icknield College. It had left him with a deep attachment to Watlington.

He married Julie when she was just eighteen. She showed me
an old black-and-white photo of the two of them emerging from
the same church he had just been buried in. They were covered
in confetti and looked impossibly young; around them were the
smiling faces of the travelling showmen community.

Julie came from a travelling family too, of fourteen children,
and had grown up in a fairground atmosphere, travelling for the
better part of the year: 'I remember the small villages being very
friendly. It was often cold when we arrived and they'd always
bring you a cuppa tea. The fair was a big thing in those times.
Light up a place for a few days.'

After marriage, Nathan and she had toured the country with
his fairground attractions: 'kiddie rides', as Julie put it, with
octopuses and double-decker buses on floats, coconut shies, darts
win-a-prize stalls and just about anything that worked with the
punters.

Later, Watlington Council gave Nathan permission to buy up
the disused watercress beds on the edge of town and for his

family and friends to put mobile homes there more permanently. Compared to the aggravation at Dale Farm that was filling the papers – Basildon Council had spent £18 million to evict travellers from land that had previously been derelict anyway – Watlington's more enlightened attitude had paid dividends.

For the showmen community had helped energise Watlington. Nathan had extended the town social centre, the Memorial Club, and organised local fairs. 'Showmen are born organisers,' said Julie: 'it's what they're good at. And they have to be.'

Not that travelling showmen were finding things easy. Government legislation on sites where they could stay, and the indiscriminate hostility of some councils to all travellers, meant that fairs had been cancelled in parts of the country. However, councils had not had it all their own way, because of ancient legislation that guaranteed 'charter fairs'.

Between 1199 and 1350 over fifteen hundred charters were issued, granting the right to hold markets or fairs. The Crown had realised that fairs were an excellent way of raising tax, and so created new ones and brought existing ones under their jurisdiction. The majority of English fairs were granted royal charters and reorganised to fall in line with their European counterparts.

For that reason Thame near by, almost a sister town to Watlington, found that when at one point noises were made about closing down their ancient fair, on grounds of the collateral damage it caused, they couldn't. Nathan had been involved in that dispute, pointing out to the town worthies and the police that the incidents they complained of – drinking in the town centre, youths getting out of control – happened all year round. The fair was too convenient and easy a target to blame.

There is still a puritan mindset at work in England. We like our 'keep out' notices. Villages have got better at installing playgrounds for children; yet facilities for teenagers are often non-existent, and most of the local bus services that took them to anywhere more exciting have folded. If you could bottle the teenage boredom of Saturday night in a country town, where the only place to meet is the disused bus shelter, then you would understand why the coming of an annual fair is still a cause for real excitement and pleasure.

✻

In Peru I usually travelled with a mule – so that it could carry my kit as well as be company of a limited sort – but that wasn't so feasible in southern England.

I had toyed with the idea of taking a dog along with me for the second half of the walk. Not that I've got one. But occasionally I walked my neighbours' sleek and beautiful rottweiler when at the barn. And my sister's family had a parson's terrier. Both were fine dogs. John Steinbeck's *Travels with Charley*, when he crossed the States with his large poodle, was one of my favourite books and an inspiration for this journey; I grew up to John Noakes's television programmes about walking the Cornish coast path with his border collie, Shep. And I was aware, not least because my children kept telling me, that a book with a dog in it would be commercially attractive.

But there were disadvantages. For a start, both candidate dogs had names I didn't feel like shouting across a crowded field of walkers: the rottweiler was called Portia (like naming a gladiator Phyllis); the terrier, even more improbably, was called Spartacus. More seriously, the way I was walking would not work with a dog – too many impromptu stops and starts and stays with friends. I met a lot of dogs along the way anyway – particularly at Iron Age hill-forts, where dog walkers were often the only other visitors. It made for a perfect constitutional circuit: once round the earthworks of a fort and no need to scoop.

I was able to borrow a dog of my own just for a day though,

as I passed Watlington, where my sister lived. Spartacus could come with me.

'You can let him off the lead,' said Alex, my brother-in-law, an incurable optimist, 'but he may not stay with you.'

Within the next hour I had dragged Spartacus out of willow ponds, hedges and just about any cover that conceivably contained a rabbit. Dog-walking was the modern equivalent of medieval falconry – it required the owner to be led into unknown territory that they would otherwise not investigate. This was fine if it was a local landscape that you were happy to explore; not if you had a whole country waiting for you to cross.

I sat down on a bench outside a pub when I got to the next village along the Icknield Way, Chinnor, exhausted by having detoured past so many rabbit burrows. A man joined me and we got talking, mainly about Spartacus, as an easy and obvious point of conversation. It took all of a minute before he made the usual joke about 'I am Spartacus'. I guessed he was about thirty-five, dressed eccentrically for the country, in pale tracksuit and trainers – more an urban look – and with an iPod looped to ostentatiously large and white Sennheiser headphones. He was very tanned. He said he had just been on holiday to Tunisia, where the clubbing was better than Ibiza.

I explained that the dog wasn't mine and that my travelling life-style made it difficult for me to have one. He was sympathetic.

'I know what you mean. And to be honest, I always think, "who needs a pet when you've already got a penis to look after."'

It was unanswerable.

✳

I arrived at Whiteleaf Cross at dusk, a late-summer dusk, alone after a happily weary Spartacus had been repatriated. There were two horses with their riders on the hilltop. A long bench had been erected above the Cross, which was fine for looking out into the valley but hopeless for seeing the Cross. The only way to get a decent view of it was to walk all the way down the hill to Princes Risborough; to be honest, at this time of evening, I couldn't be bothered, given that I would also have to walk back. I was already thinking about where I wanted to sleep, and if there was a discreet place in the woods to put up a small tent. So my view of the Cross was a bizarre, foreshortened one, looking down from the top-point.

The Cross was a much more recent carving in the chalk than the White Horse at Uffington, but still of great antiquity. The first historical reference occurs in 1742, but that does not help date it. Many antiquities were first recorded only in the eighteenth century; no one had yet used Optical Stimulated Luminescence dating to check further.

It takes the form of a small cross atop a very large pyramidal base. The entire chalk figure is some 250 feet high, visible for miles, not least because the base of the pyramid – known locally as the 'globe' – is also very wide, at over 400 feet. From early measurements taken when the Cross was first recorded in the eighteenth century, it has been growing over the years, particularly at its base, which has more than doubled in width during its regular scourings.

There have been many explanations for the Cross: that it marks a Saxon victory over the Vikings, as it was once supposed the Uffington White Horse did; that like the Cerne Abbas giant it was a phallic symbol, later bowdlerised; that it was a wayside cross for travellers along the Icknield Way, put up at any point since the West Saxons adopted Christianity in the seventh century; that soldiers in the Civil War, which raged around here while Charles I took refuge in nearby Oxford, carved the cross when they were bored (an idea that has the virtue of both ingenuity and implausibility).

More arresting is the curious fact that there are so few other chalk crosses along the Downs or elsewhere in Britain — I could think of only one, a much smaller cross at Bledlow. Given the prevalence of 'pagan symbols', you might expect the Church to counter them with symbols of its own. Then there could have been more outbursts of the sort provided by the Reverend A Baker in 1855, who rhapsodised when approaching Whiteleaf Cross:

Bursting for the first time on the eye of the traveller from the northern direction, it presents an awful and almost spectral apparition of the Sign of the Son of Man looming heavenward above the peaceful Valley, beside the ancient and everlasting hills.

My own idle thought was that because the pyramidal base on which the Cross stands is so grossly out of scale with the Cross, it may have originated as a straightforward triangle on the hill, guiding travellers, to which a cross was later added by the local monastery or church – a cross that due to the toponymy had to be much smaller as, put simply, they ran out of space at the top of the slope.

I had also just passed a more recent example of a figure in the chalk, just where the M40 slices across the Icknield Way. A giant :-) had been carved on the side of the hill, to help or irritate commuters heading down to London each day, particularly if they happened to be archaeologists. One can imagine the thesis that will be produced in fifty years time: 'The emoticon as land-scape art-form; early twenty-first-century predictive text'.

During the Second World War, so that the Cross did not guide enemy bombers to Oxford, it was covered with brushwood; on VE Day, this was ceremoniously burned on the top of the hill.

There were lovers sprawled over the grass above the Cross. A young Asian couple had set up what looked like a photographic studio so that the man could take pictures of his girlfriend with the meadow and hills behind her. He had reflector boards, para-bolic lights and enough camera kit for a full Pirelli calendar, not that there was anything unchaste about the pictures he was taking of his girlfriend, if that is what she was. She tossed her hair and gazed at the sun so as to take advantage of its soft modelling light.

I looked back at the sun myself, as it was fast setting behind the distant towers of Didcot Power Station. The towers emerging out of the orange haze looked like the lost towers of Avalon. Either that or a cooling station had gone critical.

There was very little time left to get up a tent. I headed on down the slope behind the Cross and then even further, to get away from the golf course (I didn't quite have the nerve to bed down in a bunker); but as I came over the brow of Pulpit Hill, I found what I had been looking for – Chequers Knap, a perfectly formed prehistoric barrow, just off to the side of a hollow-way lane. By now even the dog walkers had gone home, so I could set up the small tent I had first used thirty years ago in the Andes and was still serviceable: a Vango Expedition A-frame that was about as old-fashioned as it was possible to get, with the virtues of simplicity and strength. I had seen too many fancy igloo or bender tents get blown off hills to trust them.

Did the stars look brighter if seen when sleeping on a prehistoric barrow? Unlikely but true.

*

There's nothing quite like waking up under a tree to make you appreciate them. Along the ridge line of the Chilterns ahead of me ran the still surprisingly deep forests of beech.

The forests of England. Not the phrase you're supposed to use, as strictly speaking 'forest' applies only to a royal hunting ground. But the one we all do. Before consulting the archaeological research, my preconception – widely shared, I suspect – was that England was largely wooded until the arrival of the Romans. Prehistoric Britons might have made a few inroads into the densely wooded valleys, but preferred the wide-open expanses of Salisbury Plain or other high, treeless places like Dartmoor or the Berkshire Downs; the Romans cleared some lowland areas for their settlements and built connecting roads; with the arrival and gradual domination of the Anglo-Saxons during the Dark Ages, more woodland was slowly lost and a pattern of villages emerged, ready for the Domesday book to record after the Norman conquest.

This has now been shown to be wholly inaccurate. Much of England had been cleared as early as 1000 BC, some two millennia beforehand. The Bronze Age saw intensive farming on a scale that we are only just beginning to appreciate. As one academic expert put it (Oliver Rackham in *The History of the Countryside*):

> It can no longer be maintained, as used to be supposed even twenty years ago, that Roman Britain was a frontier province, with boundless wild woods surrounding occasional precarious clearings on the best land. On the contrary, even in supposedly backward counties such as Essex, villa abutted on villa for mile after mile, and most of the gaps were filled by small towns and the lands of British farmsteads.

Rackham describes the immense clearance that had been undertaken during the Bronze Age and makes the bold claim that 'to convert millions of acres of wildwood into farmland was unquestionably the greatest achievement of any of our ancestors'. He goes on to remind us how difficult it was to clear the woodland, as most British species are difficult to kill: they will not burn and they grow again after felling. Moreover, in his dry phrase, 'a log of more than ten inches in diameter is almost fireproof and is a most uncooperative object'. The one exception was pine, which burns well and perhaps as a consequence disappeared almost completely from southern Britain, the presumption being that prehistoric man could easily burn the trees where they stood: the image of pine trees burning like beacons across the countryside is a strong one. It took the Forestry Commission in the twentieth century to reintroduce large amounts of conifers, an unwelcome decision.

Some Bronze Age woodland was naturally kept and managed for what it could provide: timber for building materials, smaller wood and shrubs for fuel, acorns for pigs (which were often turned loose in the woods in autumn), hazel and other trees suitable for coppicing. But this was small scale. When the Domesday book recorded a relatively low level of English woodland – a much lower proportion than modern France, say, enjoys today – this was not a recent development, but the way it had been for millennia.

The idea that England 3,000 years ago was already as suburban as the outskirts of Basildon has not been absorbed into the popular consciousness. Nor will it ever be readily, for we suffer from what might be called Sherwood Syndrome: the need to believe that much of England – that most of England – was both wild and wooded until modern history 'began' in 1066, or indeed stayed so until much later; and that these ancient forests were the repository of 'a spirit of England', the Green Man, that could be summoned at times when we needed to be reminded of our national identity; where Robin Hoods of all subsequent generations could escape, where the Druids gathered their mistletoe from the trees, where the oak that built our battleships came from.

It is a further irony that the most heavily wooded county of England is now Surrey, thought of as the most suburban. One farmer there told me that it was the county that had the most trees and the most divorces.

There is another popular assumption that follows on from the first – that the Icknield Way I had taken so far across the high ground of Dorset, of Salisbury Plain and of the Wiltshire and Berkshire Downs had kept high because this was naturally treeless land, while many of the valleys the ancient trackway looked down onto would have been wooded and more difficult to cross. Not so. The ridgeway route kept high because it was dry all year round, a good winter road. For many sections of my walk, there had also been a 'Lower Icknield Way' that wound around the hills below in the valley, but would have been practical for livestock only in dry summers.

The landscape that Bronze Age travellers surveyed in 1000 BC, around the time the White Horse of Uffington was carved, would of course have been different: no Swindon, Didcot Power Station or M4 motorway for a start; nor, from where I now looked out, Aylesbury in the Vale that bears its name. But a cultivated system of fields and pastureland would already have been there, albeit in a different formation.

What the work of archaeologists over the last few decades does suggest is that we possessed the land very early – that England was shaped long before the arrival of the Romans, whose occupation can be seen as a brief, anomalous interlude that interrupted the continuity of British history.

The idea of England as a wild and wooded land until the arrival of the Romans is a powerful one. But like so many of the most persistent myths that survive about our country, it is as illusory as the lake from which the Lady's hand emerges to grasp the sword.

There is another surprise that I find peculiarly exciting. There may have been much less forest than we might imagine, but what did exist was of a spectacular quality. The predominant tree in southern England was not any of the ones we might expect – alder, birch, hornbeam, let alone those national favourites, the oak, or the beech that now lines the Chilterns. It was the linden, sometimes called the small-leaved lime or *Tilia cordata*, not to be confused with the large, common lime trees that are used in cities for their ability to absorb pollution and have such sticky leaves, the *Tilia vulgaris*.

The linden was the elven tree of the Bronze Age. The lovely fresh green, heart-shaped leaves created handsome rounded domes in summer. In July, it sent forth fragrant ivory-white flowers. So many insects cluster around these flowers that today, if you stand under one, it often sounds as if the whole tree is humming. Easily coppiced, the resulting offshoots could be harvested, either for burning or for carving the fine-grained wood into pots and bowls. It had a fibrous layer of under-bark called 'bast', which could be made into rope. Even the leaves of the linden were used for animal fodder, the small round fruits eaten (tasting, apparently, like cocoa) and the blossom used to make a mildly sedative tea: a tree for Titania and all her troupe.

For reasons that are not entirely clear, these wonderful trees declined as more and more invasive species of elm, birch and alder arrived – let alone the beech trees that came much later. There are only isolated pockets of small-leaved limes now in our most ancient woodlands. Many people would find them hard to recognise. They are better known in Germany, whose poets from medieval times have celebrated the experience of being '*Unter der Linden*', 'Under the Linden Trees', where lovers can crush the fragrant white flowers beneath them: Goethe's Werther is buried under one, Hermann Hesse wrote of them and Berlin's famous Unter den Linden avenue of limes is a national symbol.

A movement to replant them in England is slowly beginning, as we reassess our attitudes to woodland and move towards more broadleaf and traditional species.

But for prehistoric man travelling along the Icknield Way, as the green road entered the woods it would have become even greener: the colour of sunlight filtering through the translucent leaves of the lime trees would have been of a transcendental intensity.

*

As it was a Saturday, my children could take time off from school to join me, despite their manifold reservations about the potential enjoyment of walking a prehistoric route. They had refused to meet me at Stonehenge earlier: 'What is the point of a pile of stones?' as Daisy had put it.

But Cymbeline's Castle on the slopes of Beacon Hill can claim to be the finest small hill walk in England – and it is very small, only some 800 feet above the plain. Climbing up from the old church below at Ellesborough, it does everything right. It remains steadily in view, isolated, as the summit to climb. It is steep enough to think about zigzagging up the cattle tracks. There is a fine view from the top. And as the name suggests, it is saturated in either history or myth, depending on your persuasion.

Cymbeline – or Cunobelinus – reigned as king of the Catuvellauni from AD 9 to shortly before the Roman invasion of AD 43. The Catuvellauni were the dominant tribe in late Iron Age politics. They had led the earlier resistance to Julius Caesar, who struggled to contain them.

But during the interregnum between Caesar's invasion of 54 BC and Claudius' more successful and permanent occupation a century later, the Catuvellauni enjoyed a quasi-Roman lifestyle without having to subject themselves to Roman political control. Roman goods like wine, olive oil and tableware were imported, in substantial quantities. Roman-style coinage was issued.

Cymbeline's long reign created considerable strength. Likewise, his death in about AD 40 caused the destabilisation that allowed Claudius to invade. The subjection of the neighbouring Atrebates, continued after Cymbeline's death by his son Caractacus, was the spark, or at least the pretext, for the Roman invasion; the Atrebatan rulers fled to Rome and asked for the Emperor Claudius' protection.

If people know about Cymbeline at all, it is because of Shakespeare's play (although Hawkwind also celebrated him in a song with the terrible rhyming couplet, 'And it's high time / Cymbeline'). Critics suggest that Shakespeare made up the events in *Cymbeline* from a few scraps in old chronicles like Holinshed, much as he did with *King Lear.* But one historical aspect Shakespeare captures well is the indeterminate nature of the British court, which was not yet controlled by Rome; the characters are lured alternately by the splendours of the Roman court and the wild places of Britain: 'Let a Roman and a British Ensign wave / friendly together.' It is a curious play, a hodgepodge of different genres and cultures that cannot quite make up its mind, like the Players in *Hamlet,* whether it is tragedy, comedy, history or pastoral: a play about confusion and confused national identity.

As you walk up to it, Cymbeline's Castle stands proud in every sense from the Chilterns, jutting out from the ridge 'just like a Forwards Operation Base, an FOB', observed my older son Owen, the most military-minded of the children. 'If England was invaded, this is the sort of hill that SAS men would hide up on and launch a guerrilla operation.'

It was a perfect position for the Iron Age hill-fort that stood there and which Cunobelinus is said to have inherited. 'Said', because the odd archaeologist has waved a tar-brush of doubt over the association with Cymbeline, despite the local village also being called Kimble, the antiquity of the name, the discovery of many coins near by and the way in which the hill dominates the Catuvellauni territory.

At the rear of Castle Hill was an ugly black observation camera on a metal pole. The hill backed onto Chequers, the prime minister's weekend getaway, a brown slab of a country house that enjoys only a slightly less commanding position than Cymbeline's Castle, and is set off to one side in the woods. In recent years, walkers have been dissuaded from making use of open access legislation, if it means getting close to Chequers; not in my backyard, or estate in this case. There were signs up trying to dissuade walkers from roaming too freely over the hillside.

Just along from Cymbeline's Castle, and within sight of it,

stood Coombe Hill, a Celtic word that had somehow breasted the Anglo-Saxon invasion, just as the hill stands proud along the escarpment. At 850 feet, it is one of the highest points, which goes to show how low the Chilterns are to start with.

A perfect viewpoint had been ruined by a monument Mussolini would have been proud of: a tower grotesquely out of proportion, that reared above the hill with an ice-cream cone pinnacle covered in gilt.

My children, not usually concerned with architectural appreciation, were appalled.

'It looks so *naff*. Like one of those Disney theme-park things to show you're in the ancient world.'

The tower had been erected to commemorate the dead of the Boer War, who deserved a better tribute. This was a politician's speech of a monument, smooth-faced, inane and glib. Even its stability was suspect; there had been worries in recent years that it might fall down.

The children cheered up at the thought that we were so close to Chequers, indeed had a sniper's view of its back entrances.

'So do you think David Cameron might come up here with his family? Could I ask him for his autograph? Would he give me money?'

I explained that modern prime ministers no longer have purses from which they dispensed coins to any lucky subjects they encountered. And that no, I would not be wanting his autograph, nor that of any other recent prime ministers.

We were not far from the Getty estate where the red kites were originally reintroduced back in the 1980s, and there were some circling over Chequers below us, so that we could see their red upper wings, usually hidden. As they swooped over the hills with their unnatural, keening cry, I couldn't help thinking of what an unfair but apt metaphor it was: the scavengers released here over the last thirty years, the free-market vultures unleashed by an all-party consensus.

We retreated away from the vainglorious monument and back into the woods where we found a bowl of beech trees where someone had set up a perfect swing on a very high rope, so that first Leo and then all of us could swing out high above the trees before circling back.

The best things in life were still free.

✳

I'm writing this tucked into the nook of a convenient lone tree on the leeward side of Ivinghoe Beacon. Convenient because the Beacon protrudes north from this central block of the Chilterns, and so the wind funnels around the hill with ferocity as it sweeps across from the plains of Cambridgeshire that lie ahead. But in the protected hollow of my lone pine below the hilltop, with the setting sun falling on me from the west, even the ugly Coombe Hill monument behind me now looks atmospheric.

My children have taken the train back to Bristol, catching it with perhaps thirty seconds to spare, so I'm alone again.

I've come some 250 miles; 150 lie ahead. Edward Thomas passed drovers here taking their plump Dorset and Devon sheep on to Dunstable and East Anglia. I'm impressed again by the speed with which Thomas covered the ground: around thirty miles a day. But then poets have always been good walkers.

Much has been written describing the epic walks Coleridge and Wordsworth undertook together in the Lake District; little on why they did so. The assumption is that it was to experience the sublimity of nature at first hand – but they did not need to spend days and nights restlessly journeying for that. The poets escaped to the hills for a simpler truth: however arduous the walk, it was always easier than the alternative – having to write.

The physical labour of writing is much underestimated. When the walks ran out, and there was no escape from the desk, these fit young men in their twenties, who thought nothing of covering 100 miles in a couple of days, were laid prostrate: Wordsworth got heartburn from writing too much, together with 'an uneasiness at my stomach and side'; Coleridge, who found it even harder, needed recourse to laudanum.

> And oft, when in my heart was heard
> thy timely mandate, I deferred
> the task, in smoother walks to stray.
> (William Wordsworth, 'Ode to Duty')

Writing has always been physically exhausting – or writing at that level. Both Wordsworth and Coleridge envied, yet also deplored, the facility with which Southey could produce his epics. They were right to do so. Who reads Southey now?

The Lake Poets were not alone. Keats and John Clare drove themselves in punishing walks: Keats covered hundreds of miles in Scotland, as well as his daily commute from London up to Hampstead; the vision of John Clare tramping endlessly across the fields of Northamptonshire in search of work or sanity is one of the saddest in all English literature, but also one of the most productive.

Writing for the sternest critic – yourself – produces a bilious mix of dissatisfaction and insecurity that eats away at the stoutest constitutions. No wonder that Wordsworth got heartburn. Or that Montaigne advised potential writers to become physically fit before attempting any work of value.

There is another reason for poets in particular to walk. By setting up an unwavering rhythm in their stride, they can allow any words in their head to deviate from that rhythm and then return to it. The pleasure and power of any metre depends both on adherence to a pattern but also on breaking it. A strictly metrical poem would soon become mechanical and dull. By walking, the Romantics had a constant metronome against which to compose and to rebel. The poetic feet in a line are not called that for nothing.

Edward Thomas's and his friend Robert Frost's fondness for walking could be seen to come out of the same kitbag. Many of Thomas's poems are pieces of prose that have got up and walked out of the door.

That said, I had felt the urge to write, or even think, only occasionally when walking – otherwise I would have finished my own version of *The Prelude* from the Dorset coast to here. Most of the time the average walker goes through the usual cycle of thoughts: route-finding, the weather, clothing and wider issues of love, sex, money and the annoying tune you heard on the radio and now can't quite get out of your head. The process is a bit like meditation. The initial five miles of each day's walk just serve to clear the noise from your mind. Then random flashes of insight can start to emerge.

Kenneth Grahame, who paced many miles of these Oxfordshire trackways while composing *The Wind in the Willows*, wrote that

> Nature's particular gift to the walker, through the semi-mechanical act of walking – a gift no other form of exercise seems to transmit in the same high degree – is to set the mind jogging, to make it garrulous, exalted, a little mad maybe – certainly creative and suprasensitive, until at last it really seems to be outside of you and as if it were talking to you while you are talking back to it. Then everything gradually seems to join in, sun and the wind, the white road and the dusty hedges, the spirit of the season, whichever that may be, the friendly old earth that is pushing life forth of every sort under your feet or spellbound in a death-like winter trance, till you walk in the midst of a blessed company, immersed in a dream-talk far transcending any possible human conversation.
>
> (Kenneth Grahame, 'The Fellow that Goes Alone', 1913)

Walking on your own can set up an interior monologue of peculiar power. However, it is also necessary at times to be jolted out of your own internal rhythms.

A few summers before, I had taken the children to Switzerland for a holiday. I wanted to show them some of the wilder, more open stretches that still lay in the less frequented valleys.

Early one morning we left the ramblers' hostel on a hilltop and set off to a beautiful side valley that curled around to Mount Tounot, at only 10,000 feet a very achievable peak for young teenagers. We were alone in the valley. The air had that harsh silence you sometimes get in Switzerland, when the early sun has flash-dried the atmosphere, and the snow on the mountaintops seems to have sucked in all the moisture.

Owen put the Kaiser Chiefs playing 'Ruby' at full volume on his speakerphone. I felt like the museum guard who sees a visitor put a moustache on the *Mona Lisa*.

'Owen! The whole point of coming here is to get some peace and quiet. They can probably hear that on the Matterhorn.'

'Why not? There's no one else around. And it's boring walking in silence.'

'Yeah Dad,' the other two chorused.

We spent the next few minutes singing along to the chorus of 'Ruby, Ruby, Ruby!' I enjoyed it. Didn't Marcel Duchamp put a moustache on the *Mona Lisa* anyway?

✶

Just beyond Luton I came across some fields that had lungwort, or 'poor man's hosta', growing freely on their edges. It was a common fancy in medieval times that the leaves were spotted from drops of the Virgin's milk or tears, and the plant was known as 'Jerusalem cowslip'. Further on, there were more exotic creatures like the burnt tip orchid, moon carrot and the startling Pasque flower in the nature reserves which here as elsewhere had shot up along the Chilterns.

This was the part of the world John Bunyan had walked in, the landscape of his *Pilgrim's Progress*; he described the low hills I was walking across as 'The Delectable Mountains', a place where his pilgrims could rest: 'a most pleasant Mountainous Country, beautified with Woods, Vineyards, Fruits of all sorts; Flowers also, with Springs and Fountains, very delectable to behold'. Bunyan lived in nearby Bedford, but travelled widely as a tinker, and later as a preacher. Like Malory, he wrote much of his book in jail, imprisoned in Bedford for his non-conformist views.

I had always liked Bunyan, and the simplicity and power of

his parables. It was hard not to draw a comparison with England today, when most people were more concerned about the state of their haircuts than of their souls. The notion of grace, redemption, forbearance, patience — these were alien or at best hidden, much like the old medieval names of our familiar flowers in the hedgerows.

The virtues most trumpeted now were self-reliance and self-fulfilment, with much heavier stress on the importance of one's immediate family than of the wider community or country.

Looking back from Warden Hill, I could see the lights of Luton. An orange EasyJet plane was flying in low from the south, while the neon flicker of Sainsbury's caught my eye in the centre of the city. Below me, the banks of the prehistoric Drays Ditches gave way to a golf course, some of whose bunkers seemed to mimic and extend the earthworks.

Not for the first time, I was reminded of what a complicated country England was, of how many seams and layers it had.

I have been to empty countries, parts of Patagonia or the peninsula east of Murmansk, where you can travel in a helicopter for hours and not see a sign of human habitation. They have a wild beauty. But I prefer a landscape that has been given meaning by humans, like the Inca heartland of the Andes or the headwaters of the Ganges in the Himalaya, with their Hindu temples. The hills east of Luton, some of England's least celebrated countryside, were clearly less dramatic than the Patagonian mountains or the Kola Peninsula. But the ribbon of the Icknield Way curved beautifully over the last outlying Chilterns, past medieval villages, nature reserves and one great surprise.

Ravensburgh Castle is one of the most important and significant of all the Iron Age hill-forts, the largest in eastern England. Moreover, it's thought to be where the British mounted a heroic resistance to Caesar when he invaded.

Just to get an idea of the scale of the place: the perimeter wall is a kilometre long; it encloses eight hectares; when partially excavated in the 1960s, a thousand postholes were found, along with a rich haul of late Iron Age jewellery, like La Tène brooches.

You would have thought that it would be a national monument, lovingly tended and signposted from afar. But Ravensburgh, far from being treasured, is not even accessible to the public, let alone cared for. It lies on private land, just to the north of the Icknield Way, covered in scrubby woodland and used as a pheasant shoot.

Unless you're prepared to trespass. Which of course I was. One of my prime problems with the open access 'right to roam' legislation (which does not apply to woodland) was that it lessened the opportunity for a good trespass. But this was private woodland with a vengeance, with enough 'keep out' signs to make an American rancher proud.

It seemed prudent to go after nightfall. Luckily there was a full moon. Striking across from the fields, I entered the woods cautiously. To me, pheasants meant one thing and it was not food: they meant gamekeeper. I could imagine one coming up behind me with a lot of attitude and a 'You're not from around here, are you?' If not a baseball bat.

The wood was neglected: the white trunks of uprooted oaks that had toppled over gleamed in the moonlight, their undersides coated in the local chalk. In the past, when some of these trees had fallen, Iron Age artefacts had been found entangled in the roots.

I advanced with caution around the fort, at one point almost voiding myself when I stepped close to a pheasant in the dark and it shot up. The site was enormous. The only virtue of its complete neglect was that it was easier in the thicket of moonlit trees and shrubs to conjure up the ghosts of the Iron Age tribe who had lived here than if it had all been cleared.

James Dyer, the archaeologist who led the partial excavations in the 1960s and 1970s, made the plausible suggestion, from the scale of the fortifications and the artefacts found, that it was the base from which the Catuvellauni led the British resistance against Julius Caesar's invasion. If so, it was well chosen. Even covered by trees and at night, I could see how precipitous the slope was on the southern side, and how the fort dominated the approaches to the north and west.

Julius Caesar, writing in his customary third person, left a description that fitted well:

The *oppidum* of Casivellaunus, which was protected by woods and marshes, was not far off, and a considerable number of men and of cattle had assembled in it. The Britons apply the name of *oppidum* to any woodland spot, difficult of access and fortified with a rampart and trench, to which they are in the habit of resorting in order to escape a hostile raid. Caesar marched to the spot indicated with his legions, and found the place had a great natural strength and well fortified: nevertheless he proceeded to assault it on two sides. The enemy stood their ground a short time, but could not sustain the onset of our infantry and fled precipitately from another part of the *oppidum*.

(Caesar, *Commentari de Bello Gallico*)

Earlier that day, like Caesar, I had sized up the location and points of access while there was still some light, and also the points of departure in case I too had to 'flee precipitately'. The fort's position commanded the valley. James Dyer had commented on 'the great natural strength of the hill-fort which cannot be matched by any other in the Chilterns'. If cleared and properly maintained – let alone excavated, as Dyer could only scratch the wooded surface – it would be a fine landmark for nearby Hexton and this part of Hertfordshire between Luton and Hitchin, which was often ignored or forgotten.

After my evening venture into the wood, I felt I deserved a drink and a meal at the pub in Hexton, not least because it was called the Raven, so had some loose anthropological connection with Ravensburgh Castle.

However, there was a potential fly in my beer. As a conscientious girlfriend, Irena had informed me that walking used up only some 100 calories an hour and that if I kept eating nothing but pies as I crossed England, I would soon look like William Dalrymple. So I had promised to have more salads.

This went against the grain. A salad, as P G Wodehouse once remarked, rarely feeds the inner man. Particularly one who's been walking all day, or trespassing in woods.

I approached the bar with trepidation. The barmaid had a mass of frizzy blonde hair and was comfortably upholstered. She looked sympathetic and I need not have worried. Prominent on the menu was a 'black pudding and bacon salad'. Honour could be satisfied.

It was not a time to beat about the bush. I asked the barmaid – there was no way of putting this delicately – if the salad was 'substantial'.

'Oh yes,' she said. 'Very.'

*

As I climbed up towards Deacon Hill the next day, the path entered a delightful woodland glade. This was hardly unusual on my walk; much of the charm of the Icknield track I was following lay in how it entered and left woods right across England; in the retreat and advance of shadow and dappled light playing across beechmast before opening out again to the track across the hills.

But sometimes you arrive in a wood at precisely the right moment. The sunlight on the fields outside. Old man's beard climbing headlong among the outlying trees, searching for the sun from its shady roots. And for me, one of the greatest pleasures England can provide: the soft murmur of wood pigeons.

I've been in love with that brooding, liquid call ever since I first heard it as a boy in Suffolk where we spent summer holidays in a caravan in a wood. I would wake to hear them playing call and response from the trees above. It is too variable a sound and call to pin down that precisely – though I like Simon Barnes's attempt at a Welsh wood pigeon, 'Steal twoooo cows, Taffy.' It is too conversational to be a song, yet too melodic to be conversational. There are chromatic shifts within it that no other bird can quite manage. An oboe in the orchestra.

It came as a wonderful shock to hear it again in Peru, many years after Suffolk, when we were approaching a 12,000-foot pass that led to the Inca ruins of Choquequirao, which then still lay covered in jungle. After climbing up through an area of grassland, we arrived at a hangar of wood that guarded the pass. Wood pigeons shot out, at first startled, and then settled to give their plump, contented fluting as we made our way through the little-visited trees. One of our muleteers told me that they were called '*cucula*' locally, a wonderfully onomatopoeic word.

They were much less common there than in England; here they are seldom valued or celebrated. If wood pigeons were as rare as nightingales, or such occasional visitors, we would make pilgrimages to hear them as well. Because they are a sedentary, year-round population (unlike in Europe, where they migrate) and because we have so many of them – an estimated 20 million, easily one per household – we take them for granted.

They are also a magnificent size, the largest of all adult pigeons, weighing some half a kilogram of contented plumpness. There is that coat of grey, with just a hint of pink and mauve at the breast, like a bridegroom in his tails and waistcoat. They have a wingspan of over two feet and can fly at fifty miles an hour, with some complicated acrobatics along the way.

It may come as a shock to many city dwellers, who assume that country shooting is mainly of pheasants, to learn how many wood pigeons are added to the bag. The British Association for Shooting and Conservation (patron: the Duke of Edinburgh) estimates that a third of all wood pigeons born each year are shot – a staggering amount. That same ability to fly at speed, twisting and turning, apparently makes them a challenge for those who like to call themselves 'sportsmen', although in my book sport involves a little more energy and ethics than lifting a shotgun to your shoulder and blasting at a wood pigeon. The BASC recommends that a gun which is '12-bore, double barrelled (28″ barrels are good), choked improved and ½ firing 1 ounce (28 grams) of No 6 shot will drop pigeons stone dead at between 25–35 yards all day long'.

Why do I get annoyed at the idea of wood pigeons being shot when I'm quite happy for pheasants to grace both my pot and my table, and know perfectly well how they got there? Pheasants are bred to be shot. Wood pigeons aren't. I realise the distinction is illogical. But I still could no more kill the owner of this magnificent liquid cry than shoot a soprano on stage at Covent Garden.

Today there is another reason why I have stopped in the trees for a while to listen to the pigeons glissade above me. Because even more than associating that sound with Suffolk when I was a boy, or Peru when a young man, it's the sound I have been waking up to in my barn at Little Stoke for the last few years, and at my family house near by for nigh on thirty.

It's a reminder of having left the place for good. '*Nel mezzo del cammin di nostra vita, Mi ritrovai per una selva oscura*'; 'In the middle of my life's journey I found myself in a dark forest.'

✴

I had already found that most country districts had a certain unanimity when it came to 'who to go to' for local knowledge on farming, in the same way as it was always obvious who the village shaman was in the Amazon. Asking people around this part of rural Hertfordshire, I was quickly directed to the same person, Peter Roberts, a farmer who had over forty years of experience before recently retiring.

He had now moved out of the farmhouse to make way for his son, and lived in a cottage by the old watercress beds near Whitwell. A thoughtful, white-haired man, he was convalescing from an illness when I saw him.

'These cottages were all lived in by labourers before. Now it's just me who's had anything to do with farming.

'It's tricky soil. We're on the edge of the Chilterns in Hertfordshire. Chalk, London clay, flint, we get it all. There's a farmer I know near here has a sixty-acre field on a hill. He's always said that you could plough the bottom of the hill with one horse, but you would need two for the middle and by the time you got to the top, it would be pure clay and three horses.'

The main change he had seen had been the loss of livestock. 'There used to be eight dairy herds in this parish alone. Not any more. Not a single one. All gone over to cereals. No sheep either, apart from a few "hobby sheep". Cereals pay better, and oilseed rape. Even then, we're not really in the right part of the country. Time was when it helped being close to London. Not now. Better to be close to Felixstowe or another port. Most of the wheat goes for export so you want to keep transport costs down.'

'Also it's a heck of a job, milking. Work first thing in the morning and last thing at night. There just isn't enough money to keep people interested.

'On the farm estate I was managing, when I started we had 250 cows and 13 people working. Now there are no cows and just two or three people working, with a fair amount of casual labour.'

Peter was worried about his son, who had taken over the family farm. Not as to whether he could manage – he had diversified into light industrial units and a livery service for two dozen horses – but because 'farming now is a pretty lonely business. At least they've got mobiles so they can keep in touch more than we could when I started.' As if on cue, his son rings up. I had a vision of farmers all over the country trundling along in their tractors and using a hands-free.

'It's been a godsend, mobiles. Really helped farmers. Used to be that the only time they talked with anybody else other than their sheep was once a week in the pub, when they all got hammered together.'

Over the years Peter had become so concerned about the pressure on farmers, and their solitude, that he worked with Farming in Crisis to help those who had reached the end of their tether.

As in so many parts of the country, pheasant shooting was a big part of the local economy. 'By the time you pay for the gamekeepers, there's not a lot of profit, but it keeps them in work and gives value to the woodland cover. I'm always surprised, though, that the anti-hunting lobby don't do more against shooting. They run around complaining about a few foxes when there are hundreds of thousands of birds being blasted out of the sky all over the country.'

I went over to see another farmer close by, John Cherry, who still worked a large 2,500-acre farm based around his old family home. John was just a few years older than me and had been farming for thirty years – or, as he put it, had spent 'thirty years trying to batter the soil into submission'. An amiable, lanky man, with a mop of dishevelled hair, he hadn't let the various trials and tribulations of farming spoil his sense of humour. If anything, he had begun to take a Zen approach.

'We still don't really understand soil science. The soil is an incredibly complex organism – second only to a coral reef – and it's very easy to mess it up. Lots of chemical fertilisers can turn the sort of clay we've got here into concrete as hard as a runway.'

Like many, John had started to go easy on the fertiliser and look at organic alternatives, after a feeling that farming had lost its way in the mid twentieth century with over-intensive methods. But he had also become interested in another movement that for some farmers was, if anything, even more radical.

For millennia, the soil has always been ploughed before planting seed. Now the new 'zero tillage' movement has started to question this received wisdom. In John's view, 'The trouble about ploughing is that you can break up and destroy topsoil just as much as aerating it. What's more, if you've had a dry summer, you lose even more moisture in the ground by turning over the soil.'

The new movement of 'zero tillage' – enthusiastically promulgated in parts of the world like Argentina, which has thin topsoil – suggests that the soil is left in place to do its own, more natural regeneration, and that direct drilling is used to seed fields. In the States, 'no-till' farming has gone from an experimental acre in 1962 in Kentucky to 90 million acres across the country and growing.

If adopted worldwide, said John, it may also stop us 'going to hell in a handcart'. The erosion of topsoil has been a long-term, global problem. The Oklahoma dustbowl of the 1930s was created by ploughing up too much pastureland when prices were good. David Montgomery, whose book *Dirt: The Erosion of Civilizations* is the working Bible for the 'zero tillers', has traced the problem of 'soil abuse' from the earliest human cultivation in Mesopotamia to the American push westward and the pampas of Latin America. I had seen how prehistoric man had exhausted the topsoil in Dorset.

'Zero tillage' has some attractive side effects. Ploughing is labour-intensive and costly, using cumbersome equipment. It favours larger farms, which can justify the outlay. Direct drilling can be done with much simpler equipment on farms of, say, just 500 acres, allowing a return to smaller holdings and compacting the soil less in the process.

Despite the usual farmers' moans, John and, earlier, Peter Roberts had shared a certain optimism about the future of farming. As John said, 'It's good to be feeding the world again after so many decades of having been seen as bloodsucking leeches living on subsidies.'

✻

A country fête was taking place in a field alongside the Icknield Way and there were women everywhere: young ones gossiping with prams, older ones manning cake stalls, teenage girls hanging out with unsuitable youths.

It was the chance to make a few observations: that while the general level of pulchritude was high, the Englishwoman's natural, perfectly graceful and curvaceous pear shape is not always best suited to jeans; that there were probably rather an unnatural number of blondes around – almost impossible these days to spot a Range Rover or luxury 4x4 in the countryside without a flash of blonde hair at the wheel; and that one of the most attractive characteristics of them all, young or old, was that they laughed a lot.

It would be a rash Englishman who dared generalise too much about the characteristics of the other sex sharing the island with him. Let alone if any of them are his readers. But my sister Alice, who has more licence, told me that many of her French friends had strong views on Englishwomen. One elegant Parisienne had confided to her that she couldn't understand why Englishwomen were so obsessed by their animals and their children, and relatively uninterested in their husbands. 'You make brilliant mothers but lousy wives,' she had said to Alice. 'You need to be more mysterious to your husbands and stop sitting on the toilet in front of them.'

Another had commented on the way Englishwomen appeared to give up on sex after marriage – the theory being, apparently, that British men cheated more than their American or French counterparts because British women didn't take marital sex seriously enough; that British women didn't work at their married relationships in general and the sexual side in particular. A French friend of Alice's, by contrast, ensured that she made love with her husband three times a week – 'at an absolute minimum!'

I wasn't sure about all this, not having had too many locker-room discussions with either English or French women. Nor did a weekly quota system seem the best way forward; it sounded a bit pressurised. But it did seem unfair to put all the blame on Englishwomen for any lack of spark in their marriages. On my journey, I had met a lot of married men in pubs who looked as if they'd settled for a lifelong dependency on beer, belly and darts, and only ever smiled when they saw a pay cheque.

What was true was that in my own relationships, now that I thought about it, I had been romantically attached to wonderful German, American, and Latin ladies – and married a proudly Welsh woman – but not been involved with an English girl since leaving university thirty years before. Why was that?

And now I was walking out with Irena, who was Czech, albeit that she had lived here for decades. She also had strong views on Englishwomen: that they wore too much make-up, for a start, and that even if as a culture the English weren't having much married sex, they were obsessed by it with their tabloids, high rates of teenage pregnancy and Ann Summers shops in every high street.

She had just accompanied me on the recent journey to Peru, with a long, ambitious trek into the jungle, but had shown little interest in any walks across England, quite apart from her work commitments during the week. Like Leo, she said she couldn't quite see the point of taking a holiday to explore the country she was living in anyway. And the weather would probably be bad.

In fact the weather had been exceptional. I reminded her of this whenever I rang her up from some beautiful moor or wild place that had any reception (I was amazed how few did – one casual way in which the countryside was denigrated was that most mobile companies still couldn't be bothered to supply coverage to a surprising amount of it).

Mobile phones are constantly being denounced, for their danger to driving, wallets and the peace and tranquillity of railway carriages; but there can be few finer pleasures than talking to the person you love when gazing out on a beautiful landscape and feeling connected to them. It certainly beats talking to the sheep.

*

At Ickleford, 'the ford for the Icknield Way' across the local river, the Hiz, I stopped at the church, or rather churchyard: I wanted to find the gravestone of Henry Boswell who had been buried there. Boswell, the self-styled 'king of the gypsies' in the eighteenth century, was said to have walked every road in the country by his death in 1760, at the age of ninety – a fabulous achievement worth celebrating and commemorating.

Someone had placed wooden owls in the yew trees around the churchyard. The joke was on me as I failed to find the gravestone, despite application to a kind woman helping in the church who made further enquiries, to no avail. It seemed Henry Boswell had spirited himself away, in one final, gypsy vanishing trick.

The vicar appeared, a vague-looking man with a beard. 'Oh, I don't know much about the churchyard, I'm afraid. I'm only the vicar. You'll have to ask one of the locals.'

Maybe it was the frustration at failing to find Boswell's grave, or the cold night I had spent sleeping out on the open on a hill the night before, but for some reason this answer reduced me to an equally cold fury. 'I'm only the vicar.' It encapsulated all that most irritated me about Anglicanism and its apologetic defeatism.

The Church of England had been forged in Saxon steel and defended against the Vikings; it had built some of the finest cathedrals in Europe and, in the King James Authorised Version of the Bible, produced a prose work of unparalleled beauty and rigour; it had engaged in honourable soul-searching over the ensuing centuries, debating with thinkers from the Reformation to the Enlightenment to Darwin; and now it was sedated on tranquillisers and being put out to pasture.

For a brief moment when I was young, it looked as if the Church of England might be jolted out of its long, slow decline. John Robinson's *Honest to God* in 1963 was a brave attempt to address contemporary doubts and recast Christianity, in the way that theology had always done through the centuries. Robinson had just been made the bishop of Woolwich, an inner-city diocese, and was aware of how remote the Church of England had become. He drew deeply on the work of Rudolf Bultmann, a brilliant German theologian whose writings had not yet reached a wider English readership.

Bultmann had called for the Christian story to be 'demythologised' to give an authentic core engagement with its central premise and challenge, the crucifixion, without the accumulated trappings. Robinson wrote, in a lyrical sentence, that 'it is in making himself nothing, in his utter self-surrender to others in love, that [Jesus] discloses and lays bare the ground of man's being as love.' The original gospel message, they both argued, had been mediated through a mythological framework of the first few centuries after Jesus that was now alien to the world-view of modern humanity, and needed reinterpreting afresh.

I admired the work of Bultmann and John Robinson, and had gone to meet Robinson in the early 1980s, in his final years. He had welcomed me to his cold, austere rooms in Cambridge, and made a bachelor lunch of soup and bread, which he shared with me. By then it was already clear that the Church of England had turned its back on even the modest reappraisal he had suggested; Archbishop Runcie had more or less said that the Church would not address such issues of theology. 'Steady as she goes,' was the cry.

Instead, he and his successors moved to a more evangelical style, in the belief that if you kept repeating in an ever louder voice what previous generations had believed, this would somehow convince any doubters. Any reinterpretive theology became ring-fenced, as if contagious. Rowan Williams, the most recent arch-bishop, while admirable for his progressive social views, had still promoted a return to doctrine and liturgy, seeing *Honest to God* as 'a museum piece' and 'a transient phenomenon' of those turbulent times, the 1960s.

The only hope for the Church now lay in the welcome arrival of women priests. Perhaps they, with the energy and compassion they brought, and their capacity for awkward questions, would demand more honesty to God, and less fudging of the issues.

I remember Robinson looking at me with infinite sadness at the end of that lunch — a man who had battled courageously and who had been treated in the way the English establishment does so well with visionaries, by sidelining and ignoring them. The shadow of the cancer that was soon to kill him was already in his eyes.

He had written:

It will doubtless seem to some that I have by implication abandoned the Christian faith and practice altogether. On the contrary, I believe that *unless* we are prepared for the kind of revolution of which I have spoken it *will come* to be abandoned. And that will be because it is moulded, in the form we know it, by a cast of thought that belongs to a past age – the cast of thought which Bultmann describes as 'mythological'.

✳

The old Kayser Bonder building in Baldock, so familiar to drivers along the A505 with its striking Art Deco façade, could be a symbol of the country's changing fortunes in the twentieth century. First built by a film processing company, it later became a ladies' stocking factory (the 'Full-Fashioned Hosiery Company from Halifax') and was later diverted to producing parachutes during the Second World War. I remember passing it when it stood empty during the early years of recession under Thatcher. Then it was turned into a giant Tesco, one of the first hyperstores. As such, it attracted much opprobrium locally as a symbol of retail glitz. Nearby landowners of the more conservative sort still insist on calling it 'the Kayser Bonder', rather than 'Tesco's' like everybody else. But I've always enjoyed the Tesco – a large, cheap and democratic store in a beautiful landmark building.

That said, I'm hesitant at choosing a pie from the in-store café, which was built before the current wave of Starbucks clones, with their faux-leather armchairs; this café still has the plastic, more infantile architecture of the 1980s service station – spillproof tables and chairs, with a tray system for clearing. The pie also seems far too cheap; the old rule of thumb used to be that if the pie was cheaper than a pint of beer, there must be something wrong with it.

But this ham and mushroom pie has a surprising delicacy. The pie is remarkably fine in every sense — slender and textured.

I leave with the agreeable sense of surprise that has accompanied me for much of the walk. And with a bumper pack of boxer shorts for less than a tenner. My written instructions to the groups joining me for long trekking expeditions in South America have always included the suggestion, 'Remember, a man, or woman, can do anything if they have clean underwear every day.' And I've been on the move constantly since Oxfordshire.

The Icknield Way begins remarkably soon out of Baldock. Or at least one tendril of it does. The old low road, for dry weather, has been converted into a busy dual carriageway, the A505, thundering up and around Royston on its way to East Anglia. But the high road for wet weather, keeping to the chalk, still exists as a quite beautiful green lane, threading its way through a series of medieval villages.

The wide trackway curled and contoured intuitively over and around the slopes of the hills. Now that I had travelled the Icknield for hundreds of miles, I thought of the sheer number of travellers that must have journeyed along here over the last 5,000 years, their cattle carving a path through the landscape that had endured since Neolithic times: a monument in itself.

We have always been a restless, travelling nation. If Bruce Chatwin had taken a walk out of his front door along the Icknield Way, rather than travelling to the other side of the world to trace aboriginal paths in Australia, he could have hymned our own, English songlines.

One of the many ways we belittle the past is to assume that our ancestors were less mobile than we are today. Of course in some ways this is true: there were no EasyJets lifting off from Luton airport. But it would be wrong to think that they were sedentary. If anything, travel had a greater importance, for the movement of goods and ideas. It may have taken far longer to cross the country along such trackways as the Icknield; but this meant the experience was richer and more resonant than today's quick swing and away around the M25.

One common denominator to the archaeological investigations I've witnessed worldwide over the past few years has been the evidence of how far prehistoric man travelled: the pilgrims found buried in Maya cities who had crossed thousands of miles of Mesoamerica to get there; the grave goods in Andean tombs that had come from the Amazon or the Pacific Coast; the Viking longboats at Constantinople. Let alone the original migration by *Homo sapiens* out of Africa and along the South Asian continent to China and the Bering Strait, a migration confirmed recently by mitochondrial DNA tests.

When the bones of the 'Amesbury Archer', who lived around 2300 BC and was buried near Stonehenge, were found and analysed in 2002, they showed that he had originally come from the Alps. Moreover, along with the arrowheads that gave him his name, he was buried with artefacts from France and Spain. He might well have walked along the Icknield Way to get to the Stonehenge area, having crossed the North Sea from Europe to East Anglia.

I was approaching East Anglia now. Much of that ancient Anglo-Saxon kingdom may be flat, but it does at least mean that when you get to a hill, you can see for miles.

The East Anglians are sensitive about their lack of hills. I once had to interview Brian Eno, a task that should have been both pleasant and intriguing, but was made less so by his insistence that the interview took place at eight o'clock in the morning. He was in a filthy mood. So were my film crew, who had been forced to get up even earlier to prepare. A special rider had been added to the interview that we should not use footage of Eno when he was in Roxy Music and had long flowing hair and glitter costumes, now that he was more follicularly challenged and wore sober suits.

We began at the beginning, his family home near Woodbridge. 'Ah yes, quite flat around that bit of Suffolk, isn't it,' I murmured.

Before breakfast, my line in warm-up repartee was not as assured as it should have been.

Eno went ballistic: 'It's not flat. Why does everyone think it's flat? There are plenty of hills in Suffolk. I hate it when people say that Suffolk's flat.'

He was just warming up. Later we got to the reaction of critics when he put out his first, more conceptual, ambient albums. 'They called me an old hippie fart. All those critics who had got punk so wrong and then had to jump on its bandwagon. I can name every one of the bastards [he did, in detail]. And now they call my work classic.'

I admired the last of the hills, knowing that they would soon give way to the flat lands. A large flock of deer ran up the other side of the valley. Few people walked this way any more; it was not on the 'pretty list' of British countryside.

Certainly Wallington, the first village I came to, was largely uncelebrated. English villages are as varied as lamb chops: some are lustrous, thick cut and gleaming, inviting the pan; others are shrunken miserable affairs, where the meat has already congealed from lack of interest. Such was Wallington. There was no pub. Two large and cheerless farms dominated the place. Under normal circumstances I would have pressed on to the more attractive villages just over the hills: Therfield in particular, which promised a pub with a singing landlord, sounded more my sort of place.

But Wallington had one single lure. George Orwell had owned a house here for the last ten years of his life, when producing some of his best work.

My heart sank when I saw it. It was not a house, but a mean little cottage, of the sort that people find picturesque if they do not have to live there. It was shallow, just eleven feet deep, with small windows and an unusual sunken door that was under four feet high. I thought of the lanky Orwell stooping to get inside.

He had been desperately poor when he came here with his

soon-to-be wife Eileen (they married in the local church). To make ends meet, he wrote in the morning and sold groceries from the house in the afternoon. The rent was 'extraordinarily low', at just 7s 6d week. It was so cheap that the penniless Orwell took the cottage without viewing it beforehand. The first time he saw his new property was as its tenant, having walked the same green lane as me from Baldock, one April day in 1936.

The cottage then had no electricity, no hot water and no indoor lavatory. The outdoor cesspool frequently blocked up unless, Orwell noted in a letter, a certain sort of Jeyes toilet paper was used. The garden was full of tin cans together with − surreal touch − a dozen buried old boots. The landlord had cut costs by replacing the thatch with corrugated-iron sheeting, which made a thunderous noise whenever it rained.

The previous owner of the shop had been the local Manor Farm, whose owners had tried a more idealistic and cooperative way of working in the 1920s, at the time of the first Bolshevik experiments in Russia. The experiment in Wallington had failed, which was why the village store had been closed for a while before Orwell reopened it. The other farm in the village had continued to run in the more traditional 'capitalist' style. Orwell drew the obvious parallels and the village in *Animal Farm* is called Willingdon.

I felt enormous sympathy for Orwell and his new wife, Eileen. Life must have been cold and difficult. There was not much custom for their shop, which was fitted out as basically as they came − a few shelves and some jars with sugar, flour and other basics, and a bacon slicer. His best customers were the village children who came in asking for sweets. He needed to sell thirty shillings of merchandise per week to break even − but at least, Orwell reasoned, they could get their own supplies at wholesale prices.

The enterprise brought to mind the sad, small stores I came across in the Andes, invariably in the front room of a *campesino's* house: the tins of Peruvian tuna fish, a few packets of pasta and some dry bread. A different universe from the gleaming display back at the Tesco in Baldock with its over 20,000 retail items.

Cyril Connolly came to visit, an incongruous thought. Connolly with his more old Etonian ways had not seen Orwell since the two were at school together. Orwell told him, briskly, that it was better running a grocery store than, as he once had, a bookshop. With a grocery store, customers came in for a specific item and left fast. With a bookshop, they could chat interminably and waste a writer's time. But it was apparent to Connolly and other visitors how thin Orwell had become since school, looking 'more like a scarecrow'.

Despite the privations, it was the place where Orwell enjoyed some of the happiest years of his life. Together with Eileen, he kept chickens and goats. Eileen was an intelligent, sharp child psychologist who shared Orwell's political views and responded well to the austerity of their country living. She needed to: battalions of mice kept pushing the china off the shelves.

It was here that he wrote his career-changing *The Road to Wigan Pier*, based on the journey north he had taken the year before, with its still-current message that 'economic injustices will stop when we want them to stop'. The book made his name. His novels had sold 3,000 copies each — this sold 50,000, helped by its promotion through the Left Book Club.

Before moving to Wallington, he had struggled to shape his material and find a style. Once in the village, encouraged by the writing of 'Shooting an Elephant', his short autobiographical essay about Burma, he found a simpler and more direct approach that worked well; it helped also to be writing about the injustice and poverty of the Northern working class when living in basic conditions; although unlike the family he describes in Wigan, there was no chamber pot overflowing under the breakfast table.

Orwell uses the book to fire with both barrels: 'This nonsense about the superior energy of the English (actually the laziest people in Europe)'; 'if the English physique has declined, this is no doubt partly due to the fact that the Great War carefully selected the million best men in England and slaughtered them, largely before they had had time to breed'; 'there is at least a tinge of truth in [the Northerners'] picture of Southern England as one enormous Brighton inhabited by lounge-lizards.'

Sixty years after Orwell's *The Road to Wigan Pier*, class was still the elephant in the room. Orwell had pointed out in 1937 that it was fashionable to say class divisions no longer existed – and how wrong that was. Richard Hoggart made the same point in *The Uses of Literacy* a generation later.

Class distinctions in England don't disappear. They just change. There are as many subtle, complicated shades of class difference as there ever were – often exaggerated in the countryside, where someone in a run-down cottage lives on the estate of someone with 10,000 acres and a Palladian country house. Let alone the three Range Rovers parked on the drive.

Here are my own problems with the English aristocracy: they wear raspberry-coloured corduroys; they're often bone-stupid but think they're clever; they have more money and infinitely more land than me.

And then there's another thing I dislike about them. They can often charm me into submission.

Moreover, as I crossed the country I couldn't help reflecting that there had been a time when such wealth brought more responsibility. In the past, if an aristocratic landowner was not serving the national interest, as a politician or statesman, he would be active locally, as a magistrate or promoter of local enterprise. At the very least, landowners employed many local people from the cradle to the grave: those who had been in service with them were given tied cottages.

With a few honourable exceptions, this has changed. The wealthy in the country still have servants, but they are often Eastern European workers, to whom all responsibility ends with their contract. The landed rich feel no obligation or desire to take part in national affairs, now that they have been booted out of the House of Lords; and even in local ones, many have retreated behind their park walls. Some of the larger estates have contracted land management out to international firms that concentrate on a lucrative return (like claiming large rebates from the Common Agricultural Policy), while easing tenant farmers out.

The only responsibility felt by today's aristocracy seems to be to themselves. They concentrate on their holidays, their children and their hunting, shooting and fishing; or, for the more esoterically inclined, they go to find themselves in Bhutan or Benares or Bali.

At the other end of the scale, unemployment is still as endemic as when Orwell wrote in the 1930s. Then, some 2 million people were out of work in a population of just under 50 million. Today there are 2.5 million, and rising fast, unemployed out of a population of just over 62 million. So the percentage of unemployed has, if anything, gone up since the worst days of the 1930s depression. Yet it is no longer such a pressing national concern. We are complacent with it, comfortable with it. There is a brief flurry every year or so when new, rising figures are released. But nothing like 1972, when unemployment rose over the 1 million mark again and Edmund Heath's government declared a virtual national emergency.

Of course a welfare state ensures that the absolute poverty of Orwell's day is avoided. But what endures is what he identified so accurately as 'the deaden, debilitating effect of unemployment upon everybody, married or single, and upon men more than upon women. The best intellects will not stand up against it.' There are too many people looking at walls and counting out the hours over dead cups of coffee. Quite apart from the dead weight of their claims upon the State. Mass unemployment is the geological fault line under England: a malign slab, largely unseen, which one day may sheer off under us.

✻

From Wallington, it was a fine swoop of just a few miles across the chalk hills to Kelshall. At the centre of this village stood the water-filled base of an ancient stone cross; and a very modern one beside it, put up as a Millennium project. Both marked Kelshall's position as a staging post along the Icknield Way.

In my journey east across England, the village marked another change – a reminder that, coming out of Hertfordshire and into East Anglia, I was crossing the historical boundary into the lands the Vikings colonised. The name Kelsall was one the Vikings had given, meaning 'cold stream'.

In the fourteenth-century church, there was a memorial to one of the figures from Anglo-Saxon history who interested me most: King – and St – Edmund the Martyr, who ruled East Anglia before the arrival of the 'great army' of Danish Vikings in 869. Edmund was then still a young man of just twenty-nine, having been king since a boy of thirteen.

He was killed by the Vikings – which in itself was not unusual. Kings of Northumbria and Wessex had been slain or fatally injured in battle with the invaders. But a legend attached itself to Edmund: that he had chosen martyrdom at the Vikings' hands; that, in the words of his later biographer, Abbo of Fleury, he had let himself be taunted by the Vikings, shot full of arrows, like St Sebastian, and then brutally beheaded.

As a legend, it plays to two dominant themes in late Anglo-Saxon history as they tried to withstand the Viking raids. One is the more familiar, that of the Vikings as brutal and merciless thugs, the 'slaughter-wolves' as they are described in *The Battle of Maldon*.

In recent years, there has been much wringing of hands and soft shoe shuffling by historians about this traditional portrayal of the Vikings as storm troopers in longships. 'We need to understand,' they intone from the academic pulpit, 'that they were traders as well as raiders – that history, written by their opponents, has been one-sided in its portrayal – it is far too easy to talk of invasions – we should be talking about assimilation – any large-scale "Migration Theory" is seductive but implausible.'

Well, up to a point. Certainly there is recent archaeological evidence from York, among other places, of Viking trading after they had conquered half the country and held it under Danelaw. But no amount of sophistry and revisionist history can disguise the brutality of the Viking raids – nor the length over which they were sustained. From the devastating attack on Lindisfarne in 793, when, as the Anglo-Saxon Chronicle recorded, 'the ravaging of heathen men destroyed God's church', right through to the Norman conquest of 1066, which the Norwegian king Harald Hardrada did so much to facilitate, the Vikings were an intermittent, anarchic presence that was about as subtle as an axe in the face.

What interests me most about the story of St Edmund is not the familiar tale of Viking brutality, but the Anglo-Saxon response. At times, the English reacted to the Viking threat with force themselves – as Alfred and his successors did, or the heroic warriors at the battle of Maldon a century later. But more often than not, they responded with that trademark English emotion: guilt.

The Viking raids, wrote Alcuin at the time of Lindisfarne, were God's punishment of England for its sins. The martyrdom of Edmund, the way in which King Ethelred insisted on hearing mass before the battle of Ashdown, the increasing insistence on ever tighter canonical laws – like not marrying your fourth cousin – all came from a deep sense of Anglo-Saxon guilt, a guilt that had to be extirpated before the Vikings could be defeated.

We think of the Anglo-Saxons – if we think of them at all, which is rare, despite their 500-year control of the country at a crucial and formative time – as licentious immigrants from northern Europe with a fondness for mead. But after their conversion to Christianity, they became some of our most austere rulers: far more so, say, than the Victorians, perhaps yet one more reason why Alfred the Great was so revered in the nineteenth century.

That the Saxons should understand the Viking invasions as in some way *their own fault*, a judgement on their loose moral behaviour, was only compounded later when it really did become their fault: for paying the Vikings to go away, the Danegeld that kept them coming back for more.

Danegeld was first paid after Maldon in 991, a century after Edmund's death and another battle at which the Vikings were victorious. The poem *The Battle of Maldon* initially celebrates the fighting quality of Earl Byrhtnoth and his men, as they try to withstand the invaders at the end of a narrow causeway on the Essex coast; this is when one of the men lets his hawk fly to the wood.

But someone has blundered – in this case Earl Byrhtnoth who, whether from naivety or hubris, allows the Vikings the free passage they ask for across the easily defended causeway and onto the more open mainland: an early example of the English playing cricket when their opponents are playing hardball.

> Then the battle,
> with its chance of glory, was about to begin.
> The time had come for all the doomed men
> to fall in the fight. The clamour began;
> the ravens wheeled and the eagles circled overhead,
> craving for carrion; there was shouting on earth.
> (*The Battle of Maldon*, translated by Kevin Crossley-Holland)

In the ensuing mêlée, Byrhtnoth is killed, as are many of his men. But while the poem celebrates their heroism, it is also self-lacerating about an English shame – the cowardly desertion from the front of Godric and his brothers, compounded by Godric's use of his dead commander's horse, which makes the English foot soldiers, unaware their leader is dead, think that Byrhtnoth himself is abandoning the fight. Godric and his brothers 'flee for the woods/ Fled to the fastness, and saved their lives'. What is more, this treachery, or at least failure, has been predicted by one of their number before the battle, Offa, when he foresees that the English may not live up to their fine words when it comes to the crunch.

In many ways, the Anglo-Saxon reaction to the Viking violence was the classic one of a victim: hatred and dislike of a brutal antagonist, but also a confused culpability in which they blamed themselves as well as their attacker.

St Edmund the Martyr's death exemplifies this. No wonder that his burial place should become 'Bury St Edmunds' and be so visited as a shrine; or that a culture of guilt and of an obscure sense of failure should reside deep in the English psyche even after seemingly confident periods of expansion and Empire.

A woman in Kelshall church, of the kind and thoughtful sort who have kept the Church of England going, had come in to arrange the flowers. She told me that a few years previously there had been a local campaign in East Anglia to get St Edmund adopted as England's patron saint in place of St George – or more correctly, readopted, as George had usurped him at the time of the Crusades.

The idea was attractive: St Edmund's brave and gentle sacrifice as opposed to George charging after dragons. Moreover, Edmund had the advantage of being English (you can't be more English than an Angle), unlike the Middle Eastern George, and sported a subtler and more attractive flag, of three gold crowns on a field of azure blue. But I knew that such a campaign was ultimately doomed to failure. George with his flag is as red-faced and bold as we would like to be, even though, in our heart of hearts, we know that we are not.

Chapter 5

A Circle in the Sand

'The Sun Machine is coming down
And we're gonna to have a party, uh, huh, huh.'
David Bowie, 'Memory of a Free Festival'

The walk on towards Royston and Cambridgeshire beyond was delightful, helped by a lengthy stopover at the Fox and Duck in Therfield. I was sorry to find that the singing landlord performed only in the evening, so could not regale me over a lunchtime pint. A fellow walker stopped by who had so much ground to cover that he drank his meagre half-pint at the bar and went straight out again. I felt quite spoiled for time as I lingered over a generous burger in front of the fire, washed down with equally generous quantities of Theakston's Old Peculier, and rolled over the last of the hills towards Therfield Heath. I passed two memorial benches in a quiet grove of birches with views out over the plain beyond. Both had inscriptions: one said, 'Enjoy yourself, it's later than you think'; the other, 'Above the clouds it's always sunny'.

Therfield Heath was littered with Neolithic and Bronze Age barrows and had been an important mustering point for tournaments and armies in the Middle Ages. In 1455, right at the start of the Wars of the Roses, the Yorkist party gathered here together with Richard Neville, Earl of Warwick, 'the Kingmaker', before going on to fight the first battle of the campaign at St Albans. It is probable that Sir Thomas Malory, a known supporter of Warwick, was part of that group, with the reckless, heady excitement that must have come at the start of hostilities; that is if he wasn't in prison at the time on one of his numerous charges.

The battle took place in May. Did Malory remember that feeling of a war beginning in the spring when he wrote his final book about the collapse of the Round Table?

In May, when every lusty heart flourisheth and bourgeoneth, for as the season is lusty to behold and comfortable, so man and woman rejoice and gladden of summer coming with his fresh flowers; for winter with his rough winds and blasts causeth a lusty man and woman to cower and sit fast by the fire. So in this season, in the month of May, it befell a great anger and unhap that stinted not till the flower of chivalry of all the world was destroyed and slain.

Past Ickleton I approached the outskirts of Cambridge and the curiously named Gog Magog Hills, which would have given Brian Eno much pleasure. Although they are only about 250 feet high, Daniel Defoe referred to them as 'mountains'. Here the Icknield Way crosses a Roman road, the Street, probably built to control the troublesome Iceni after their insurrection under Boudica.

When the land is ploughed and the light is right, you can see numerous dark lines on the soil, all converging on Mutlow Hill [a Bronze Age barrow]. These are the old hollow ways of the Icknield Way and the Street. At the point where they meet the Fleam Dyke, the vallum of the earthwork has been 'slighted' in ancient times. Part of it has been thrown back into the ditch. But the hollow ways pass both under and over the slighted bank.

This is the 1957 description of the site by T C Lethbridge, then the keeper of Anglo-Saxon Antiquities at the Cambridge

University Museum of Archaeology. It is much as you might expect from the holder of such a post: a dry, observant, slightly technical account, written in crisp Cambridge prose by the author of several well-received books. Over the previous thirty years, Lethbridge had conducted many excavations of barrows and prehistoric sites in his other capacity as Director of Excavations for the Cambridge Antiquarian Society.

But what he discovered near by at the Iron Age hill-fort of Wandlebury, my next destination, was to send his distinguished career into a strange tailspin that is still highly controversial. 'Poor Tom,' a colleague told me, 'he went slightly mad towards the end.'

> I began to notice from the faces of other archaeologists that they were seriously disturbed by my interpretations of my excavations.
>
> (T C Lethbridge, *Gogmagog: The Buried Gods*)

Lethbridge had painstakingly tracked down historical accounts of early chalk figures carved onto the banks of Wandlebury hill-fort, much in the manner of the Uffington White Horse or the Cerne Abbas giant. These Wandlebury figures were no longer to be seen; without regular scouring, and in a region of wet fertility like Cambridgeshire, they would soon have grown over. One Elizabethan account forbade Cambridge students to go to Wandlebury for any 'festivities', because of its pagan associations. The names Gog and Magog, given to the hills, suggest that it was regarded as a place rich in just such prehistoric and therefore pagan associations. Lethbridge speculated that these festivities might have included the scouring of chalk figures.

He decided to conduct excavations at Wandlebury to see if they could be traced, spurred on by the account of an old man who had once worked with him at the Archaeology Museum in Cambridge, in the restoration department, and claimed to have heard reports of the figures when he was a small boy in the nineteenth century.

It was enough to pique a red-blooded archaeologist's interest. Using a technique he had employed many times before, and similar to that used by farmers when they check their fields for drainage pipes, Lethbridge went probing all over the slope at Wandlebury with a six-foot, stainless-steel pole to see if any of the turf had once been cut away, much, in his words, 'like using a lead line at sea' (Lethbridge had written about early maritime traffic and often used nautical terms and methods). He and his small team then marked up any resulting discrepancy with poles.

His excitement at finding what he thought were the outlines of three chalk figures is understandable. For any archaeologist it would have been the find of a lifetime, let alone one approaching the end of his career: Lethbridge was fifty-three. Yet his account in the forthcoming book, *Gogmagog: The Buried Gods*, was remarkably calm.

He described the figure of a horse, with a curious beak-like head that matched the iconography of other Iron Age horses; another figure of a man with a sword; and a final, dramatic image of a large female 'giantess'. The head of this final figure he excavated and photographed, revealing a quite remarkable face.

Critics claimed that he had not taken account of the natural dips and depressions that might be formed in chalk by rainwater, or by the coprolite mining practised in this area of Cambridgeshire. Some even hinted that he had engineered the face himself by 'creative excavation', or suggested that students might have carved the figures as a prank.

Lethbridge was already disliked by some of his colleagues. He enjoyed a private income and had an attractive, much younger wife, neither factors which make for academic popularity. He was also prickly at times, as archaeologists can be. In many ways he was very like Hiram Bingham, the discoverer of Machu Picchu, who similarly managed to make enemies of his colleagues at Yale after marrying a Tiffany heiress.

I have met many archaeologists over the years. The only other profession that can be remotely as cantankerous are minicab drivers, with whom they have much in common. The minicab driver sits in isolation, waiting long periods for a fare, while hearing on his radio about other drivers being assigned lucrative destinations.

Archaeologists never quite reach their Robert de Niro *Taxi Driver* moment, but a simmering, repressed violence is often only a short dig away from their surface. The long periods spent in relative isolation, along with the frustration of digs that may not reveal much (but still have to be written up and published), are not good for the soul.

In addition, while Lethbridge's description of the excavation had been straightforward and detailed, his interpretation of the findings was difficult for colleagues to stomach. Lethbridge was ahead of his time in being fascinated by anthropology and folklore. Archaeologists of that era were often suspicious of anthropology. I can remember a distinguished old-school archaeologist telling me, with casual and revealing misogyny, that 'Anthropologists were like old women: they never stopped talking; and, worse, they paid far too much attention to what everyone else told them.'

In Peru, I was used to the running battle between archaeologists and anthropologists that was almost the leitmotif of Andeanist studies. Archaeologists resented the short cuts by which anthropologists could simply talk to people rather than spend years digging; unless, that is, they happened to come up with a bit of evidence that corroborated the archaeologist's own conclusions. Meanwhile anthropologists felt that archaeologists had their heads stuck down holes and couldn't see the bigger picture.

Lethbridge speculated widely (his colleagues said wildly) about the possible significance of the figures he had found. Drawing on a compendious knowledge of comparative archaeology, and with reference to Frazier's *The Golden Bough*, the same work that had so fascinated T S Eliot, he made analogies right across the prehistoric world. Were the figures of prehistoric Iron Age deities? Did they bear some relation to the names Gog and Magog? Could they be 'the lost gods of Albion'?

It was heady stuff. But the doubt cast by colleagues over his findings, which led to a Council of British Archaeology inquiry in 1956, and the aspersions cast on his excavation methods, sent Lethbridge into a spin. He resigned his post at Cambridge – he had always disliked what he called 'academic trade-unionism' – and went with his wife to live in Devon. There he started to write books of counter-culture that investigated areas way off left field, on the paranormal, dousing and suchlike, which have recently been acclaimed by Julian Cope and other New Age voyagers.

These helped relegate his earlier findings at Wandlebury yet more to outer academic darkness. When I went to look at the outlying slope of the hill-fort where he had dug, now called the 'Hill Figures Field', the grass had grown back over his fifty-year-old excavations; moreover, the lower part of the slope was now covered with small trees.

But having seen the photographs of the quite extraordinary head he uncovered, and doubting that it was in the man to have fabricated such a find, I wondered if it was not time for further, more calm analysis of the phenomenon.

✻

It was a cold day when Cambridge came into sight across the plain, ringed by the motorways and science parks that now surround it; no longer is there that sense of the college towers shimmering up out of nothing.

My feelings about Cambridge were complicated. I owed it a great deal. But in some ways I also resented it.

I come from a family of Cambridge scientists. Both my grandfathers won the Nobel Prize for Physics. So did their fathers. This was not good when I was at various schools. Physics teachers would observe me expectantly, as if I was a test tube that must surely start to glow red with successful combustion. Genetically the odds were stacked in my favour. But try as I might, physics remained a mystery as arcane as Babylonian cuneiform.

I somehow got through exams by rote – and the maths at least I managed – but failed to grasp fully how the simplest concepts of physics like mass and gravity interrelated, let alone the particle physics that my great-grandfather's discovery of the electron had initiated. I was a disappointment. My parents took me to the Christmas Lectures at the Royal Institution; I was bored. The models of DNA at the Cavendish laboratories in Cambridge made me think of candy on sticks and had an abstract beauty I appreciated, but could not understand.

The only time my scientific genes looked remotely like bearing fruit – or seed – was when a sperm bank suggested I could supplement my student grant by getting a premium rate for my genetically attractive product.

I walked into Cambridge along the Trumpington Road, past the small flat that my widowed grandmother had lived in; when a student – of English literature, not science – I had often biked out to visit her. Past the medical-industrial complex of Addenbrooke's Hospital. And past the new Judge Business School which symbolised Cambridge's brash new twenty-first-century face, as a centre of excellence and of money, with its post-modern façade that mixed classical elements with colours out of a child's paintbox.

There was something about Cambridge that always prompted the same reaction in me, as it had when I was an undergraduate. Not respect for its learning, scholarship or antiquity – although in theory I felt all that – but the need for the warmth of another human body.

Whether it was the cold wind blowing in from the Urals over the East Anglian plains, or the rigour of its Puritan past, my reaction was always the same; the only other city where I had a similar response was Cusco at 10,000 feet in the Andes, where the nights were also cold.

The more my teachers tried to instil in me a sense of academic rigour, of reasoning, the more I abreacted by wanting emotion, and the restless abandon and commitment of a love affair. My first term I was taught by an English Fellow who had iced water for blood. We were reading *Romeo and Juliet*, a case study for the dialectical tension between reason and emotion. At one point I blurted out that I liked one scene because it was 'so true'.

The professor pursed his lips. 'The truth, Mr Thomson, is a very naive critical concept.' Which of course it was.

Critical concepts would become far from abstract in the years that I was at Cambridge. The early 1980s saw a heated battle in the English Faculty that at the time both excited and amused the students, and was covered in the national press. Dons threatened to sue their colleagues; many refused to talk to each other; mass protests were held outside Senate House.

The ostensible cause for all this was the refusal to give tenure to a young academic called Colin MacCabe, an avowed structuralist. But this was just the tipping point. The real argument, which had been building for a decade, was over how English was taught. Should it follow the traditional model, in which, said its critics, an established canon of Great Writers were anointed and dissected like the bodies of Catholic saints? Or should Cambridge English acknowledge the French ideas of what was loosely called structuralism — although that term, like just about everything else, itself came to be deconstructed — in which what mattered was the text, not the author, and in theory (everything being now 'in theory') one could do as much critical analysis of a shopping list as of Shakespeare's *Sonnets*?

The two most senior professors disagreed violently. In the blue corner, Christopher Ricks, who was able to riff exquisitely for an hour on the way Cleopatra said 'Oh', and had a quicksilver mind suspicious of any dependence on theory; in the red, Frank Kermode, author of the best-titled book of literary criticism ever written, *The Sense of an Ending*, and open to change. Both bounced around the ring trying to position themselves as the radical contender.

It was a fight without referee, judge or time limitation and rumbled on in the academic jungle long after a disgruntled Christopher Ricks had departed for Boston and bit players like MacCabe had moved elsewhere.

But what at the time could be discounted as a literary rattling of cages, and of overexcited academics, seems in retrospect to have presaged a far greater change in the decades to come. The carpet was pulled under our feet. Structuralism encouraged a postmodern approach in every discipline from architecture to museum curatorship, in which the concepts of originality and truth became redundant and everything could be fictive, elusive and playful. Which of course was fun, for a while. Chippendale pediments on New York skyscrapers, *Flaubert's Parrot* and the growth of music sampling (no point in recording your own when there was already a James Brown drum break). So pervasive was its influence that the next decade would be summarised by another brilliant book title: Michael Bracewell's *The Nineties: When Surface was Depth*.

Authors became fictional characters in their own narration. Martin Amis began the trend with *Money*, appearing alongside the fictional John Self. Will Self – not another Martin Amis construct, although many at first assumed so – followed suit, as did J M Coetzee and others. Literature became a hall of mirrors. There had always been writers and artists that way inclined, from Laurence Sterne to the Dadaists; now they took over the Academy.

In my own chosen profession, television documentary, the

consequences were radical. Where once producers had been encouraged to go out and engage with the world, the remix became king. Why go to the bother of filming expensive new material when you could repackage and rewrite old archive? Originality became as outmoded a critical concept as truth had been. Whole evenings of repeats were scheduled – 'white wine television', Channel 4 called them. If there was nothing new under the sun, as structuralism suggested, then you might as well just rearrange the furniture. (As if on cue, the BBC scrapped their anthropological series *Under the Sun*, which had filmed remote and different cultures around the world, and scheduled yet more repeats.)

Travel documentary was one of the few areas where they still occasionally needed 'new product' and so I was able to film in India, Bhutan, South America and elsewhere. And at least if we had to cannibalise the past, I could do a ten-hour history of rock and roll, and go to interview all my old musical heroes in the process, for a series called *Dancing in the Street*.

Now, as I walked along King's Parade with hundreds of other summer tourists, I was struck by how sunny and busy it was. In my mind's eye, Cambridge had always been an austere, empty place. A dark place as well. I remembered coming back late at night along Garrett Hostel Lane and hearing the slow creaking wheels of the poet J H Prynne's bicycle as he came lugubriously into sight, looking like a character out of *Gormenghast*. The University Library had been a bleak monument to the overpowering might of published academia, every book ever published going onto its shelves. If you wanted a pastry, you had to bicycle to Fitzbillies at the other end of town.

No longer. Trinity Street was prematurely lit up as if for Christmas – a retail Mecca with clothes shops, expensive cafés and boutiques sprinkled along its length. It seemed unfair when most students had little money to spare with the rapid increase in their fees; kids in a candy store with no change.

Back as a student myself, I had written for *Broadsheet*, which was not the official University newspaper, the pompous *Varsity*, but a scurrilous and photostatted arts magazine by young gunslingers who fancied themselves as critics.

I was the theatre reviewer, among other things. As a critic I was frequently myopic. It was easy to get it wrong. The actors who we all thought would go on to be the Hamlets and Ophelias of our generation, the ones who got the big, serious parts, ended up later as prep-school teachers in Wales, or nurses. The 'character' actors we thought of as charming but inconsequential – Stephen Fry, Hugh Laurie, Emma Thompson, Simon Russell Beale – were the ones who became famous.

Although there was one exception to this. I can still remember the first night when an actress wearing nothing but long red hair stood in the middle of the stage and revealed herself in *'Tis Pity She's a Whore*, with a performance of blazing integrity and scarily translucent white skin. I cleared the central pages of *Broadsheet* for a double-page spread on Tilda Swinton's debut.

Some of the other writers on the magazine were exceptionally good, like Tom Lubbock and David Sexton. And the stellar talent was the young don who, by chance, became my own teacher when he moved to Trinity College: Eric Griffiths.

He arrived with a trail of rumour and innuendo swirling around him – that he was a loose-living, drug-taking, Machiavellian figure. Eric has always attracted controversy. Years later, the papers claimed that he had discriminated against an applicant from a state school because she knew little Greek. Unlikely, given Eric's own background as a Welsh scholarship boy. He did, however, discriminate against what he perceived as obdurate stupidity or narrow-mindedness.

As the most charismatic teacher of his generation – the *Guardian* described him as the cleverest man in England – he could be frightening to his students, not least because he was so partial; you were either part of his coterie or shunned as an anoraked sad case: 'Can you believe it, he's doing his thesis on Tolkien,' he complained of one of his students, consigning him unfairly to the mines of Moria.

He deplored my loose habits, heterosexuality and lack of cigarettes, but we became good friends. He was only a few years older than me. My abiding vision of Cambridge was of Eric in his rooms drinking and holding forth at length on Pope or Julie Kristeva and grabbing books from the shelves to prove a point.

My academic career at Cambridge up to that point had not been good. Awarded an exhibition (a junior scholarship) to go there, I was therefore supposed to work even harder to merit it, but hadn't. The teacher who had commented on my naive critical concept had not lit my fires. I had lost all my notes on a plane to go partying in Majorca when I was meant to be revising in a windowless room. Just to rub salt in the wound, my beautiful girlfriend Emma worked far more diligently than me, pointed out the fact and could quote Dante in Italian.

Eric changed that. He was inspirational. He took his mentor Christopher Ricks's fluency and supercharged it with a younger, protean energy, in which, like Ricks, he could riff and play on a concept until the strings bent. But he was also vulnerable: to doubts about his faith – he became a Catholic while he taught me – and about his own writing, which was less prolific than it might have been, partly because of his heightened self-criticism. His cherished friendships also sometimes led to cherished enmities.

By my last year, I was exhausted by three serious relationships that had begun well but ended unhappily. I exhausted myself yet further with a major dissertation on Robert Lowell's sonnets, the literary equivalent of finding a lost city in the jungle. Lowell was famously prolific. Not only had he written hundreds of sonnets, he had published them in multiple versions. Helping me navigate the maze was my supervisor, the young poet Michael Hofmann, who sent me to Christopher Ricks for further guidance.

This was an intimidating moment. Made worse when Ricks,

having reviewed my draft dissertation, paused in embarrassment: 'I think that at one point you may have misquoted T S Eliot.' It was not a question. I had misplaced a comma in a line of the poetry. Ricks let the moment hang. It was at that moment I realised I would never become an English academic.

Ricks had once, as a conceit, suggested that the entire English course be organised around T S Eliot's criticism. He had edited Eliot's verse. He could probably recite, comma perfect, whole paragraphs of Eliot's prose. I might as well have urinated in the presence of the Pope.

I had already started to turn to film – or rather to television, to 'broadcasting' in the fullest sense of the word, finding a wider audience outside what seemed the petty arguments of literary criticism.

Late at night, I went to tell Eric of my decision. I heard him pacing in his rooms as I went up the stairs. He came to the door looking wasted, having been writing a review. I could tell he was struggling because, uncharacteristically, there was no music playing: usually Talking Heads were at full volume, tearing down the house.

'I keep hearing all these voices in my head,' he said. 'Voices of writers.'

Wittgenstein famously urged F R Leavis to 'Give up literary criticism!' Despite English being one of the largest faculties at Cambridge and other universities, I felt like agreeing. Of course there was much to be grateful for: the chance to spend three years studying literature was a wonderful gift, which I drew on later. But it was not an altogether healthy discipline. Many of those who studied it became introverted – or even more introverted. As a way of engaging with life, spending your time in an ivory tower reading dead writers with only the odd break for a one-to-one tutorial with an equally introverted professor living in a smarter ivory tower; well it led to strange behaviour. One friend of mine was unaware of the Iranian hostage drama for eight months. Another didn't know where the faculty lecture rooms were after three years at Cambridge, because he had hardly left his room.

And now I went to see Eric again. He had recently suffered a terrible stroke and was confined to a wheelchair. His sister and the physiotherapists who had been treating him at Addenbrooke's had told me of his determination to recover. Unable to speak clearly, he could still manage three very characteristic expressions: of approval, with a smile; of dismissal, for those writers or critics like Julie Kristeva he considered beyond the pale; and, most characteristic of all, an ambivalent waving of the hand signalling that his critical jury was still out on the case. What I'd always liked about Eric was this last capacity for uncertainty, so attractive in a critic.

I found seeing him again very affecting. As it happened, I arrived on the day he moved into new college rooms, specially fitted out with wheelchair access. Someone was helping to fill his shelves with the books that had been in storage while he was in hospital.

Everything that had been best about Cambridge English came back to me. What Eric had tried to teach his students was critical honesty. Truth might be a naive critical concept, but you had to be honest to your own initial reaction to any work of art, without falling back on Flaubert's 'received ideas', and stay counter-intuitive when all around you might be falling for the party line.

Eric had a magpie mind. He had shared my enthusiasm for Cambridge's least-known museum, the Anthropological Faculty's cupboard of a space in the corner of Downing Street, with its displays of aboriginal shields and Inca headdresses. Of all the loosely described structuralist critics, the one who had most caught my fancy was the anthropologist Claude Lévi-Strauss, with his *Tristes Tropiques* and tales of the Amazon and its tribes.

The cold rigour of Cambridge's climate and puritan endeavour had made me crave not only the comfort of women, but sun and southern skies. I had already spent time in Mexico; I wanted to go further south of the border, to Peru. The lure of travelling, together with that of filming, meant that it was many years before I returned to Cambridge.

But now, I found, to my surprise, that I was enjoying myself. Irena had come down from London, so we could sample the excellent restaurants that had grown up in Cambridge since the days when there were just a couple of kebab joints and no one had heard of a cappuccino. We had a guest room overlooking Trinity College Great Court, one of the finest views in England. Best of all, we spent the weekend just wandering the streets, without any worry about an essay to be completed.

Looking back at it, that was the real problem about being a student at Cambridge. You had to work so hard, or at least, in my case, worry that you weren't working hard enough. There was a perpetual anxiety. It would have been a great place to be on holiday.

Seeing the place with Irena's eyes helped. She had left what was then still Czechoslovakia in the early 1980s. The communist state had gone into one last deep-freeze before the thaw of the Velvet Revolution in 1989. It was a repressive place where she was once sent home from school for wearing a T-shirt with a 'USA' logo.

When she arrived in England, Cambridge had represented intellectual freedom. She had married her first husband in one of the Cambridge colleges and frequently returned to the place, perhaps also because it was also the home of Pink Floyd, adored by Czech intellectuals, who from Václav Havel and Tom Stoppard downwards had a fondness for progressive rock. Irena had escaped across the Iron Curtain with her mother and came to England not speaking a word of English (the Czechs still taught Russian in their schools). One part of the ensuing culture shock was that by the 1980s no one was playing the music she had expected:

Genesis, Pink Floyd and Led Zeppelin. It was all post-punk and new romantic.

Now, as she drove me back to Wandlebury to take another look at Lethbridge's mysterious chalk figures, she kept singing the chorus from Black Sabbath's 'Iron Man', convinced that this was Ozzy Ozbourne's view of prehistoric England. I was less sure, suspecting that it might be something to do with the *Marvel* comic of the same name. Either way, the lyrics were not deep: 'Iron Man: is he alive or dead / has he thoughts within his head.' Nor did they stand much repetition.

There was a drizzle of rain over the Gog and Magog Hills when we got there. The Iron Age hill-fort at Wandlebury is an odd monument anyway: it must be the only hill-fort in England to have an eighteenth-century complex of buildings and a walled garden within its circular ditch.

Irena's general interest in English prehistory was low, verging on complete indifference. So I was surprised by the enthusiasm with which she helped identify the outline of Tom Lethbridge's chalk figures on the grass slope. Using Lethbridge's old photographs as guidance, we could clearly make out the shape of the central chalk face under the tussocks.

A park warden came over to see what we were doing, perhaps puzzled why a long-haired blonde woman was singing 'Iron Man' and playing air guitar as we tried to trace out the shape of the goddess's head.

'Ah yes,' she said, regarding us with the kindly indulgence the English afford to anyone pursuing an unfathomable but harmless pursuit, like brass-rubbing or breeding llamas. 'I have heard about the chalk figures. We're closing in ten minutes.'

*

It was ten miles or so from Cambridge up to Ely. First thing on Monday morning, I set off with renewed energy along the towpath beside the Cam, remembering times when I had jogged along it as a student to work off the excesses of the night before, my head full of writers like Thomas Malory, or plays like *Cymbeline*, or things I should have said, but hadn't, to a girl.

I had visited Ely once before as a student. A day out, with my cousin Rachel Bell and her friend Elspeth Thompson, to get away from the claustrophobia of Cambridge. We had eaten in the Old Fire Engine House and taken great pleasure in winning some goldfish at a travelling showman's stall on the common. You needed to hit a large balloon with a dart to win a fish. Three Cambridge undergraduates took some while to realise that the ticket for trying cost far more than the price of a goldfish.

It was an innocent time. Since then, Rachel and I have each been through matrimonial vicissitudes and poor Elspeth, who became a fine writer on plants and gardens, took her own life a few years ago, but the shock of entering Ely Cathedral felt much the same now as then: a wave of cold air, like entering a larder, or elevator shaft; the sparseness of decoration, together with an impossible elevation; above all, a repository of silence after the noise and intellectual confusion of Cambridge. Even if you didn't share in the certainty of faith, it was calming to be with a congregation that did.

For me, Ely is the most striking of all the English cathedrals. It may not have the fine treasures of Durham or Canterbury, nor be as tall as Lincoln, but it has one wonderful advantage: scale. The town of Ely is so small that the cathedral dwarfs the place.

As I walked on, looking back across the Cambridge plain, the spire seemed even taller than the Burj Khalifa I had seen in Dubai just a few months previously, with its field of fountains playing in a desert, although that is the world's highest building.

The last stretch of the walk lay ahead: I was detouring from the Icknield Way, whose route was indistinct over the plain (far easier for ancient trackways to be preserved in the hills). But I would end at the same point on the Wash and the coast.

I crossed the county boundary into Norfolk. Depending on their age, stage and inclination, people associated Norfolk with Cromer crabs, Alan Partridge or the Queen at Sandringham. It had only one association for me: a music festival held at a supposedly 'secret location', although a secret shared by many thousands. Friends of mine had organised the festival for many decades in the grounds of a large and rambling country house. They started with just 100 guests – an expanded party. The next year friends brought friends, those friends came back with theirs, and within a few more years they had to put on a cap at 2,000 tickets.

The reasons for this rapid success were simple: the presiding spirit, DJ and actor Benedict Taylor, together with his extended family, spread a warmth and enthusiasm to the entire project that enthused all who came; the owners of the house were an intriguing and genial bunch who were prepared to let their house and gardens be invaded each year; admission was by invitation only, which some claimed led to elitism, others to a sense of community and that, like any 'tribal gathering', as the first Californian festivals were called, you needed to be part of the tribe. Either way, it was a hot ticket if you could get one.

I went to the very first event that took place there in 1982, while still a student at Cambridge, driving through the Norfolk night in the rain with a male friend who had just been through a life-changing religious experience and was telling me about it; in the way you can share such thoughts when it's pitch black outside and you're driving and can't see each other's faces.

Arriving at the bulk of this large old house, which was deserted on the ground floor, we wandered across the empty reception rooms towards a spiral staircase leading down to the basement. The staircase was lit up with strobe lights and the Gap Band's 'Oops Upside Your Head', which had just come over from the

States, the first trickle in the deluge of dance and House music that was to follow.

There were two bowls of fruit punch as we entered the basement cellars. One was a straightforward, if potent, alcoholic blend of the usual brandy and wine, with the odd bit of fruit; the other was the same, but with added magic mushrooms. Having always liked psychedelia, and after two hours' driving through the rain and plain of Norfolk with my friend sounding like a Johnny Cash song, I had a healthy glass of the magic mushroom cup. Many others appeared to have done the same; at some stage the bowls of punch had been switched, whether by accident or design. The rooms were full of outrageous costumes out of the Funkadelic and Bootsy Collins mail-order catalogue: gold lamé, leopardskin and feathers, with diamante sunglasses.

This was some years before 1989 and the rave 'summer of love'. Ecstasy was still just a twinkle in the chemist's eye. But already there was a realisation that at a time of recession and graduate unemployment, matched only by today's figures, at least you could get out and dance.

I had just bought a winter coat with which I was inordinately pleased. Cambridge in winter was cold. I left it in one of the rooms as I arrived at the house, then remembered the car keys and my wallet were both still in a pocket. I went back to retrieve them before the magic mushrooms gained too much of a hold. The coat had gone.

Magic mushrooms can induce a floating sensation of calm and ease; but in the wrong circumstances, they can produce deep and traumatising paranoia. These were the wrong circumstances.

I started to sweat. I also started compulsively to ask all the other guests, repeatedly, if they had seen my coat or my wallet or my car keys. I can't remember where I slept; I'm not even sure I did sleep. It was a long night.

The next day it emerged that someone, after a glass too many of punch, had gone off by accident with my coat, which they duly returned. A rational explanation, which in calmer waters I would have reached myself. But by then I had gone through a night of paranoid, mushroom-fuelled uncertainty in which I thought that my car, money and, worst of all, brand-new coat had disappeared up the chimney of this huge Norfolk house.

As the festival has grown over the years, and stretched over a long weekend rather than just a night, I've enjoyed the way a conventional part of the Norfolk landscape is turned for a few days each year into a musical epicentre with its own energies – a fraction of the size of festivals like Latitude, also in East Anglia, with its 35,000 capacity, let alone Glastonbury in the West Country with its 150,000, but with an intensity and warmth that are hard to beat.

Over the last thirty years we have become a nation of festivalgoers. Glastonbury was a joke at the start of the 1980s, a hippie leftover. There was the odd big festival at Knebworth or Crystal Palace (Steve Harley built a scaffold just under the lake there, so that he could jump off the stage at the climactic moment of his set and 'walk on water', like any self-respecting rock star). But these were more big concerts to support headliners rather than places where, ultimately, 'it's not about the bands'.

Today there are more than 400 music festivals around the country, quite a few in similar 'secret locations' shared only with subscribers – like the 6,000-capacity 'Secret Garden Party' in Cambridgeshire, which proclaims itself 'a massive playground for slightly daft adults, with boat races, emotional baggage lockers, science experiments, burning art installations, fire circles, floating sculptures, mobile sound systems, pillow fights and the alternative Olympics'. Emotional baggage lockers? What happens if you lose the key?

Festivals like Glastonbury now fulfil a latent need. We have always been fond of tribal gatherings. Archaeologists profess themselves amazed at the amount of feasting that took place in

Bronze Age sites or hill-forts: pork in particular was consumed in abundance, an advance on the bacon sandwiches and hot dogs of today's festivals. The medieval chartered fairs continued that legacy. It comes back to a central proposition about the English character: that we have the boldness of the very shy. For most of the year we refuse to talk to anybody else on trains and, the national mantra, 'mind our own business'. But given the chance for a few days to lose our identities in the mix, to be communal, libidinal and Bacchic, we seize it with both suddenly hennaed hands. Just so long as we can go back to being normal on Monday for the office.

✳

As always when entering Norfolk, I felt like one of Napoleon's foot soldiers entering Russia. The county stretched out for ever. When I was young and foolish at Cambridge, I did very little walking to the north of the city, as I imagined it to be dull and flat. Now that I was older and supposedly wiser and actually walking it, I realised that I had been completely right. There were stretches of the last haul to the Wash when I thought wistfully of the Karelian peninsular in northern Russia, where at least they greeted you with a glass of vodka in every village across the tundra.

Or if not Russia, the plains of America, a landscape that likewise has no curves. Norfolk is bisected by straight lines of poplars and canals. Its fields are like aerodromes. Outside of commuter range from any large city, and with a fishing industry dying on its feet, the county's density of population now is less than it was in the eighteenth century, when Daniel Defoe was startled by how many people lived in Norfolk. There may well be fewer today than in the surprisingly populous Bronze Age.

Yet Norfolk has a wide-open, empty, frontier beauty – and a

buried secret. Under the peatlands to the north of the county, near the border with Lincolnshire, lie the remains of a fascinating civilisation.

After a long slog to get there, I found myself making one of the strangest time shifts in England. I was walking out of the New Town of Peterborough, past the light industrial units of Fengate with all their peripheral bric-a-brac of twenty-first-century urban living – the furniture stores, garages and drive-in plumbing depots – to appear suddenly in the Fens, an ancient landscape of dykes and straight roads and horses looming at me out of the mist.

Stranger still to come to Flag Fen, the country's most significant Bronze Age ceremonial centre, just a mile or so outside the city's edge.

Despite lasting almost 2,000 years, from 2500 to 800 BC, the Bronze Age is somehow less visible than either the preceding Neolithic Stone Age or the Iron Age that followed. Stonehenge and the other stone circles are easy and obvious symbols of the Neolithic; the Iron Age has the hill-forts I had followed in a line across the country all the way from Maiden Castle, a very public affirmation on the landscape. But the Bronze Age can get lost, despite in many ways being the most appealing and formative period of all.

The introduction of bronze around 2500 BC, and the beginnings of intensive agriculture around 1500 BC, coincided with a demographic explosion that took the British population to a level archaeologists are continually having to revise upwards as they make fresh discoveries, but may have been as high as two million.

Two million is a quite astonishingly high figure, if one remembers that the rural population today is no more than some five million. Given that it now seems most of the country was not only being farmed, but was deforested by 1500 BC, the whole way we view the Bronze Age has changed.

The old Ladybird version of our history, and the one I was taught at school, ran like this: that after a slow and backward evolution on the edges of Europe, through the evolving technologies of stone, bronze and iron implements, we were fast forwarded by the arrival of the Romans; then, after a period of darkness following their departure, the incoming Anglo-Saxons slowly embraced Christianity, cleared the forests and established the village pattern that the Normans and 'modern history' inherited. It is a historical model that relies almost entirely on written evidence, which is why the Romans, the first to write that history, figure so prominently.

But a far more radical and interesting way of telling the story has emerged strongly in just the last decade, as archaeology has made an exponential leap with its own new evolving technologies like LIDAR and DNA testing. It is one that I had become fully aware of only as I visited the prehistoric sites along my route.

In this model, history would be retold as follows: the Neolithic found us as part of a wider Atlantic community embracing Spain and Brittany, with an adventurous enterprise that saw monuments built as part of a ritual landscape from the Orkneys to my ring of stones on the Dorset coast; the arrival of the Bronze Age precipitated a period of activity like the Elizabethan or Victorian – one of enormous and confident expansion. We were at the top of the European commodities market, as we had unrivalled access to bronze, with the copper mines of Wales, the tin of Cornwall and the lead of the Somerset Levels allowing us to produce far more than anybody else. Bronze was not just a material but a currency, with bronze axes used for barter, and it is again not until recently that we have realised what an industrial quantity was being produced. It is now estimated that the Great Orme mine in Wales alone provided some 200 tonnes of copper, almost ten times more than was previously thought.

We were in effect printing money, and this golden age – symbolised by the fabulous Mold Cape made of fine beaten gold held by the British Museum – spurred the population growth and intensive clearance of the landscape.

For many years it has been known that the outlines of Bronze Age field systems can be seen on land that modern agriculturists regard as marginal, such as Dartmoor or Exmoor. It was assumed that these areas were farmed only because the wooded valleys were unavailable to prehistoric man. But now almost the reverse is thought – that at no other time in our history was so much land farmed; that Bronze Age farming had extended right across the area of southern England that I had just walked through, from the valleys to the highlands, and that the reason the field systems can still be seen on the moors is simply because more modern agriculture has retreated from such Bronze Age ambition.

The arrival of the new technology of iron in around 800 BC, far from being an advance, prompted the biggest recession in our history, one that lasted almost two centuries from 800 to 600 BC, beside which any eighteenth-century bubble or recent financial crises pale. Iron had been developed in the eastern Mediterranean. It was not a commodity with which England was particularly blessed. The arrival of Celts from Eastern Europe (or at least Celtic culture from Eastern Europe, as it is still difficult and tendentious to track the actual migration of peoples), and a lack of resources, led to population pressure and possible internal warfare, with the Iron Age hill-forts a product of that strife.

Then the Romans arrived. A study of the Catuvellauni and other tribes shows that the contrast Caesar liked to celebrate between the civilisation he brought and the barbarians he found was greatly overstated. Iron Age Britain already enjoyed many of the advantages of Mediterranean trade – and 'the Roman Interlude' was a less dramatic change than the classicists who first told our island story liked to make out.

Flag Fen was a rare reminder of that Bronze Age glory. It had been preserved by accident, unlike other wooden monuments in the country, because deposits of peat had settled around it, so preserving the wood that would otherwise have rotted. We are familiar with the idea that bodies can be preserved in this way, like the 'bog people' Seamus Heaney commemorated in his poetry; less so with wood.

It was discovered in 1982 by Francis Pryor. He had followed a technique established by fellow archaeologists in Holland: when a drainage dyke is cleared, a natural cut is usually scooped out of the side which gives investigators the chance to see down below the surface, without the labour and cost of digging themselves.

Francis applied the same idea to the fens and literally stumbled – he hit his foot against a post – upon the Flag Fen site, a momentous find. The post was the first of no less than 60,000, which stretched across this wet meadowland as a ceremonial causeway to an artificially constructed platform at its centre, and then on towards the light industrial units I had passed at the edge of Peterborough.

The word 'ceremonial' must be used with caution. It is the first that archaeologists reach for when they either don't understand or wish to aggrandise their findings – but in this case is justified by the remarkable amount of offerings found at the site, a range of bronze swords and jewellery unified by their delicacy of composition.

I once tried to explain the difference between the Bronze and Iron Ages to some young children, with difficulty, until one of them said, 'So was the Bronze Age the time of the elves, and the Iron Age the time of the dwarves?' Well, not quite. But the delicacy of Bronze Age art and artefacts is extraordinary: at Flag Fen there were small bronze razors, rare glass beads, jewellery like tiny gold ritual rings, too small for a finger, and elegant bronze sickles, daggers and swords. I was much taken by an exquisite pair of bronze shears, kept in a wooden box that had been hollowed to fit them, like a guitar case. There was also the earliest wheel discovered in Britain, made of alder with oak axles and braces for extra strength.

I went to see Francis Pryor and his wife Maisie Taylor, who lived not far from Flag Fen on their farm – for Francis, as well as being an archaeologist, is a farmer, and looks like one in a satisfying, whiskery way. Perhaps this has given him more bonhomie than some of his peers; certainly he's the only archaeologist I've ever met who offered me a drink without telling me at length about his fieldwork first.

Francis was putting up a gate when I arrived. His farm was small, at just 50 acres, and supported about 150 lowland Welsh sheep, a breed called Lleyn (described admiringly by *Farmers Weekly* as 'quiet in nature, prolific, has great maternal instincts, milky, & will not eat you out of house and home').

'They keep me sane,' he told me.

Much of Francis's work has been about the importance of a direct connection with the land, like *The Making of the British Landscape*, a reworking of W G Hoskins' classic account, so he lives what he preaches. And what he preaches most, understandably, is the chronic lack of awareness of the Bronze Age.

'The Bronze Age was far more revolutionary than the Industrial Revolution,' he told me over a lunch of cheese and cider. 'We went from a country of scattered communities who farmed where they could and came together for ceremonies at a few great monumental henges, to a country that was largely inhabited as it is now. If we were to go back to 1000 BC, we would recognise the culture and the landscape – but go back to 3000 BC and the Neolithic age of Stonehenge, and we would be entering a different, alien world.'

Francis had studied archaeology with the eminent Andeanist Geoffrey Bushnell at Cambridge – at one point he had wanted to concentrate on pre-Columbian cultures in South America – so was sympathetic to the idea of ritual landscapes as a way of interpreting the Nasca lines or the Inca ruins around Machu Picchu, or for that matter ancient Britain.

His main complaint now was that we were so 'monument-specific'; that we tended to focus far too much on individual monuments, like Stonehenge, and neglect their setting in a far wider landscape of associated sites that give them meaning.

Sometimes, though, a monument came along that was devoid of such a setting. Together with his wife and fellow archaeologist, Maisie Taylor, Francis had been present at the uncovering in 1999 of what was surely the strangest of all the prehistoric monuments I would come across – what the press dubbed 'Seahenge', a Bronze Age circle right on the coast where the Icknield Way ended. But that lay ahead, at the very end of my journey.

'I don't do any more digging. It's a young man's job. When I was young, old men – and women – hung onto their jobs and grants. It was difficult to get started. I don't want to be like that. And also I want to be proved wrong. I want new archaeologists to come along with new theories. And it's not as if there's much work around for archaeologists anyway. The credit crunch – or bankers' balls-up, as I call it – has stopped a lot of the developer-led archaeology that boomed after the 1980s.'

Although it hadn't stopped it all. Francis and Maisie were excited by a find that had only just happened close to Flag Fen, at a site called Must Farm quarry, thanks to the brick manufacturer Hanson, which had sponsored an archaeological dig before extracting clay from Jurassic age levels. The result was spectacular:

six boats hollowed out from oak tree trunks at the centre of what was clearly a well-used Bronze Age river channel.

Along with the boats came fish and eel traps in the form of big woven willow baskets, and votive offerings of fine bronze swords and spears, tossed into the river in perfect condition. Preserved by the peat, the site was already being heralded by Francis and other leading archaeologists in the know, for the discovery had yet to go public , as 'the largest Bronze Age collection ever found in one place in Britain'.

It was hard not to suspect that we stood at the very beginnings of a supremely exciting time for Bronze Age archaeology.

Right away, I felt I had to go and see the Must Farm quarry site for myself. It wasn't far from Flag Fen as the oystercatcher flies, but the water made it difficult around that part of the world, so I had to go back into Peterborough and then out again. At one point, I walked around yet another of the roundabouts with which New Towns like to stud their outer belts, and came face to face with a building as representative of the early twenty-first century as Flag Fen was of the Bronze Age: a gigantic Amazon UK storehouse, big enough to launch a rocket from and a symbol of the Internet age. Clad in white tiles, it looked functional and clean and faceless. Inside, it was vacuuming up the retail business from bookshops and high-street stores, many of which would soon go to the white-tiled wall.

Did I call it a storehouse? My apologies. According to Amazon it is not a distribution warehouse, as the innocent observer might suppose, but, I discover, a 'fulfilment centre'. George Orwell couldn't have made it up.

Compared to the clinical environment of Amazon, the quarry when I reached it looked like something out of Iraq. Hanson had scooped meteorite-sized chunks out of the ground in their quest for Oxford clay, and as far as the eye could see, there were teams of archaeologists and quarry workers in hard hats and hazard-jackets wandering over the desolate site or using Land

Rovers to negotiate the mud. Above them, and making the scene even more surreal, a wind turbine farm loomed over the horizon.

By definition archaeology moves slowly. I've been to many digs around the world and watching turtles race would be more exciting. It's not a spectator sport. Every ten or twenty years there is a major discovery, but just as with fishing or surfing, the good days never happen when you're there: 'You should have been here yesterday, mate. The waves/fish were fabulous.' Or rather, in archaeology: 'You should have been here five years ago, *Señor Profesor*.'

So I couldn't quite believe my luck that a chance encounter with Francis had led me here. I immediately took to Mark Knight, the red-haired project leader of the Cambridge Archaeological Unit doing the work. He was almost hyperventilating with excitement.

'To find one intact Bronze Age boat would be remarkable. To find two close together was beyond my wildest dreams. To find six is just . . .' His voice tailed off. Understandable, given that the find has at one stroke more than doubled the known number of Bronze Age boats in the whole country, and these have that vital archaeological commodity, 'provenance', the context within which they have been found.

The boats were lying on the bottom of deep pits, as if they had been in a lake that had been drained — as in some ways they had. Normally they would have disintegrated, but again the peat had preserved them at a considerable depth underground, some twelve to fifteen feet.

To give some sense of comparison: at Stonehenge you might get thirty centimetres of topsoil, most of which has been ploughed and disturbed at some stage anyway; here you get three to four *metres*, more than ten times as much. Peat accrues fast in deep layers. Such depth brings its own problems. It is well beyond the range of aerial or radar surveys from the surface. These boats would never have been found if they had not been in a quarry.

Mark had found his voice again. 'And it's not just the boats: it's everything that goes with them. The swords, the fishing gear, the jewellery . . .' So far, in his excitement, he had been talking in conversational English. Now he lapsed back into archaeology-speak: 'You could say it's a whole articulated 3-D Bronze Age landscape!'

What he meant was that the peat gave very precise layers of data: the six boats were deposited over an approximately 600-year timespan, from the first to the last. The dendrologists had yet to do a full analysis on the precise dates, but the early estimate was that the range lay between 1300 BC and 700 BC.

The boats were narrow, like punts, made of oak and decorated with curious criss-cross markings on the sides. Many had been heavily repaired. It was unclear whether they had been abandoned (perhaps when the repairs got too much), or more deliberately left as some form of offering, like the swords and jewellery that were thrown in the water close by.

The longest of the boats, at some twenty-five feet ('big enough for an entire family and the granny,' said Mark), had interesting scorch marks at one end of the deck. Mark speculated that the boat family may have kept a fire going on board; oak is so difficult to burn that the boat itself may never have ignited, as you might expect if you burned wood on wood.

Mark led me over to another adjacent quarry pit that was even deeper. 'Look down at that. That's the Mesolithic. That's the level of the North Sea. It's incredible to be getting down to these depths.'

The archaeologists had been lucky. If there was not a rich vein of Oxford clay for bricks, lying under the peat, at Jurassic levels, Hanson would not have invested the huge amount needed to dig down so far. And the interest in the clay coincided with the 1980s regulations requiring companies to get a site cleared by archaeologists before and while such work was happening. Not that Hanson needed forcing. I was impressed by the enthusiasm with which they had collaborated with the Cambridge team.

'To be honest,' one Hanson manager told me, 'digging for clay is a dull and messy business. Having something like this keeps the digger operators interested. What would have been annoying is to pay a lot of money to the archaeologists, and then have them find absolutely nothing.' The Cambridge team had been working on and off the site for the previous fifteen years, so it was not surprising they had become so excited on finding something of such value.

Mark explained to me how the landscape along the old course of the River Nene had changed considerably as sea levels rose. 'At the start of the Bronze Age, around 2500 BC, this was still a dry valley, with the usual monuments and barrows [he waved a map at me that marked them all]. But then the sea levels rose and the area became wetlands. The inhabitants had to adapt. People turned to fishing and used these riverboats to get around.'

He conjured up an attractive picture of life at the time: 'We've found fish and eel traps near the boats. The eel traps are remarkably like the ones still used. There's a platform house close by. These banks were lined with willows, and there was probably an abundance of wildlife like otters and pelicans.'

The offerings his team found show how substantial was the trade overseas. The boats weren't big enough to go offshore themselves — they were for river traffic — but some of the offerings, like a sword, looked Mediterranean. It suggests there may have been some trading posts (or, as Amazon would put it, 'fulfilment centres') on the nearby coast, where goods were distributed from ocean-going craft.

Mark gestured over to the fens that stretched out beyond the quarry. 'The likelihood has got to be that there is more of this as far as the eye can see. We just happen to have found these boats here because this is the only place where anyone is digging to such depths. But this isn't a unique event.

'The fens must be the best place for prehistory in the whole of the country. I keep seeing colleagues flying out from Cambridge to sites in Mesoamerica and Africa. They should be just driving up the A1. This is where the action is.'

He shared Francis's feeling that we were only just on the cusp of further discoveries that will reveal a huge amount about the Bronze Age in the years to come: 'In the past, it felt as if we were looking at the Bronze Age through a very narrow window, with the curtains partly drawn or slightly misted over. Now it's as though someone has opened the windows.'

*

The last stretch lay ahead of me, to the coast and the sea.

I was excited by the revelations about the Bronze Age. I also felt tired. Walking long distances may make you fit — and that's questionable, because it makes you fit for nothing other than walking — but there comes a time when a hot bath and a cold pint are the only things luring you ahead.

By chance, I had brought some coca tea back from my last

trip to Peru. Strictly speaking, this was not something that the US Food and Drug Administration endorse – indeed they arrest people for it at airports – as coca leaves are the raw ingredient for cocaine. I hadn't thought it sensible to ask what the policy was at Heathrow, if they had one. But the tea was herbal and gave a sustaining energy that helped Andean Indians through long nights on the mountains; I had taken it for years, particularly when walking long distances. This was a good moment to brew up with my thermos.

I sat on the side of the track, sipping at the acrid coca tea, looking out over the endless plain of Norfolk and thinking about everything I had seen on my 400-mile journey.

Some things in England had improved immeasurably. Pubs, pies and Premiership football for a start. Perhaps because Norfolk reminded me so much of Russia, which I had recently travelled across, I was struck by one contrast in attitudes: in Russia, the whole idea of 'relationship issues' had been considered for so long a bourgeois decadence under the Soviets that there was now widespread family dysfunction, with alcoholism and divorce rife; England was by no means perfect – and it was easy to poke fun at the 'touchy-feely culture' in which prime ministers kept apologising and everyone was 'finding themselves' before 'moving on' – but there seemed to be a far greater concern for other people's feelings than in other countries I had travelled through.

Underneath the brash and flash of tabloid Britain that had reached parts of the countryside – I had a mental image of Jordan driving a black Range Rover as she went to ride her horses on the North Downs – there was still a residual modesty, a kindness that was there if not always spoken. That said, while being increasingly connected by the distorting prisms of cyber-space, we were disconnected on the ground: we don't walk and talk enough.

England was also a phenomenally beautiful country. How often had I come back to Heathrow from abroad and marvelled at the sudden green of the fields as I drove home. We are complacent about its beauty, which we assume to be natural, but is highly managed by our farmer custodians, in whom we show little interest. You need to walk large stretches of England to appreciate its subtle gradations; changes that can be missed when speeding past on motorways or A roads.

My walk had taken me within the baleful orbit of London, a reminder that there were two countrysides: the one close enough to London or a big city for house prices to have risen steeply and villages to be empty during the week, when the inhabitants were sucked into commuter trains; and the older countryside, like Dorset or Norfolk, too far out, where the problem was often the reverse — a lack of public transport meant no one could leave during the day at all. Many of the East Anglian villages I passed had been left with bus services so reduced they had just one daily departure and arrival, if that.

It was also less secure living in the countryside than one might think: more gun crime than in the cities, according to statistics; more divorces; too many car crashes on small country lanes (more dangerous than motorways or urban traffic, and with a ridiculously high speed limit of sixty miles an hour, as I knew from my Speed Awareness Course); and, towards King's Lynn and north Norfolk, one of the highest rates of suicide in the country.

I was sure this last, unexpected, statistic had something to do with everything being so flat. I've always needed hills. They don't have to be the Lake District, Alps, Andes or the Himalaya — although some of my happiest journeys have been made in those mountains — but some slight rise in the landscape doesn't half lift the spirits. All the way from the coast, I had been travelling along the spine of the country, with its gentle undulations of down and valley; by comparison, Norfolk was flat-chested. Sorry, Brian Eno.

I rarely listened to my iPod when walking. It was better for dozing off to if I slept out in the open. But crossing Norfolk was so dull that I saw no alternative. I should have been listening to Mozart or Vashti Bunyan, or for that matter Eno's ambient musings — something calm and reflective. But instead I was listening to Ryan Adams's guitar-driven *Rock N Roll* at full volume, the only way to relieve the tedium of the East Anglian steppes.

The pretty village of Ringstead came as a welcome relief. There was the faint flush of a hill — the Ringstead Downs off to one side, with their beech trees and chalk grasslands, a very last whimpering sigh of the Chilterns; the Gin Trap, a seventeenth-century coaching inn, which served an excellent bangers and mash; and some farm buildings reassuringly in the centre of the village.

It was just a few miles to Hunstanton, a curious Victorian resort that had been built up by the L'Estrange family, the local landowners since the Norman conquest (their hereditary title of 'Lord High Admiral of the Wash' sounded straight out of Gilbert and Sullivan).

Hunstanton had much that was bad and much that was good about England. The bad was more obvious. A grim set of plastic amusement barns had been put up along the seafront, with slot machines; there was an 'Ancient Mariner Inn', with the sort of restaurant that sandwiches go to when they die, and another pub that had proudly put up a sign to say there was 'a real log fire'. You expected everything to be fake. It had none of Blackpool or Weymouth's exuberance or charm. There were bossy notices from the L'Estrange Estate telling you not to do any of the things you might normally want to do at the seaside.

But beyond, on the beach, I found some huts that Maisie Taylor had told me about, spread out below the cliff. These were not the polite little beach huts that change hands for over £100,000 at the front on Southwold, but more ragged, bleached affairs, scattered across the dunes and sometimes, I was told by locals, overwhelmed by them. On a bad year whole huts got submerged by the drifting sand. One was called Sea Holly, in turquoise; another, Ocean Drive, looked like it had been a wooden caravan that had got to the beach and just stopped. Both were the sort of places to write a book in and look out to sea, as the winds shored the dunes up against you.

I'm a sucker for bleached wood, whether on a beach hut or the driftwood that was scattered over the sand. And across the wide beach, flecked with flint, kite surfers were racing at a fabulous speed, matched only by those who were out on the water.

A little down the coast too were the remains of St Edmund's Chapel, built in 1272 in memory of the martyr king, who was thought to have landed on Hunstanton beach in AD 855 'to claim his Kingdom of East Anglia', some fourteen years before his death at the hands of the Vikings.

If he did land here — and the historical jury is still out on the case — he would have found that it all looked very familiar. It reminded me strongly of the wide Jutland and Danish beaches from which the Angles had come.

But what I had always known would be the end of my journey lay just a mile ahead along the shore, at Holme-next-the-Sea, the north-eastern edge of the Wash, and a departure point since prehistoric times to cross both that water and the North Sea to Europe.

*

In the spring of 1998, a special-needs teacher called John Lorimer found a Bronze Age axe on the beach at Holme. Not that he knew what it was at first; the crescent-shaped blade required identification by the county archaeologists. While they were looking at it in Norwich, John returned regularly to the same spot on the beach to look for more artefacts. He noticed a strange piece of wood in the peat beds that the incoming sea was slowly eroding – strange because of its weirdly contorted branches. Then on later visits he realised that a neat circle of posts around the tree were becoming exposed – at which point it was clear the structure was man-made.

John called in the experts, who by this time had dated his axe. It was when they realised that the 'branches' were strange because they were in fact the inverted roots of an oak tree buried upside down that the world stood up and took notice. Or, in Francis Pryor's words, 'picked it up, ran with it, tossed it around in the air and devoured it'.

The wood had been preserved by the same peat that had kept Flag Fen causeway and the boats at nearby Must Farm quarry in such good condition. Wood can be accurately dated, unlike a stone circle. The date the experts came back with was 2049 BC, in the early Bronze Age.

The papers needed a catchy name. 'Seahenge' was obvious but misleading – for when it was constructed, it was not on the beach, but inland, and was not strictly speaking a henge. But no matter. The growth of the coastline had, over four millennia, brought the sea to the site. That it had exposed the circle now rather than at any other time over the past few thousand years – when it might well have been ignored or missed – was sheer luck. It was also an indicator that there might well have been many more such sites which have not survived.

One reason the press loved it was that the Druid and New Age community didn't. As could have been foreseen, they objected strongly to the timbers from Seahenge being removed; for English Heritage decided the only way to save the circle from the incoming sea was to take it away for preservation.

Rollo Maughfling, the self-styled 'Archdruid of Stonehenge and Glastonbury', was just one of many who protested. He has described the first time he saw the circle, as the tide retreated over the wooden posts and they began to emerge from the waves with, at their centre, 'the magnificent upturned central tree formation, seawater pouring off it and lapping around it. A shiver ran down my spine.'

Many of the archaeologists were affected as well. Francis Pryor described what it was like to enter the circle when Channel 4's *Time Team* built a full reconstruction:

> I can only say it was profoundly moving and peaceful. Somehow the thick timbers excluded nearly all sound from outside. I was also strongly affected by the strong smell of freshly split oakwood. You could almost cut the tannin in the air. The cleft-oak interior harmonised with the de-barked tree trunk in an extraordinary way. It was as if this special enclosed space had truly been cleansed and purified . . .

Some protesters tried to stop the archaeologists' work by throwing away their sandbags; the police were called. A legal challenge in the courts to halt the removal of the circle, which the protesters argued should be allowed to stay in its natural and spiritual site, failed when it was clear English Heritage carried too much establishment and academic backing to be beaten.

The circle and the central oak were finally removed. After restoration at the specialist tanks in Flag Fen, they are now on display at the Regional Museum in King's Lynn. The central inverted oak, in particular, retains all its power, even behind glass.

The press controversy surrounding its removal, with photos of Druids bearing staffs confronting bulldozers and archaeologists, overshadowed the fact that Seahenge was such an extraordinary creative achievement.

For me, entering the mindset of those who made the circle was in some ways as challenging as anything contemporary art could offer. Here was a tree that had been stripped of its bark – a cumbersome operation which Francis has described as 'completely senseless and pointless' – and then, even more oddly, planted upside down, an idea that was beyond the irrational. Around it had been positioned a dense circle of fifty-five oak posts, forming a palisade: these too had their bark stripped, but only on the inward-facing side. The bark had been left on the exterior, so that to an observer the original monument would have looked like an enormously wide tree trunk, which one could then step inside to find the inverted oak tree at its centre.

The only entrance was through one of the posts that had split, so offering a narrow V between which to slip; as a child, climbing in the oak tree-house that we built in a wood in Suffolk, I remember the feeling of getting stuck between such forking branches; and of the subsequent entrance to a special place.

Because the bark had been stripped from the inside of the posts, the interior, once gained, would feel worked and cleansed. And inside this giant artificial tree, what would we have found?

The trunk of another oak tree, but inverted so that its one-tonne mass disappeared into the ground and its truncated roots waved in the air. The world turned upside down.

We think of the oak as an image of our national stability. Our steadiness under fire. Hearts of oak. The French have their long lines of high, thin poplars, the Spanish their cork trees, the Italians their olive groves, the Russians wide forests of silver birch: all trees of great practical use, of value.

We like our oaks for their steadfastness, their age and the way they spread about themselves with a wayward sense of ownership; that they also provide acorn-feed for pigs and our beloved pork is collateral benefit.

I find it intriguing that what archaeologists call 'the Great Central Stump' of an oak tree should have been used with such lightness, such finesse, although those seem to have been the trademarks of the Bronze Age.

The one-tonne trunk was lowered upside down into the ground using woven honeysuckle rope: not a natural choice of material. We know, because some of the abandoned honeysuckle rope was found wrapped around and under the oak, preserved by the peat, the first such prehistoric rope ever to have been found. Maisie Taylor, Francis Pryor's wife, had helped make the identification, and I had talked to her about it at their farm.

To give honeysuckle that tensile strength, it would need to be soaked first, and then woven with great skill. There are other naturally occurring materials that would lend themselves much more easily to making a rope. So the choice of honeysuckle was a symbolic one, just as was the oak, which might possibly have been brought some distance to the circle to transfer a sense of place, like the Stonehenge bluestones brought from Wales.

In 2049 BC, at the time the oak was lowered into the ground, the transition to a deforested Britain was beginning. The trees were starting to be felled. Bronze axes and tools could work the wood in a way impossible in previous Neolithic times. On just this one upturned trunk of oak, the marks from some fifty different axe-heads have been distinguished.

Francis had suggested one possible explanation for the site, and one that made sense to me intuitively: that it was a mortuary ring. The tree, a symbol of life, had been turned upside down to show death; the body of the deceased was then placed on the upturned roots of the tree so that scavenger birds could descend to strip away its flesh – excarnation, as had happened to the skeletons of those found near the Iron Age hill-forts I had visited; the outer palisade created a private and hidden space within which this could happen. In his view, 'The tree could have provided a superb excarnation platform, but I cannot prove it.'

Whatever the explanation, to see the great blackened trunk of the upturned oak tree at the nearby King's Lynn Museum is a primal experience. As with Damien Hirst's shark, *The Physical Impossibility of Death in the Mind of Someone Living*, the glass case the trunk is kept in only adds to the feeling that this is an emotion we once knew but have since anaesthetised.

*

And now I had come to the beach where it had been found. There was of course no sign of 'what I'd come to see', or rather respect the memory of. I knew exactly where Seahenge had stood only because Francis and Maisie had given me accurate directions. Black waves swirled over the spot.

The beach was completely empty, aside from a few distant dog walkers. Beyond the bar of shingle at Gore Point, oyster-catchers, one of my favourite birds, were wheeling with their bold, confident cries. Grey plovers were walking on the shingle. The marram grass had woven the sand together to form dunes along the beach tough enough to withstand the North Sea winds and tide, for the while at least; a duck-boarded path led across them to allow birdwatchers access to the shore.

I liked the view of local historian and archaeologist Matthew Champion, who, while sympathetic to the reasons for the removal of Seahenge, had commented that 'perhaps we should have let the cold waters of the North Sea finally take it away once and for all. The circle was after all a place of boundaries, a symbolic structure on the cusp between sea and land, life and death, the land of the living and the land of those who gone before. Perhaps it would be no bad thing if we had simply let it slip over the boundary for one last time.'

> This royal throne of kings, this scepter'd isle,
> This earth of majesty, this seat of Mars,
> This other Eden, demi-paradise,
> This fortress built by Nature for herself
> Against infection and the hand of war,
> This happy breed of men, this little world,
> This precious stone set in the silver sea,
> Which serves it in the office of a wall,
> Or as a moat defensive to a house,
> Against the envy of less happier lands,
> This blessed plot, this earth, this realm, this England . . .

John of Gaunt's speech in Shakespeare's *Richard II* is a familiar way of framing our island story, a Churchillian way. The sea as our defence, our moat, that protects us from invaders and gives us our strength.

But there is a different way of looking at it. The sea makes us open to other influences. As a nation, we are one gigantic port, absorbing the language, cultures and rhythms of the world. We have always done so from the earliest of prehistoric times. That is our strength. We are not landlocked, immobile.

Empire didn't suit us. It brought out the bossy, inflexible, hierarchical side of our national character. But being more on the edge of things again, that will suit us fine — a fluid, swirling mix of energy, like the sea around us, which can absorb people and ideas from across Europe, whether music, food, architecture or technology, and transform them with mercantile energy.

Elizabethan England was a minority power, running before the heavy galleons of Spain and the Habsburg Empire in Europe. We are better as the world's pirates than as its policemen. We are a liminal country, on the edge of things. Which is a great place to be.

I looked down at the wide sands of Holme, with their black pools, the low tide sucking across the beach. Seahenge was a reminder of the changing line of the coast and our country's mutability; of the many secrets that still lay buried waiting to be discovered, which, if archaeological techniques continue to improve so exponentially, will surely happen; of how many other such wooden mortuary rings might have been scattered across Bronze Age England, and the miraculous survival of this one.

Above all it was a reminder of flux, of change. Nothing about England is solid: its people, its culture, its language, its coastline. All are constantly changing, and have been from our earliest prehistory.

Rather than trying to hold onto some outmoded notion of national identity, like a piece of the driftwood out in the ocean, we should just let go and have the waves take us where they will.

I looked out to sea. In the far distance there was the faintest white line of wind turbines on the distant horizon, like the white foam of waves breaking. A flock of plovers rose up to join the oystercatchers wheeling above me. A huge and empty sky was lit to the west by the descending sun.

The end of one journey inevitably meant that soon I would embark on a new one. I didn't know where I would next be travelling. There was talk of taking a boat around Cape Horn and the lower coastline of South America.

Whatever happened, I felt I was ready to go abroad again; although I was not sure I would find anywhere quite as strange and foreign as England.

Timeline

BC

4000–2500	**Neolithic Age**
3700–3400	Wayland's Smithy
3630–3375	Cursus near Stonehenge
3000–2000	Different phases of Stonehenge
2600	Avebury
2500–800	**Bronze Age**
2049	Seahenge
1350–1000	Flag Fen
1300–700	Must Farm quarry boats in use
1400–600	White Horse carved at Uffington
800 BC–AD 44	**Iron Age**
600–450 BC	Construction of Maiden Castle, and other hill-forts throughout Iron Age
300 BC	Grim's Dyke
54 BC	Julius Caesar's initial invasion of Britain
c.AD 9–AD 40	Reign of Cunobelinus (Cymbeline) as king of the Catuvellauni
AD 43	Successful invasion of Britain under Emperor Claudius
AD 43–410	**Roman Interlude**

| 410–550 | **Romano-British giving way to Anglo-Saxon [supposed 'Arthurian' period]** |
| c.500 | Battle of Mount Badon. Romano-British defeat Anglo-Saxons |

AD 550–1066	**Anglo-Saxon period**
556	Cynric, the leader of the West Saxons, defeats Britons near Barbury Castle
595	St Augustine begins conversion of Anglo-Saxons to Christianity
793	First Viking raid at Lindisfarne
871–899	Reign of Alfred the Great
871	Battle of Ashdown
878	Battle of Eddington [Ethandun], Guthrum defeated by Alfred
991	Battle of Maldon, Vikings defeat English
1066	Norman invasion

1066–1485	**Norman and Medieval England**
1455	Start of the Wars of the Roses; Battle of St Albans
1471	Battle of Tewkesbury brings the Wars of the Roses to an end. Edward IV regains throne
1485	Battle of Bosworth. Richard III defeated by Henry VII
1485	William Caxton publishes *Le Morte d'Arthur* by Sir Thomas Malory

| 1485– | **Tudors, Stuarts and modern history as we know it** |

All prehistoric dates are approximate and subject to constant revision. Those given for monuments refer to their construction, not their period of use.

Disclaimers and Acknowledgements

This is emphatically not a guidebook. If it intrigues people into making journeys of their own along the older paths of the country, then those making decisions over stiles and hills and bridleways should consult the many gazetteers that set out routes.

By far the best and most inspirational for the Icknield Way are *Ancient Trackways of Wessex*, by H W Timperley and Edith Brill (1965) and *The Icknield Way* by Anthony Bulfield (1972), although both are old enough to need supplementary maps; or the useful booklet publication by Ray Quinlan and the Cicerone Press, *The Greater Ridgeway*, which is small enough to fit in a pocket.

Julian Cope's wonderful and eccentric *The Modern Antiquarian* (he uses his rock-star girlfriend in the pictures of megaliths to give scale) is too big to fit most coffee tables, let alone pockets, but details many prehistoric sites, as does Aubrey Burl's *Rings of Stone*, illustrated by Edward Piper.

The word 'Celt' has occasionally been used. This is the archaeological equivalent of smoking in a restaurant and I should make the disclaimer that I am well aware that it is a loaded and tendentious term — but there are times when no other word will quite do and the reader can add their own judicious pinch of salt. The alternative is to say 'Brythonic', but that sounds as if you're lisping.

Nor have I bothered to put Iron Age 'hill-forts' in inverted commas the whole time. Their use may well not have been exclusively or even partially military, but that is the common name we know them by, and archaeological pedants can add their own ironic quotation marks.

Barry Cunliffe has studied hill-forts extensively and produced many excellent publications on the Iron Age, just as Mike Pitts has on the Neolithic in *Hengeworld* and other works. I am also grateful to John Blair for his *Anglo-Saxon Oxfordshire* and to John Peddie for *Alfred: the Good Soldier*.

Eminent writers like John Steinbeck and Peter Ackroyd have attempted modern versions of Sir Thomas Malory's *Le Morte d'Arthur*, but nothing can match the cadence of the original text in Vinaver's edition of the Winchester manuscript: *Malory: Complete Works*, edited by Eugène Vinaver (Oxford University Press).

There are fine biographies of Malory, William Cobbett, Kenneth Grahame and Richard Jefferies by Christina Hardyment, Richard Ingrams, Peter Green and Edward Thomas respectively, and an equally fine biography of Edward Thomas himself by Matthew Hollis. Despite many biographies of Orwell, the best source about his life remains his own writing: *Collected Essays, Journalism and Letters* (four volumes, Secker & Warburg).

✻

My thanks to those who offered hospitality or guidance along the way: Jeremy and Paula Lawford, Richard and Clare Staughton, Kevin and Rachel Billington, Tim Copestake, Chris and Jane Somerville, Peter and Eleanor Buxton, William and Aliya Heath, the Rainbow Circle, Roger and Maha Thomson, Andy and Heather Martin, Adrian Poole, Maisie Taylor, Matthew Champion, Laurie

Gwen Shapiro, Nicola Keane, Benedict Taylor, Barry Isaacson, Bob Colenutt, Mick Conefrey and numerous pub landlords.

Simon Keynes for advice on the Anglo-Saxon period, Francis Pryor for similar advice on the Bronze Age, and Oliver Rackham on prehistoric woodland, with the usual disclaimer that nothing I have included is in any way their responsibility.

My agent Georgina Capel, my editor Trevor Dolby at Preface and all those at Random House who helped with the production of the book, along with Adam Burton for the illustrations and John Gilkes for the maps.

Irena and my children for sharing some of the walking and all of my life.

Appendix

'Thunderer' article for *The Times* on Stonehenge.

Stonehenge is vital to the nation.
It should be spared the cuts

Stonehenge was given to the nation in 1918. So far, almost a century later, the nation has done a remarkably bad job at looking after it.

The situation at the site is currently, as its custodians English Heritage put it, 'severely compromised' and as others like leading archaeologist Mike Pitts would say, 'an embarrassing, abominable, inexcusable mess'. For decades, plans have been put forward to improve the site and then postponed.

Two main roads not only thunder past but divide the circle of stones from the Avenue that should lead to it. The findings from Stonehenge are scattered piecemeal between some sixteen different museums and private holdings around the country. For the almost one million annual visitors drawn there, it can be a dispiriting experience, with the stones themselves fenced off and the current 'visitor centre' resembling a British Rail station built in the 1970s. Overall, it can be a bit like having a picnic in a car park.

Just last week the Government announced that it would no longer help finance the proposed new landscaping and visitor centre which Labour had announced last October.

On the face of it, this might seem perfectly reasonable. A saving of £10 million would result. We all know that cuts have to be made; the Government claims that Labour committed to projects that were never affordable.

What no one has pointed out is that they have left in place a whole raft of other projects that Labour committed to at the same time: £50 million towards the extension of Tate Modern, £22.5 million towards the creation of the British Museum's World Conservation and Exhibitions Centre, and £33 million to secure the future of the British Library's newspaper archive in new premises in Yorkshire.

While all these projects may be worthwhile, they are certainly more expensive and show a strange sense of priorities. Stonehenge is a quite unique prehistoric monument that has Unesco World Heritage status. We are supposed to be conserving it not just for the nation but the planet, and at present are failing dismally.

You don't have to be a paid-up pagan or druid to appreciate that this circle of megalithic stones represent an extraordinary imaginative and creative effort of our prehistoric fathers that compares well with our own Millennium Dome of 5,000 years later – and how much better it would have been to divert some small change from that grandiose project to Salisbury Plain.

Surely it behoves us to spend what little money we have left in the public purse on preserving one of our greatest monuments before embarking on far more expensive new projects? Or, as a Conservative Party obsessed with home-owners might put it, perhaps we should fix the roof before we build an extension?

Hugh Thomson

*

Letters to the Editor of *The Times*

Stonehenge

Sir, Hugh Thomson [yesterday in *The Times*] rightly questions the wisdom of the coalition Government's decision to cut its support for improving the setting and building of a new visitor centre at Stonehenge, an icon of our national heritage and the centrepiece of the 'cultural offer' pitched to the International Olympics Committee for 2012. The casual saving of £10 million places Stonehenge under threat as a World Heritage Site of outstanding universal value.

The news is felt all the more painfully since this is now the third time the project has been cancelled and it is estimated that £45 million to £55 million has already been spent abortively in developing these proposals. More than £25 million has been promised from other sources including the Heritage Lottery Fund. Added to this, the visitor centre has already received planning permission. So to make a saving of £10 million at this advanced stage makes no sense, either financially or strategically. It would be cheaper to finish the job now, rather than cancel and have to start again.

We invite the Government to seek an effective solution to the problem.

Professor Maurice Howard
Professor Geoffrey Wainwright
Professor Colin Renfrew
Professor Timothy Darvill

From: John Pettifew Clark
To: Crowmarsh, Eustace
               [mail to:ecrowmarsh@randomhouse.co.uk]
Subject: Hugh Thomson

Dear Eustace

Thank you for sending me the MS of Hugh Thomson's *The Green Road into the Trees*.

I will post you the copy-edited manuscript by surface mail. I have followed normal UK publishing practice and Random House house style in my editing and instructions to the typesetter.

Meanwhile, in addition to the usual solecisms and stylistic quirks that I see all too often from writers who have not had a classical education, I did want to raise a few concerns.

You should be aware that along the way, on what is ostensibly a walking book across England, Thomson manages to alienate a great many of his potential readers.

To be specific, and listing them in order of occurrence, he insults or makes gratuitous reference to: vegetarians, William Dalrymple (who is the favourite writer of most aunts in England), Paul McCartney, the Prince of Wales, publicans with beards, model aeroplane groups, the custodians of Stonehenge, all three of the major political parties (comparing the Liberal Democrats at one point to Pagans), rentier farming landlords, the Church of England, the neo-pagan group 'Dragon Order', gastropubs, bird-watchers, the army on Salisbury Plain, aristocrats, archaeologists, minicab drivers, hunters of wood pigeons, the Vikings (who, we should remember, have living descendants), postmodern architects, Amazon and Katie

Price (also known, I believe, as 'Jordan'); along with numerous others.

It is possible that there is some overlap between these groups (vegetarians, for instance, may be Paul McCartney fans, given his association with Linda; many aunts who read William Dalrymple are likely to be members of the Church of England), but it still seems a high-risk marketing strategy, and risks offending many.

Moreover, just to ensure that he makes a clean sweep of the majority of the population, he takes a sideswipe at married Englishwomen – and their husbands as well.

Nor has he taken his own advice and travelled with an animal (a dog, or perhaps like Stevenson, a donkey), which would have ensured commercial success; the British public like to read about animals, and they are less liable to involve contentious issues of class or history.

I would suggest that in future it might be safer to commission him to write a book about a less populated part of the world, or at least one that has fewer special interest groups, or readers. I see from the author biography that he has travelled to Afghanistan. Why not send him there? Or even better, the Empty Quarter of Arabia. It worked for Thesiger.

Best wishes – and thank you again for that excellent lunch at the Garrick.

Yours
John

John Pettifew Clark

PS I will enclose a hard copy of this with the manuscript. Remember to take it out!

Index

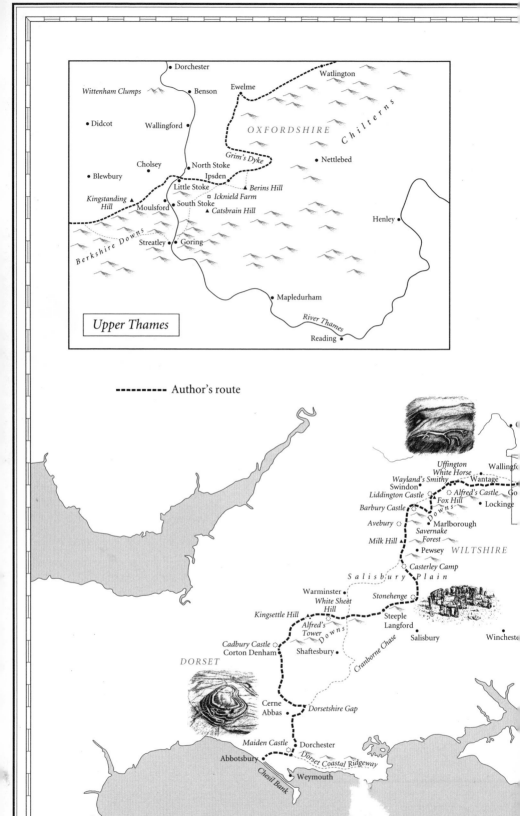

Upper Thames

------- Author's route

Wittenham Clumps

• Dorchester
• Benson
• Ewelme
Watlington

OXFORDSHIRE

Chilterns

• Didcot
• Wallingford
Grim's Dyke

• Nettlebed

• Cholsey
• North Stoke
• Ipsden
• Berins Hill

• Blewbury
• Little Stoke
□ *Icknield Farm*

Kingstanding Hill ▲
• Moulsford
• South Stoke
▲ *Catsbrain Hill*

Berkshire Downs

• Streatley
• Goring

• Henley

• Mapledurham

River Thames

• Reading

Uffington White Horse
Wallingfo[rd]
Wayland's Smithy
Wantage
• Swindon
☼ *Alfred's Castle*
Liddington Castle ☼
Fox Hill
• Lockinge
Barbury Castle ☼
Go[ring]
Avebury ☼
• Marlborough
Savernake Forest
Milk Hill
• Pewsey
WILTSHIRE

☼ *Casterley Camp*
Salisbury Plain
Warminster •
White Sheet Hill
Stonehenge ☼
Kingsettle Hill
• Steeple Langford
Alfred's Tower
Downs
• Salisbury
• Wincheste[r]
• Shaftesbury
Cadbury Castle ☼
Corton Denham
Cranborne Chase

DORSET

• Cerne Abbas
Dorsetshire Gap

Maiden Castle ☼
• Dorchester
• Abbotsbury
Dorset Coastal Ridgeway
Chesil Bank
• Weymouth